40 YEARS

# Dick Vitale's
## MOUNT RUSHMORES
### OF
## COLLEGE BASKETBALL

# SOLID GOLD
## Prime Time Performers
## From My Four Decades at ESPN

# DICK VITALE

### with Dick Weiss

Research by **Howie Schwab**

Foreword by **Bob Ryan**

"Nobody has seen more great teams, players and coaches in college basketball than Dick Vitale and Dick Weiss. Dickie V and Hoops have been the Gold Standard in this game for over 40 years. There is nobody better suited to chronicle the excellence they've seen at courtside."

- Jay Bilas, ESPN

"I was excited to hear Dickie V is doing a new book. I respect his opinion and look forward to his Mount Rushmore teams. I know he has several players on it currently serving as coaches. It is great that stars like Patrick Ewing, Chris Mullin, Danny Manning, and Steve Alford give back to the sport."

- Tim Brando, Fox Sports

"No one loves the sport of college basketball more than Dick Vitale. It shows in his trademark passion and enthusiasm. I've seen it up close and it is incredible. After four decades sitting courtside for ESPN, he is perfectly suited to document the best of the best for this new book."

-Doris Burke, ESPN

"If there were a Mount Rushmore for college hoop announcers, Dick Vitale would be on that mountain -- probably with his mouth wide open. There's never been anyone who invested more enthusiasm into the game, and that sometimes has overshadowed his excellent understanding of talent and strategy. I value Dick's insight into the game as much as anyone I've encountered and believe there is much of value in his proclamations regarding the best of college basketball."

- Mike DeCourcy, The Sporting News

"There is no one who has done more to promote basketball over the last four decades than Dick Vitale. He is definitely on the Mount Rushmore of sports analysts. I can't wait to see who made his Mount Rushmore. No opinion is more valuable and informative than his."

- Mike Greenberg, ESPN

"Can't wait to see Dick's new book, *Dick Vitale's Mount Rushmores of College Basketball*. No one has seen more college basketball than he has over the last 40 years. It should be a great read."

- Dan Shulman, ESPN

"If college hoops fandom, basketball on TV, or ESPN had a Mt. Rushmore…Dickie V would be front and center on all of them!!! No one has been more supportive and generous to all of us who have come in touch with the game. It is his 40th anniversary on the air and he is giving us a great gift."

-Mike Tirico, NBC Sports

"You can argue about who is on the Mount Rushmore of college hoops fanatics, all I know is there are only three spots open. Dickie V has one locked up. What I love most about his passion for the game is that I never have to let go of mine."

-Scott Van Pelt, ESPN

"One of the reasons I am a college basketball broadcaster is because of Dickie V's encouragement. Since the first time I met him in college, his enthusiasm and passion transcended the game. I am truly honored to be mentioned among his Mount Rushmore elites of college basketball."

- Jay Williams, ESPN

"If anyone should be on Mount Rushmore, it's Dick Vitale. So who could be more qualified to pick legends for the ultimate hoops mountain."

- Rece Davis, ESPN

Paperback ISBN: 978-1945907364
EBook ISBN: 978-1945907388
Library of Congress Control Number: 2018959473

Published by Nico 11 Publishing & Design | Mukwonago, Wisconsin
Publisher: Michael Nicloy
Marketing Coordinator: Reji Laberje
Quantity order requests should be emailed to: mike@nico11publishing.com

*Dick Vitale's Mount Rushmores of College Basketball*
*Solid Gold Prime Time Performers From My Four Decades at ESPN*

Author: Dick Vitale
Contributing Author: Dick Weiss
Research: Howie Schwab
Foreword: Bob Ryan
Contributing Editors: Howie Schwab, Reji Laberje
Associate Editors: Michael Nicloy, Lyda Rose Haerle
Cover Design/Layout: Michael Nicloy
Cover Painting: Philip A. D'Amore; D'Amore Artistry
Interior Layout: Michael Nicloy

All images courtesy of Dick Vitale unless otherwise indicated.
Front cover image of Dick Vitale by Phil Ellsworth / ESPN Images

"DICK VITALE 40 YEARS" photo collage:
Layout: Michael Nicloy
Images: Tom Christie, Tom Ford, Fred LeBlanc, Mark Murrary, Aubrey Wiley, John Atachain, Mitchell Layton, Scott Clarke, Darren Abate, Rich Arden, Joe Faraoni, Peter Lockley, Jeff Camarati, Bruce Schwartzman, Mike Smeltzer, Phil Ellsworth; all courtesy of ESPN Images.
Every reasonable attempt has been made to determine the ownership of copyright and proper credit of images used in this book.

Printed in Canada

# DICK VITALE'S
# MOUNT RUSHMORES
# OF COLLEGE BASKETBALL

*Solid Gold Prime Time Performers
From My Four Decades at ESPN*

Published by Nico 11 Publishing & Design
www.nico11publishing.com

Be well read.

I want to dedicate this book to all of these beautiful young kids who have or their families have been to my gala over the years. They will be missed, but certainly not forgotten.

- Dick Vitale

**Benjamin Gilkey**
December 22, 2007-
February 11, 2017

**Julia Mounts**
October 8, 2002-
April 23, 2016

**Chad Carr**
September 26, 2010-
November 23, 2015

**Austin Schroeder**
August 13, 1999-
April 28, 2015

**Lauren Hill**
October 1, 1995-
April 10, 2015

**Luke Kelly**
January 27, 2010-
January 19, 2015

**Lacey Holsworth**
November 30, 2005-
April 8, 2014

**Justin Miller**
April 21, 1992-
April 3, 2013

**Dillon Simmons**
November 2, 1998-
April, 25, 2014

**Eddie Livingston**
September 3, 2006-
November 24, 2013

**Adrian Littlejohn**
February 4, 2010-
May 1, 2011

**David Heard**
May 5, 2000-
February 10, 2011

**Johnny Teis**
August 1, 2002-
April 11, 2011

**Tony Colton**
October 18, 1999-
July 30, 2017

**Lucy Weber**
June 8, 2009-
November 20, 2010

**Payton Wright**
May 7, 2002-
May 29, 2007

**Caleb Jacobbe**
February 4, 1998-
May 10, 2006

This book is dedicated to Dick Vitale, from ESPN, who will always be the voice of college basketball to me and has devoted his life raising money for the V Foundation to help children with pediatric cancer.

     - Dick Weiss

To my parents, who always inspired me and taught me right from wrong.

                                                          - Howie Schwab

# TABLE OF CONTENTS

# FOREWORD
## By Bob Ryan

The book is about Mount Rushmores of college basketball.

There's lots of good reading and lots of fodder for great sports arguments. In the end, none of this is quantifiable. It's about opinion. And, oh boy, does Dick Vitale have opinions.

Who can shoot the rock. Who can pass the rock. Who shouldn't shoot the rock. Who shouldn't pass the rock. Who's the best Diaper Dandy. Who's a definite PTP'er. Who's on the All-Impact Team. Who's a Windex Man Supreme. Who needs a TO, baybee, and right now!!! The man is not shy in dispensing his opinions.

He has had ESPN as a forum since December 5, 1979, when he and Joe Boyle did the very first ESPN college basketball broadcast, a 90-77 DePaul victory over Wisconsin. At the time he was, well, distraught. He had, as he himself would say, gotten the Ziggy from his job as head coach of the Detroit Pistons. There was always going to be a job coaching at some level, but nothing was certain. And then came this opportunity to broadcast basketball on this strange, ambitious network dedicated to sports. Who knew if it would last?

Guess what? Dick Vitale made it work. He did so by the simple expedient of being himself. Anyone who knew him—and I had made his acquaintance during that Pistons' tenure—knew that his middle initial should have been "E." That's "E for "Enthusiasm.""

In the beginning the mechanics were elusive. Why is this producer yelling in my ear? Who needs this production meeting? What? I've got to make my point in fifteen or twenty seconds? Gimme a break!!!

But Dick always had one thing going for him. Well, maybe not one. First of all, he was a basketball junkie. He oozed hoop-ness from his every pore. He had good basketball thoughts. But lots of guys have good basketball thoughts. Lots of guys learn how to synthesize their thoughts to make good TV. Competent color men are in plentiful supply.

What set Dick Vitale apart from the start was not specifically the *What*, but the *How*. He could not conceal his obvious enthusiasm for the game. He didn't analyze a game as if it were Physics class. He called a game as if it was a fun-filled circus, full of spectacular athleticism and artistry. And the trick is not one syllable of it was ever forced. It was pure. It was him. It was AWESOME, baybee!

The year 1979 was a pivotal one in the history of college basketball. In March, Michigan State and Indiana State played for the NCAA championship. It was the first collision of Messrs. Magic Johnson and Larry Bird, and it brought more people under the tent than any college game, before or since. The second big thing was the debut of Dick Vitale as a college basketball broadcaster.

An exaggeration? Uh-uh. Dick Vitale would prove to be the greatest ambassador of broadcasting goodwill the game has ever known. It didn't take long before the arrival of Dick Vitale at your campus was a major happening. He would chat up everyone. He would shoot free throws. He would pose for pictures, perhaps wearing a goofy hat. And then he would sit down and bring added life to whatever was happening on the court.

He was a total force of nature. He was also a very hard worker. He made it his business to keep up with the game, from Maine to California and from Washington state to Florida. He knew the high schoolers. He was not just a colorful announcer, he was a certified authority. There was no one quite like him.

He would have to be on any Mount Rushmore of college basketball announcers.

There is another Rushmore on which Dick Vitale would be a charter member. That would be the Mount Rushmore of Humanitarians.

Ever hear of the V Foundation? It was founded to perpetuate the memory of the late Jim Valvano, the beloved coach and close friend of Dick, who left this world far too soon as a victim of cancer. The V Foundation for Cancer Research raises awareness, and, more importantly, money for pediatric cancer research, and it has had few more dedicated patrons than Dick and Lorraine Vitale.

For the last thirteen years Dick Vitale has been the host of a spring Gala in Sarasota, Florida. During that time the event has raised a staggering $25.2 million, including $3.7 million in 2018 alone, all to benefit pediatric cancer reasearch. The kids. The books he writes, the sporting events he hosts or attends, the gala he holds…it's all for them. At the gala, there is a dazzling list of impressive honorees, representing the coaching and broadcast professions. The guest list is full of sport A-listers. The 2018 attendees included all four Final Four coaches.

But the highlight comes each year when Dick Vitale introduces some of the young pediatric cancer patients who have been served by the foundation. He runs down each one of their individual histories and back stories as if they were his own children. He truly knows the people and their families. He brings the same enthusiasm to this task as he's done to his broadcast career. Nothing is forced. It's all genuine.

It's all Dick Vitale. And it's awesome, baybee!

And do you know what this book is? Fun, that's what. It will start arguments. Just keep 'em clean and think of the kids whose lives have been changed by Dick Vitale.

# OPENING THOUGHTS

One day, I was sitting with a bunch of my buddies and, as usual, the conversation was all about sports. We began to battle back and forth about whether anyone would supplant Michael Jordan as the greatest of all time in the world of basketball.

It has been generally felt by many experts that Jordan has not had anyone equal his stature. The fun began as I said, wait a minute, what about King James, LeBron James!

Then the battle began.

Names came flying out, fast and furious. Jordan and LeBron, Bill Russell, Wilt Chamberlain, Elgin Baylor, Jerry West, The Big O, Larry Legend, Magic Johnson. The hits just kept on coming. It was an intense back-and-forth, baby!

Well, that gave me an incredible idea. I went to bed that night, tossing and turning, thinking about picking the best of the best in my four decades behind the microphone at ESPN.

Then I simply said, I will call it my Mount Rushmores, the best four in various categories, Yes, the best coaches, players, etc. I think you get the picture.

I love sports because there are so many diverse opinions about athletes and teams. Growing up in New Jersey, I remember the heated discussions over baseball. My mom and dad each had nine brothers and sisters and they were all sports lovers. It was especially true of those on my mother's side. Every Sunday morning, after Mass, my mom and dad would have the bagels, donuts, coffee, and juice ready and then the debate would start. My uncle Frank would say Mickey Mantle, number 7, was the best center fielder ever. That would get me going. I would come back and say number 24, the "Say Hey Kid", Willie Mays, was in another league.

Immediately my uncle Tom would burst out, "The Duke!" Duke Snider. He loved the Brooklyn Dodgers and number four.

That would immediately get my dad in an uproar. You guys are all out of it, the best of the best was the Yankee Clipper, Joe DiMaggio. My pop would say that Joe D. was the only Hall of Famer who didn't have to make a spectacular catch because he was waiting for the ball.

Those were fun moments as it is always a blast to battle with buddies over who is the best.

I enlisted the help of Hall of Fame writer Dick "Hoops" Weiss and former ESPN research guru Howie Schwab to help come up with categories for our All-Mount Rushmore teams. Together we developed this concept and I put together my lists for each group.

My friends, let the debates begin. I know you can make a case for different people in several categories. That's the fun part, like being at a sports bar and debating who you liked more.

I could have gone with a number of people for coaching and playing honors. At the end, I made some tough decisions.

I do want to be very clear that all of my Mount Rushmore players and coaches are only from my era at ESPN, which began on December 5, 1979, when I worked the very first major college basketball game on ESPN, which was between De Paul (Number One in the Nation!) vs. Wisconsin. That is the only reason I did not include greats like Magic Johnson, Larry Bird, and the legendary John Wooden. They were just before my time at ESPN. I have the utmost respect and admiration for those guys!

I hope you enjoy my latest book. It was a lot of fun putting these All-Mount Rushmore teams together.

**As with most of my projects, this book is really special to me because all of my proceeds from the sale of it will go to the V Foundation for pediatric cancer research. Please spread the word, as we must all unite to help kids battling cancer.**

**I would appreciate it so much if you would make a donation by telling friends about this book and by going to: www.dickvitaleonline.com. All donations will go through the V Foundation for Cancer Research.**

# *Dick Vitale's*
# MOUNT RUSHMORE
## OF
# COACHING ROYALTY

### MIKE KRZYZEWSKI

### BOB KNIGHT

### DEAN SMITH

### ROY WILLIAMS

# Mike Krzyzewski
## (1975-Present)

Phil Ellsworth / ESPN Images

When talking about the crème de la crème of college coaches, the name that has to come to mind is Mike Krzyzewski; he has dominated his sport. Duke's Krzyzewski is today's face of American basketball and he is one of the most respected, influential coaches in basketball, globally.

## Carved in Stone

Since 1980, "Coach K," as he's known, has served as the head basketball coach at Duke University, where he led the Blue Devils to five NCAA championships, twelve Final Fours, twelve ACC regular season titles and fourteen ACC Tournament championships! Among men's basketball coaches, only John Wooden has won more NCAA championships. Krzyzewski has also been the head coach of the United States' men's senior national team, which he led to three gold medals in 2008, 2012, and 2016. In addition, Krzyzewski coached the American team that won gold medals in the 2010 and 2014 World Championships. He was even an assistant coach on the famous 1992 Olympic Dream Team.

Krzyzewski is a two-time inductee into the Naismith Hall of Fame: in 2001 for his individual coaching career and in 2010 as part of the Dream Team. He was inducted into the US. Olympic Hall of Fame in 2009.

On November 15, 2011, Krzyzewski led Duke to a 74-69 victory over Michigan State at Madison Square Garden to become the coach with the most wins in NCAA Division I history. His 903rd victory set a record, breaking the old one set by his former coach, Bob Knight. He wasn't done! On January 25, 2015, when Duke defeated St. John's 77-68 at the Garden, Krzyzewski became the first men's Division I coach to reach 1,000 wins.

## The Career

Krzyzewski was born in 1947, on the Northwest side of Chicago, in a working-class neighborhood. His father, William, was an elevator operator. His mother was a cleaning woman. The family shared a two-story home with relatives. Krzyzewski attended Archbishop Webber High, a Catholic preparatory school, where he emerged as a star and caught the attention of a young Bob Knight, who signed him to play for West Point.

Krzyzewski became the captain of the Army basketball team in his senior season in 1969, leading his team to the National Invitation Tournament (NIT) before graduating. Krzyzewski served in the U.S. Army from 1969 to 1974, rising to the rank of Captain; he directed service teams for three years. He was discharged from active duty in 1974 and started his coaching career as an assistant on Knight's staff at Indiana in 1975. After one year, Krzyzewski returned to his alma mater, where he became head coach at West Point for five years from 1975 through 1980. He led the Cadets to a 73-59 record with one NIT berth.

He was coming off a 9-17 season in 1979 when Bill Foster left Duke for South Carolina. Krzyzewski was a surprise choice for the head coaching job, but his mentor, Bob Knight, convinced then-Athletic Director, Tom Butters (a good friend), to take a chance on the young coach.

"If you like me as a coach, you'll love Mike," Knight said. "He has all of my good qualities and none of my bad ones."

When Krzyzewski was introduced at the press conference, no one could pronounce his name ("sha-chef-ski," to American ears). "You can just call me Coach K," he said.

After three rocky rebuilding seasons, Krzyzewski and Duke became a fixture on the national scene. They went on to have thirty-two NCAA appearances in thirty-eight years and twenty-three consecutive bids from 1996 through 2018. Overall, Coach K has taken his program to post-season play in thirty-four of his thirty-eight years at Duke. In addition to being the winningest coach of all time, he is the most winning coach in NCAA *tournament play* with ninety-four victories. Krzyzewski's best stretch came from 1989 through 1992 when the Blue Devils, with rock stars Christian Laettner, Bobby Hurley, and Grant Hill, went to four Final Fours and won back-to-back national championships in 1991-1992 by upsetting the until-then-unbeaten UNLV in the 1991 semi-finals, followed

*Phil Ellsworth / ESPN Images*

by Michigan's Fab Five in the 1992 finals. He also won championships in 2001, 2010, and 2015.

23

Krzyzewski had unprecedented success coaching Team USA after he was selected as the U.S. national coach. Before Coach K, the program had gone through a bronze medal meltdown in 2004. Former Phoenix Suns' owner, Jerry Colangelo, the newly-named managing director of Team USA, called a summit in Chicago that included great Olympic coaches and players like Chuck Daly, Jerry West, Lenny Wilkins, Larry Bird, Michael Jordan, Pete Newell, Magic Johnson, and John Thompson.

Colangelo's first order of business was to select a national team coach. The candidates included Greg Popovich, of the San Antonio Spurs, Mike D'Antoni, of the Suns, and Nate McMillan, of Portland, along with a shorter list of college coaches like Krzyzewski, Rick Pitino, of Louisville, and Jim Boeheim, of Syracuse.

At one point during the discussion, respected former UNC coach Dean Smith spoke up, voicing loud support for his long-time rival, Krzyzewski. "There's only one guy who can do the job," Smith said. "And that's coach K."

Colangelo finally chose Krzyzewski over Popovich. Picking a college coach was a gamble, but Krzyzewski was the right choice. He coached the 2008 Redeem Team with LeBron James, Kobe Bryant, Carmelo Anthony, and Jason Kidd to a gold medal in Beijing and another gold at the 2012 games in London when James and Kevin Durant were the stars in a win over Spain in the finals.

Krzyzewski announced his retirement after the games, but Colangelo convinced him to come back for the 2016 games in Rio and the U.S. won again when Durant established himself as the best player in the tournament under Coach K's leadership.

Krzyzewski's success did not go unnoticed. He was given the opportunity to coach in the NBA at least five times with the Boston Celtics, Portland, the Los Angeles Lakers, the Nets, and the Minnesota T-Wolves. The Lakers were willing to give Krzyzewski forty million dollars over five years *and* part ownership in the franchise that Phil Jackson left in 2004. Krzyzewski chose to stay put with his Blue Devils and the basketball court at Cameron Indoor Stadium was renamed "Coach K Court" in honor of the man who honored them.

Phil Ellsworth / ESPN Images

Krzyzewski, his wife Mickie, and his family founded the Emily Krzyzewski Center in 2006 to inspire students from kindergarten through high school to dream big and reach their potential as leaders in the community. The family has also been active for years in fundraising and support for Duke's Children's Hospital, the Children's Miracle Network, and the V Foundation for Cancer Research.

His is a life well spent.

# Bob Knight
## (1965-2008)

Photo courtesy of Malcolm Emmons/USA Today

Early in my coaching career, back in the late 1960s, I would go to coaching clinics to enhance my knowledge of the game I love. I will never forget going to a clinic and being mesmerized by the young coaching sensation from West Point. His teaching ability just blew me away and his confidence in sharing his basketball wisdom was unbelievable. He could be charming with friends, combative with enemies, and was known for his loyalty and dedication to those he admired. He was often controversial, always passionate, and never one to disappoint. That's the Bob Knight I know. Regardless of how he was personally considered, no one can ever take away from the fact Knight was one of the most brilliant minds in the history of college basketball.

## Carved in Stone

Knight is a Naismith Hall of Fame inductee who won what was then an NCAA Division I record of 902 games during his forty-two-year career at Army (where he was given the nickname, "The General"), Indiana, and Texas Tech. He valued education, graduated ninety-eight percent of his four-year players, and donated money to school libraries. Knight never cheated, and dominated the college basketball landscape for a large portion of the time he coached at Indiana from 1971-2000.

While at Indiana, The General was inducted into the Naismith Hall of Fame, establishing his credentials by winning three national championships in 1976, 1981, and 1987. He coached the Hoosiers to a perfect 32-0 record in 1976, the last time a Division I team finished unbeaten. The seventy-seven-year old Knight also won one NIT championship and eleven Big Ten championships in twenty-nine years. Knight was named national Coach of the Year four times and was named Big Ten Coach of the Year eight times. The Hoosiers won 662 games, including twenty-two seasons of 20 or more wins, while losing 239, a .735 winning percentage.

In twenty-four NCAA tournament appearances, the Hoosiers won forty-two of sixty-nine games and advanced to the Final Four five times. In 1984, The General coached the men's Olympic team to a gold medal, becoming one of only three basketball coaches to win an NCAA championship, an NIT title, and an Olympic gold medal.

Knight's distinguished coaching tree includes Hall of Fame coach Mike Krzyzewski, of Duke, Steve Alford, of UCLA, Chris Beard, of Texas Tech, and NBA coaches Randy Wittman, Keith Smart, Isiah Thomas, Mike Woodson, and Lawrence Frank.

Isn't it ironic that the guy who passed Knight as the winningest coach of all-time was his point guard at West Point, and one of his own former assistant coaches! What made Mike Krzyzewski's (Coach K's) record-winning day special was that Knight as doing color commentary as student surpassed teacher breaking the record of most wins by a single coach.

## The Career

Bob Knight grew up in Orrville, Ohio. He played for Fred Taylor as a reserve forward on a national championship team at Ohio State in 1960 and graduated in 1962. Knight coached junior varsity basketball at Cuyahoga Falls High, Ohio, for a year, then enlisted in the U.S. Army and accepted an assistant coaching position with Army in 1963. Two years later, he was named head coach at the age of twenty-four. In six seasons at West Point, he won 102 games, but developed a reputation for his explosive temper. Following a 66-60 loss to BYU under Hall of Fame coach Stan Watts in the 1966 NIT semi-finals, Knight lost it, kicking lockers and verbally blasting officials. He later went to Watts' hotel room and apologized. (That part of the incident didn't receive the same national attention.)

In 1971, Knight left Army for Indiana. In his second year, the Hoosiers won the first of four consecutive Big Ten championships and advanced to the 1973 Final Four. Knight's finest hours as a coach came in the 1975 and 1976 seasons. In 1975, the Hoosiers swept the entire Big Ten by an average of 22.8 points per game. However, in a late-season win against Purdue, they lost consensus All-American forward Scott May to a broken left arm. May's injury limited him to just seven minutes of play time. The top-ranked Hoosiers lost to Kentucky, 92-90, in the NCAA Midwest Regional finals.

The Hoosiers were so dominant that four starters—May, Steve Green, Kent Benson, and Quinn Buckner—made first team All-Big Ten. In 1976, with a healthy May and basically the same cast, the Hoosiers were perfect, defeating Michigan, 86-78, in the title game at Philadelphia.

Immediately after the game, Knight lamented, "It should have been two."

Knight won his second title when sophomore guard, Isiah Thomas, led IU to a win over North Carolina in the championship; his third was in 1987, when Keith Smart drained a jumper in the final seconds to give Indiana a victory over Syracuse.

The General had another strong run, between 1991 and 1993, when the Hoosiers, with All-Americans Damon Bailey and Alan Henderson, as well as national Player of the Year, Calbert Cheaney, won eighty-seven games. It was the most wins by any Big Ten team in a three-year span, breaking his own record of eighty-six set by his teams from 1974-76. The Hoosiers won two Big Ten titles in 1991 and 1993 and advanced to the Final Four in 1992. During the 1993 season, IU finished 31-4 and was ranked number 1 in the final AP poll, the trusted standard, but unfortunately lost to Kansas in the Elite Eight.

Knight was one of college basketball's most successful and innovative coaches, perfecting the motion offense and building a reputation for his tenacious man-to-man defense. He was just as known, though, for throwing a red plastic chair during a Big Ten game against Purdue in 1985, after he expressed disgust following two quick fouls on his players. He was immediately hit with a technical. When Purdue's Steve Reid stepped to the line, Knight tossed a chair across the floor toward the basket in front of Reid. He was hit with two more technical fouls . . . and ejected from the game. He apologized to the fans the next day, but he'd already been given a one-game suspension and a two-year probation by the Big Ten. Knight later joked that he saw an old lady standing on the sidelines and threw her a chair so she could sit down. In 2000, CNN Sports Illustrated ran

a piece on Knight in which former player Neil Reed claimed he had been choked by Knight in practice. Knight denied the story. Less than a month later, the network aired a tape of the practice, and he was eventually fired by school president Myles Brand for violating a no-tolerance policy on violence when he got into an altercation with a student.

Following his dismissal from Indiana, Knight took a year off, then accepted the head coaching job at Texas Tech. He quickly improved the program and led the Red Raiders to three NCAA appearances and an NIT bid in his first four years. Shortly after setting the record for most wins by a Division I coach in 2008, Knight retired, handing over the job to his son, Patrick.

He went on to work as an analyst at ESPN until 2015, when he and the network decided to go separate ways. Knight wanted to spend more time fishing and hunting. In 2009, he shared insights about why he was no longer coaching. Knight believed there was a lack of integrity going on in the coaching profession. It certainly did not go over well in Big Blue Nation when he said the game has a coach in Kentucky who put two schools on probation and is still coaching.

Knight stated, "I cannot understand that."

J.P. Wilson / ESPN Images

Bob Atashian / ESPN Images

Knight will always be acknowledged as one of the greatest coaches ever, but I only wish he would go back and share a moment of celebration with the fans at Indiana. He has refused to return since being fired by Myles Brand.

On a personal note, I know a little bit about the loyalty of Robert Montgomery Knight. I had been nominated several times for the Naismith Basketball Hall of Fame…but was rejected on each occasion. One day, my phone rang after being nominated for the third time. I received a call from The General.

Knight said, "Listen to me. I feel you will be shot down again. The Hall of Fame voters lean strongly to people with achievements in the NBA."

Knight blew me away when he then stated that he gathered letters from every living Hall of Famer endorsing me for induction into the Hall of Fame.

"This is going to be your Hall of Fame year," he said. "I will send you all of the letters to treasure for the rest of your life."

One letter in particular jumped out at me. It was from the Wizard of Westwood, John Wooden, and it really touched me. Needless to say, I was touched by Knight's loyalty and his personal support. That year, 2008, I received the call from John Doleva, the Director of the Naismith Hall of Fame, informing me that I had made it. When inducted, my presenter for this great honor was none other than my friend, Robert Montgomery "The General" Knight.

# Dean Smith

## (1961-1997)

*UNC Athletic Communications*

In my four decades at ESPN, I have never seen a coach who is so revered and loved like Dean Smith of North Carolina. I loved sitting and sharing basketball stories with the coach I labeled "The Michelangelo" of coaching. Smith was a genius at winning time. Throughout his career, he was able to bring the Tar Heels back from sure defeat to the winner's circle, again and again. Even more importantly, Smith had that one attribute that coaches strive for: ULTIMATE RESPECT from everyone involved in the UNC basketball program.

## Carved in Stone

Dean Smith was a "coaching legend" and was inducted into the Naismith Hall of Fame in 1983.

Smith coached the Tar Heels for thirty-six years, from 1961-1997, and retired with 879 victories; it was the NCAA Division I record at the time. Smith won 77.6 percent of his games. During his tenure, UNC won two national championships and appeared in eleven NCAA Final Fours.

From 1966 onward, Smith's teams never finished worse than tied for third in the ACC. The team won four consecutive regular season and ACC tournament titles in the late 1960s, and went to three straight Final Fours, losing to Lew Alcindor and UCLA in the 1968 championship game. Smith coached UNC to twenty-seven straight 20-win (or more) seasons from 1970 through 1997; twenty-two of those seasons had at least 25 wins. He earned seventeen ACC regular season titles, thirteen ACC tournament titles, and twenty-seven NCAA appearances.

My Michelangelo recruited twenty-six All-Americans and twenty-five NBA first round draft picks. Four of his players—Michael Jordan, James Worthy, Larry Brown, and Billy Cunningham—have been inducted in the Naismith Hall of Fame, along with former assistant and current North Carolina coach Roy Williams.

From 1970 until his retirement, Smith's teams shot over fifty percent for all but four years.

## The Career

Smith attended Kansas on an academic scholarship and played college basketball, winning a national championship in 1952 as a smart, role-playing guard for Hall of Fame coach, Phog Allen. After graduating from Kansas, Smith went into the Air Force, eventually landing at the Air Force Academy as an assistant coach. He went into coaching, against the advice of Allen, who urged Smith to seek a medical degree. In 1958, Frank McGuire arrived at the Final Four looking for an assistant. Air Force coach Bob Spear recommended Smith. He spent three years as an apprentice to McGuire.

Among other things, Smith helped integrate Chapel Hill in 1959 when he walked into a segregated restaurant with Dr. Robert Seymour, the pastor of the Binkley Baptist Church, which Smith attended, and a black theological student. The three men were served and integration was born on Chapel Hill.

Smith's big break came in 1961 when McGuire was forced to resign by Chancellor William Aycock in the wake of a major recruiting scandal and a two-year probation. McGuire left to coach Wilt Chamberlain and the NBA Philadelphia Warriors. Smith was hired the next day.

Smith's elevation occurred amid rumors of a point-shaving scandal involving UNC players. Smith was told wins and losses didn't matter as much as running a clean program. North Carolina, which had won a national championship in 1957, de-emphasized basketball by cutting their regular season schedule to seventeen games. North Carolina finished 8-9, the only losing season in Smith's career. The Tar Heels were fair during his first three years. The fourth looked like it might be worse. In 1965, after North Carolina lost to Wake Forest, 107-85, on the road, angry students burned Smith in effigy in front of Wollen Gymnasium. When the team arrived back on campus, Billy Cunningham, a senior on that team at the time, ran off the bus roaring and ripped the effigy down. UNC went on to win nine of its next eleven games and a dynasty was born.

In addition to his college coaching career, Smith coached the U.S. Olympic team—which included three of his starters: Tom LaGarde, Walter Davis, and Phil Ford—to a gold medal in 1976. He had to wait until 1982 to win his first national championship. A team composed of Michael Jordan, James Worthy, and Sam Perkins defeated Georgetown, 63-62, in New Orleans, when Jordan drained a jump shot with sixteen seconds to play and Worthy intercepted a pass from Freddie Brown on the next possession. Smith won his second title in 1993 when the Tar Heels defeated Michigan, 77-71. The Tar Heels led by just two points in the final seconds when Wolverines' star Chris Webber called a timeout his team didn't have.

Smith announced his retirement on October 9, 1997, saying if he ever felt he could not give his team the same enthusiasm he had given it for years, he would retire. The announcement came out of the blue. Bill Guthridge, Smith's assistant, succeeded Smith as head coach, but—in 2003—Smith convinced Roy Williams, then of Kansas, to come home to his alma mater and coach the team.

Sadly, in 2010, Smith's family announced he was suffering from a progressive neurological disorder. Eventually he had trouble remembering the names of his players, but they will never forget him. Smith was one of the great innovators in the history of the game. He is most associated with the implementation of John McLendon's four corners offense, a strategy for stalling with the lead at the end of the game. He also created the "tired signal" in which a player would raise a fist to indicate he needed to come out for a rest. He kicked off huddling at the free throw line before a foul shot, encouraged his players who scored a basket to point a finger to the player who had the assist, and he instituted a variety of defensive sets in the game. Smith's fast-break style, a half-court offense that emphasized the passing game, and an aggressive, trapping defense that forced turnovers and led to easy baskets, helped to make so many young men into star players. For Smith, though, stars and less-known players, alike, were equally honored as seniors in the last game of each season, Senior Day.

Smith, who died in 2015 at the age of 83, was best known for running a clean program and graduating 96.6 percent of his players. He was more than just a coach. His legacy also includes his work with civil rights. Smith helped promote desegregation in the state when he signed Charlie Scott, the school's first black player and he used his influence to push for equal treatment of blacks by local businesses.

He is and will always be one of the faces of equal rights and *the* face of North Carolina basketball.

# Roy Williams
## (1988-Present)

Phil Ellsworth / ESPN Images

Dynasties lead to more dynasties. The General gave us Coach K. Roy Williams would be the first to tell you that his coaching success, which led to induction into the Basketball Hall of Fame, was due to his mentor, the Michelangelo of coaching, Dean Smith. Williams lights up with incredible pride when sharing stories about his tenure working under Smith, but he earned his way on this list because of his own accomplishments.

## Carved in Stone

Williams, who has won 842 games at Kansas and North Carolina and coached the Tar Heels to three national championships in 2005, 2009, and 2017, modeled his exceptional thirty-year coaching career after his legendary Hall of Fame mentor.

Williams has taken his teams to nine Final Fours. He is the only coach in NCAA history to lead two different programs to at least four Final Fours apiece and the only basketball coach in NCAA history to have 400 or more victories at two NCAA Division I schools. In twenty-eight of his thirty seasons as a head coach, Williams has coached his teams to twenty or more wins. In his forty years as an assistant *or* head coach, he has been on a team that reached the NCAA tournament thirty-eight times.

## The Career

Williams, who grew up in Asheville, North Carolina, enrolled at the University of North Carolina and played on the freshman team with the thought of studying under Smith. When Williams was a sophomore at North Carolina, he asked Smith if he could attend his practices; he said he would sit in the bleachers taking notes. He volunteered to keep statistics for Smith at home games and work in Smith's summer camps.

Williams took a job as head basketball coach at Charles D. Owen High in Black Mountain, North Carolina, and he spent four years there before coming back to UNC, serving as an assistant to Smith from 1978-1988. During those years, North Carolina went 275-61 and won a national championship in 1982. Williams gained a measure of fame when he was instrumental in the recruiting of Michael Jordan.

In 1988, Kansas was looking for a new coach after Larry Brown left the school for a job with the NBA San Antonio Spurs, and Smith, who played for Kansas, recommended Williams for the job. Weeks after he was hired, Kansas was placed on probation for violations that took place prior to his arrival. As a result, the Jayhawks were barred from postseason play for the 1989 season. Williams, inspired by the "clean-play" modeling of his mentor, turned a bad situation around quickly, coaching Kansas to fourteen consecutive NCAA tournaments, two national championship game appearances in 1991 and 2003, and a 418-101 record (an 80.5 winning percentage), winning nine Big 12 championships in the final thirteen of his fifteen years in Lawrence. He was selected AP national Coach of the Year in 1992 and Big Eight/Big 12 Coach of the Year seven times. His teams went 201-17 (a 92.2 percent winning percentage) at Allen Field House and won 62 consecutive games at home from February, 1994 through 1998, reaching the number one ranking in six different seasons.

In 2001, Williams had an opportunity to return to North Carolina when Bill Guthridge retired as head coach. After national media sources announced Williams would take the job, they quickly backed off; Williams had made a campus visit and left without signing a contract. After a week of soul-searching, Williams held a press conference at Memorial Stadium in Lawrence, where he announced he was staying at Kansas. This decision would last only two years before he chose to return to UNC.

*Phil Ellsworth / ESPN Images*

Williams took the 2003 Kansas team to the NCAA championship game against Syracuse, losing 81-78. The end of the season brought another cloud of uncertainty about Williams' future because his relationship with Athletic Director Al Bohl was poor. Chancellor Robert Hemenway fired Bohl in what many felt was a desperate move to keep Williams. The respect

Williams had for Dean Smith played a role in his return to his alma mater, replacing Matt Doherty who had held the position after Bill Guthridge; Doherty had been Williams' former assistant at Kansas.

Two years after his return to UNC, Williams won his first national championship. Sean May scored twenty-six points as the Tar Heels, who finished 33-4, defeated Illinois, 75-70, in the NCAA championship game at St. Louis. Five members of that team—May, Raymond Felton, Rashad McCants, Jawad Williams, and freshman Marvin Williams—went on to play in the NBA. After the season, the top seven scorers left, either by graduation or declaring for the draft early. Williams reloaded quickly with 6'10" tall center, Tyler Hansbrough, guards, Wayne Ellington and Ty Lawson, and forward, Deon Thompson; they won three straight ACC championships from 2007 through 2009.

UNC advanced to the Final Four in 2008, losing to eventual champion Kansas, Williams' former team, in the national semi-finals. Two nights after the loss, Williams showed up to watch Kansas defeat Memphis in overtime, wearing a Jayhawk sticker on his shirt. Classy. In 2009, Hansbrough—a four-time All-ACC selection and the consensus national Player of the Year—led the Tar Heels to a second national championship with an 89-72 victory over Michigan State in Detroit. Williams won a third title in 2017 when guard Joel Berry scored twenty-two points during a 71-65 victory over Gonzaga in Glendale, Arizona, a year after UNC lost to Villanova, 77-74, on a 3-point shot by Kris Jenkins at the buzzer.

All told, Williams has won eight Atlantic Coast Conference titles at Carolina, one AP national Coach of the Year and two ACC Coach of the Year awards. He is third all-time leader for most wins at Kansas, behind Phog Allen and Bill Self, and second all-time leader for most wins at UNC, behind his mentor, Dean Smith.

In 2007, Williams was inducted into the Naismith Hall of Fame.

# *Dick Vitale's*
## MOUNT RUSHMORE
## OF
## ALL IMPACT PLAYERS

## PATRICK EWING

## RALPH SAMPSON

## CHRISTIAN LAETTNER

## MICHAEL JORDAN

# Patrick Ewing
## (1982-1985)

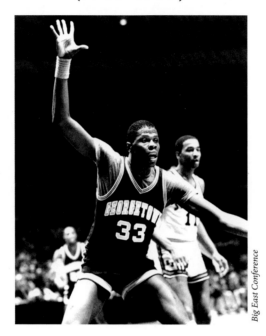

Big East Conference

## Carved in Stone

No player had a bigger impact on Eastern college basketball than the Jamaican-born Patrick Ewing, who got a late start in the game. Ewing excelled in cricket and soccer as a youngster on the island before moving to the United States as a twelve-year-old and joining his family in 1975. Ewing learned how to play basketball at Cambridge Rindge and Latin School in Boston. The game would stay a part of him and he would stay a part of the game from every moment after.

The original Big East Conference was founded in 1979, when Providence College basketball coach and future Hall of Fame inductee, Dave Gavitt, had the vision to assemble an East Coast basketball-centric conference capable of competing for national championships. The core of this made-for-TV league consisted of Eastern College Athletic Conference (ECAC) and Yankee conference teams: Providence, St. John's, Georgetown, Syracuse, Seton Hall, Boston College, UConn, and—eventually—Villanova and Pittsburgh.

The Big East enjoyed immediate success, winning its first NCAA championship five years later when 7'0", 245-pound center, Patrick Ewing – the league's first superstar—led the Hoyas to the NCAA tournament title in 1984. He would lead two more NCAA finals during his brilliant college career. Ewing was a three-time All-American, a star on the 1984 Olympic team, and—in 1985—the national Player of the Year.

## The Impact

Patrick Ewing became an intimidating presence who was considered the best prep prospect in the class of 1981, because of his size and his team's dominance. Sadly, he suffered backlash in the form of racially-fueled taunts. He constantly played in front of hostile crowds. On more than one occasion, rival fans rocked the team bus when Ewing arrived for a road game.

Ewing was good enough to follow in the footsteps of Darryl Dawkins and Moses Malone, jumping to the NBA directly out of high school, but he promised his mother he would become the first member of his family to graduate from college and even took courses at an Upward Bound program at MIT-Wellesley to prepare to see his promise through.

As a senior in high school, Ewing came close to signing a letter of intent with North Carolina, but—while on a recruiting trip—he witnessed a Klu Klux Klan rally, which dissuaded him from going there. He eventually signed a letter of intent to play for future Hall of Fame coach, John Thompson, at Georgetown. When it was time for him to make his announcement, the room was filled with fans hoping he would play for local schools, Boston College or Boston University. After his announcement, the room emptied out.

Ewing made Georgetown a national name, often drawing comparisons to Celtics' great Bill Russell. Thompson, who had been a backup to Russell in the NBA, was the perfect father-like mentor for Ewing, protecting him from the media.

Ewing, who averaged 15.3 points and 9.2 rebounds during his career, was not called upon to be a huge scorer, but his intimidating, physical presence alone impacted the game at both ends of the floor.

The Hoyas' us vs. the world mentality, known as Hoya Paranoia, reached its zenith during the 1982 Final Four in New Orleans. Thompson kept his team 90 miles away in Biloxi, Mississippi after Ewing received a death threat. In a loss to North Carolina in a star-studded national championship game that year, freshman Ewing set the tone when he was called for goaltending five times during the first eight minutes, making his presence felt. The Hoyas led late in the game before Michael Jordan knocked down a sixteen-foot baseline jumper to give the Tar Heels a 63-62 lead with 16 seconds to play. James Worthy secured Dean Smith's first national championship when he picked off a bad pass by Freddie Brown on Georgetown's final possession.

It would take two more years before Ewing got his national championship ring. The Hoyas won the Big East regular season, the Big East Tournament championship, and then blew through the 1984 NCAA Tournament, shutting down Kentucky, 53-40 in the national semifinals before defeating Houston, 84-75, in the championship game. Ewing scored 10 points, grabbed nine rebounds and outplayed Hakeem Olajuwon. Ewing was selected the Most Outstanding Player in the tournament as Georgetown won its first and only NCAA championship in school history.

Ewing was the dominant player in college again as a senior for the Number 1 team in the country for most of the season. He won the Naismith national Player of the Year and was again named Big East Player of the Year; the team won the Big East tournament again.

Thompson made sure Ewing got his degree and Ewing was the first player selected in the NBA draft of 1985 when the New York Knicks, who won the league's first ever lottery, drafted him. Ewing went on to make the All-NBA team seven times, to play in the 1992 Olympic Dream team, and to be inducted into the Naismith Hall of Fame. He was an NBA assistant for fifteen years before returning to become head coach at his alma mater, Georgetown, in 2018.

# Ralph Sampson

## (1973-1983)

*Virginia Athletics*

### Carved in Stone

Ialways get a kick when I think of Ralph Sampson. I will never forget doing a magical game between North Carolina and Virginia. At the end of the contest, Jordan made big plays to spark a stunning comeback. It was at that moment I stated that Michael the Magnificent was the best player, pound-for-pound, in the college game.

The next time I saw Ralph, when I did a Virginia game, he came up to me and stated, "Here is Michael Jordan's PR agent." We both laughed hysterically.

I have seen Ralph several times since, and we laugh when we think about that moment.

Sampson is as good a big man as ever to play in college basketball.

At 7'4", 215 pounds Ralph was bigger than life as Virginia's center. His impact on the Charlottesville campus from 1979 through 1983 may have been greater than any one person since President Thomas Jefferson, who founded the school.

Sampson, who was characterized as the most graceful center since Kareem Abdul-Jabbar, may have had more impact on a school than any player in ACC history.

Sampson was a superstar from the time he was a freshman and left college as a three-time National Player of the Year and a three-time ACC Player of the Year. Sampson led the Cavaliers to an NIT championship in 1980, a Final Four appearance in 1981, a Number 1 ranking in 1982 and 1983, and a 112-23 record over four seasons. Sampson and Virginia either shared or finished first in the ACC regular season standings three times.

The larger-than-life center fought through double and triple teams to average 16.9 points and 11.4 rebounds during his career. He left the school as Virginia's all-time leader in career rebounds with 1,151 and blocked shots with 462.

Ralph Sampson became "Must-See-TV."

## The Impact

Before Sampson arrived on campus with the eight-foot bed he brought with him from his Harrisonburg, Virginia, home, expectations were sky high. Giddy undergrads painted "Ralph's House" in black letters on top of University Hall. The Cavaliers were ranked 9th and 13th in two pre-season polls.

Before Sampson, Virginia basketball had never even been on national TV. By the time he left, the Cavaliers were a regular showtime and many of the Cavaliers' intersectional games (like Ohio State when Sampson scored 40 points and gathered 16 rebounds in a 68-63 victory) were specifically arranged for prime-time TV.

The biggest made-for-TV matchup in Virginia history occurred when Sampson and Virginia defeated the Patrick Ewing-led Georgetown Hoyas, at the Capital Centre in Landover, Maryland, in the most-hyped confrontation since Lew Alcindor and Elvin Hayes battled in the Astrodome in 1968. Sampson, who scored 23 points and grabbed 16 rebounds, got the best of Ewing, who had 16 points and 8 rebounds. Virginia walked away with $85,000 after it split TV rights with the other ACC schools.

Virginia Athletics

The painfully-shy Sampson lived in a fishbowl. It appeared everyone wanted a piece of him. He was on the cover of every major newspaper and magazine, and wasinterview fodder for all three major networks. He did not deal well with instant celebrity. He resided briefly on Thomas Jefferson's historic lawn, in a room custom-fitted with a larger doorway, but ended up staying in coach Terry Holland's basement when his residence became a tourist attraction.

"You got people coming by to bang on his door at midnight, two in the morning, just to get a picture," Holland said. "It was like he was an animal in a zoo."

Sampson let his actions speak louder than words on the court.

Fans flocked to University Hall, where nearly every game during his four years was sold out. "Stick," as Ralph became known, didn't disappoint. He led the Cavaliers to twenty-four wins as a freshman and was selected MVP of the NIT. During Sampson's sophomore year, the Cavaliers began 23-0 and rose to Number 1, winning the ACC regular-season title and advancing to the Final Four for the first time in school history. Sampson averaged 17.7 points and won the first of three Naismith awards.

In the 1981-82 season, with key players, Jeff Lamp and Lee Raker, gone, Sampson took on a bigger role as a junior, winning twenty-seven of their first twenty-eight games and sharing the regular season championship. When he turned down a one million- dollar offer to play for the Los Angeles Lakers after his junior year, entrepreneurs printed up popular T-shirts that read, "Good News for the 'Hoos. Ralph's back."

*Virginia Athletics*

Virginia had a strange season during Sampson's senior year, beating Georgetown before losing to Chaminade, a tiny NAIA school, in Honolulu, then recovering to share the regular-season ACC title, and then just missing a second trip to the Final Four when they lost to eventual champion North Carolina State in an NCAA Final Eight game in the West Regionals.

Sampson, who was selected by the Houston Rockets with the Number 1 pick overall in the 1983 NBA draft, left campus with 2,225 points, and 1,511 rebounds. Virginia was 50-2 at home and ranked in the Top 10 for forty-eight straight weeks. Sampson's great accomplishment was creating more buzz than any big man in the history of the league.

Sampson had a successful NBA career, but he was the first player since Bill Walton, in the modern era, to be elected to the Naismith Hall of Fame primarily for his work as a college player.

*Virginia Athletics*

# Christian Laettner

## (1989-1992)

*Duke Athletics*

### Carved in Stone

Christian Laettner was one of my favorite players to watch, because he was a flat-out winner.

Laettner's brilliant play led the Blue Devils on an awesome run to four consecutive Final Fours from 1989 to 1992. The Dukies cut down the nets as national champions in 1991 and 1992. And his ability to make clutch shots over the course of his career made him the greatest player in the modern history of March Madness.

### The Impact

Laettner got his name from Hollywood! That's right, baby! His mother named him after Christian Diestl, the German soldier played by Marlon Brando in the movie "The Young Lions."

Laettner looked like a prep when he attended the prestigious Nichols School in Buffalo, but he hardly fit the stereotype. Laettner was the son of a printer for the Buffalo News, and his family lived in a lower middle-class neighborhood of Angola, thirty miles south of the city. Laettner got up at 6:00 every morning to make the forty-five-minute bus trip to school and had an inherent blue-collar personality, with an edgy side that made him ultra-competitive when he came to Duke.

The 6'11" Laettner was both confident and cocky. He looked at big games as challenges and he always seemed to step up when Duke needed him the most. He never saw a big shot he didn't think he could make. Time and time again, you could put it in the book that Mr. Laettner would come through.

Laettner is best known for the shot he made as a senior against Kentucky in the 1992 NCAA East Region finals at Philadelphia. With Duke trailing the Cats by one with 2.1 seconds left in overtime, Laettner cemented his legacy with one of the most memorable moments in tournament history.

Teammate Grant Hill, left unguarded on the baseline, threw a seventy-five-foot pass to Laettner, who caught the ball above the foul line between two Kentucky players. He took one dribble, faked right, turned to his left and drained a seventeen-foot jumper at the buzzer to give the Blue Devils a 104-103 victory in a game many still regard as the best tournament game ever.

Krzyzewski recalled the scene in the huddle before the historic shot when Laettner told the team he would catch the ball if Hill threw it. "Some people would call that bravado or cocky, but it made us believe we were going to win. His confidence rubbed off on his teammates."

Laettner was the perfect player that night. He finished with 31 points and did not miss a shot, making ten out of ten, from both the field and the foul line. His play propelled Duke to the Final Four, where they defeated Michigan's Fab Five, 88-85, to win their second straight NCAA championship. Laettner, who averaged a career-high 21.5 points along with 7.9 rebounds and shot 57.5 percent from three-point range was named consensus National Player of the Year and was selected as the only amateur to play for the 1992 Olympic Dream Team.

A three-time All-American, Laettner was used to the spotlight by then.

He started for much of his freshman year, shooting an astonishing 72.3 percent from the field. He scored in double figures in every NCAA game, making the All-East Regional team after scoring 24 points, grabbing 9 rebounds and outplaying Alonzo Mourning, as Duke defeated top-seed Georgetown to advance to the Final Four.

Laettner had both tremendous range and a soft touch from the line for the Blue Devils, shooting 80 percent for his career, including 83.6 percent as a sophomore. He had a breakout season that year, averaging 16.3 points, making third team All-American. He liked being both the villain and the hero for the Dukies, with last-second shots. Against Connecticut, he drilled a game-winning, last-second jump shot, with less than one second to play in overtime, as Duke broke the Huskies' hearts, 79-78, in the East Regional finals, eventually advancing to the national championship game against University of Nevada, Las Vegas (UNLV).

As a junior, Laettner led the Blue Devils in every statistical category, averaging 19.8 points and 8.7 rebounds, while shooting 57.5 percent. He was named Most Outstanding Player in the Final Four after scoring 46 points and grabbing 17 rebounds as Duke upset top-ranked and previously unbeaten UNLV. He broke a 77-77 tie with two free throws and 12.7 seconds left, then defeated Kansas to win the school's first national championship.

Laettner was the ultimate winner in college basketball.

# Michael Jordan
## (1981-1984 . . . and beyond)

UNC Athletic Communications

### Carved in Stone:

It was absolutely electrifying to watch Michael the Magnificent perform his high-wire act in Chapel Hill. Jordan became, in the eyes of many, the greatest of all-time, after leading the Chicago Bulls to six NBA titles. Early in college, he demonstrated the greatness that would follow.

When Jordan was young, he was a huge fan of North Carolina State's sky-walker, David Thompson. He even rooted for Marquette when the Warriors defeated the University of North Carolina (UNC) Tar Heels in the 1977 national championship game, but he had a change of heart when he visited Chapel Hill to participate in the Carolina basketball academy the summer before his senior year.

### The Impact:

Jordan had been cut from his team at Lacey High in Wilmington, North Carolina, as a sophomore. Then, as a junior, he sprouted up from 5'11" to 6'3" and his game exploded.

Smith and his assistant Roy Williams arranged for Jordan to participate in the late Howard Garfinkel's (The Garf's) fabled Five-Star camp in the Poconos in order to make a final determination whether they should offer Jordan a scholarship. It almost backfired. Jordan was the best player in the camp, dominated on the outdoor courts, and suddenly Carolina, which thought they had discovered the ultimate sleeper, had to battle North Carolina State, Maryland, and South Carolina for his signature.

All the pre-season magazines were about to go to print with their high school superstars—including the top five players in the country—and The Garf called me. He couldn't wait for me to see Jordan since I had been a guest lecturer at the camp.

As soon as he got off the phone, he called Bob Lapidus, his buddy at Street and Smith's. "Who's in your top five?" he started screaming. "They can't compare to this guy."

Leave it to Garf to try to stop the presses. Sadly, the story had already gone to bed.

Jordan signed with North Carolina because of Smith's reputation for producing NBA players like Phil Ford and Walter Davis. The world would have to wait until that winter to discover what Garf knew. Michael the Magnificent averaged a modest 17.7 points and 5.0 rebounds during his three-year career. He went on to become a first team All-American the next two years.

Jordan averaged 20 points as a sophomore and led the ACC in scoring as a junior with 19.6 points and 5.3 rebounds while shooting 55.3 percent. He was selected consensus National Player of the Year that season and went on to become the star of the U.S. national team that won a gold medal in the 1984 Olympics in Los Angeles.

Photo courtesy of Malcolm Emmons/USA Today

It took a little longer for the legendary Dean Smith to determine how good Jordan could be. Jordan was his best in clutch situations.

Jordan led the Tar Heels to a 1981 national championship as a freshman when he made a game-winning baseline jumper to give UNC a 63-62 victory over Georgetown.

He punctuated his final year with a steal and a last-second jumper to force overtime in a victory at Tulane.

He blocked a last-second shot by Chuckie Driesell to preserve a victory over Maryland.

He led the Tar Heels on a 16-point rally against Ralph Sampson and Virginia at Carmichael Auditorium.

He locked up the game with a steal off Rick Carlisle and a breakaway dunk.

Jordan's college play was just a preview of coming attractions for one of the greatest players in the history of the sport.

# *Dick Vitale's*
# MOUNT RUSHMORE
## OF
# ALL MARCH MADNESS

## DANNY MANNING
## CHRISTIAN LAETTNER
## KEMBA WALKER
## GLEN RICE

# Danny Manning
## (1984-1988)

*Kansas Athletics*

### Carved in Stone

Larry Brown was a great college coach, and the versatile 6'10" Manning, who had some Magic Johnson in his game, was single-handedly capable of lifting a team to unseen heights. He took the Jayhawks into rarefied air in 1988 when it was least expected.

### The Madness

Danny Manning grew up in Greensboro, North Carolina and appeared destined to play for North Carolina after leading Page High to a 26-0 record and the state championship as a junior. That all changed when Larry Brown accepted the Kansas coaching job and offered Manning's father, Ed, a long-time NBA and ABA player, an assistant coaching position prior to Danny's senior year. The family moved to Lawrence, Kansas, and Manning, the best prep prospect in the country, signed with Kansas. Just like that, the Jayhawks became a national contender.

Manning, who had helped take Kansas to a Final Four as a freshman, was coming off a junior year where he averaged 23.9 points and 9.5 rebounds and was a first team All-American. Manning looked ready to make the leap to the NBA, but he came back for his final season because he felt Kansas could win it all.

Phil Ellsworth / ESPN Images

The best laid plans unraveled, beginning in October, when Joe Young was ruled academically ineligible. Sophomore forward, Mark Randall, decided to seek a medical redshirt. Senior guard, Archie Marshall, suffered a season ending knee injury. Then, junior center, Marvin Branch, was ruled academically ineligible. Two top junior college guards—Otis Livingston and Lincoln Minor—never made any major contributions.

Kansas was left with Manning and a patchwork lineup that started the season 12-8 and looked like they might not even make the tournament bracket after blowing a six-point lead and losing to Nebraska in the last game of the regular season. The Jayhawks got in as a sixth seed with 11 losses.

The Jayhawks last won a national championship in 1952 behind a Player of the Year, Clyde Lovellette. This time they depended on another prime-time player, Mr. Manning.

"We have the greatest player in the game," Brown said. "With a great player, you've always got a chance."

Manning, who averaged 24.8 points and nine rebounds and made first team All-American for a second straight time, wouldn't let them lose in postseason. This was his team–Danny and the Miracles. Manning averaged 27 points during Kansas' six-game run.

The Jayhawks defeated Xavier, 85-72, in the first game, then got by Murray State, 61-58, when the Racers missed a go-ahead shot and Manning hit two free throws with 1 second left. Manning scored 38 points as Kansas raced by Vanderbilt, 77-64, in the Sweet 16, and then added 20 more when Kansas defeated in-state rival, Kansas State, 71-58. It was made extra sweet because the rival had beaten them twice in the regular season.

After the Jayhawks arrived in nearby Kansas City for the 50th anniversary of the tournament, Manning turned it up a notch. He carried some bitterness with him in his game against Duke in the national semis. When he was a freshman, Duke defeated Kansas in the same round, 71-67, and Manning was limited to four points. This time, he took no prisoners, scoring 25 points, grabbing 10 rebounds, blocking six shots, and getting four steals, as Kansas defeated the Blue Devils, 66-59.

Manning had his crowning moment, scoring 31 points and adding 18 rebounds as Kansas defeated top-seeded Oklahoma, a team that had beaten them twice in the regular season, 83-76, to win the title game. Manning was bringing the ball up the court, pulling Oklahoma's big men out, and confusing Billy Tubbs' team on defense. He put the game away with four straight free throws in the final seconds.

Manning was voted the Most Outstanding Player in the tournament. He finished with 2951 career points and, to no one's surprise, was a consensus choice for National Player of the Year. He was also selected as Big Eight Player of the Decade.

Danny and the Miracles were simply awesome, baby, with a capital A!

# Christian Laettner
## (1989-1992)

*Duke Athletics*

## Carved in Stone

Duke's two-time All-American forward, Christian Laettner, in addition to being a top All-Impact player, is arguably the biggest star ever to shine in the modern era of March Madness. The Blue Devils' 6'11" matinée idol, who played with an intensity and swagger at both ends of the court, scored 407 total points in four NCAA tournament appearances and played in 26 of 24 possible games during his four-year career that culminated with him being named consensus National Player of the Year and being selected as a member of the 1992 Dream Team.

Laettner will always be known for his perfect game, as a senior, against Kentucky, in the 1992 NCAA Eastern Regional finals in Philadelphia, when he shot a perfect 10-for-10, made 10 of 10 free throws, finished with 31 points, and made the game-winning shot at the buzzer, to give the Blue Devils a 104-103 overtime win against the Wildcats. Christian set the stage for Duke to win a second consecutive national championship

## The Madness

Laettner had other dramatic moments before he blossomed into a college superstar.

Laettner had his first shot to be a hero when he was just a freshman. Duke was playing Arizona at the Meadowlands. The Wildcats had a 77-75 lead, but Laettner had a chance to force overtime if he converted a one-and-one at the end of regulation.

He missed the front end and was consoled afterwards by his teammates, not to mention former President Richard Nixon, a Duke law school graduate.

That was one of the few times Laettner missed a big shot.

Laettner took a giant step forward at the end of his freshman year when he scored 24 points, grabbed nine rebounds, and outplayed Georgetown's 6'10" Alonzo Mourning as the Blue Devils defeated the Hoyas, 85-77, on the same court where he missed the free throw against Arizona three months later.

Laettner loved the Meadowlands.

He found himself in another make-or-break situation the next March with the game and another trip to the Final Four on the line. Duke was playing Connecticut in the 1990 NCAA Eastern Regional finals. Laettner's family had come down from upstate New York to watch him play.

Connecticut looked like it might be in position to spoil the Devils' Final Four run. The Huskies had a one-point lead in overtime and looked like it had the ball after Duke point guard, Bobby Hurley, threw a pass for Phil Henderson in front of the University of Connecticut (UConn) bench. UConn guard, Tate George, initially had the steal, but he lost control of the ball and it went out of bounds with 2.6 seconds to play, giving Duke one more chance.

Coming out of a timeout, Mike Krzyzewski could see the inbounds pass was well-guarded, so he switched plays and called "Special"—a quick-hitter in which the ball was inbounded and immediately reversed back to the player who inbounded it, which—in this case—was Laettner.

"I kind of got a little anxiety in my stomach," Laettner said. "Once the whistle blew, it was gone."

UConn did not have a man on Laettner, who threw the ball to Brian Davis, who quickly returned it. Laettner dribbled once, double pumped, and then drained a jumper as the final buzzer sounded to give Duke a 79-78 victory that propelled the Blue Devils to the second of four Final Fours.

"In our ecstasy in winning, it can't be complete because of the people you play against," Laettner said afterwards. "Either team that lost would have been crying in the locker room. We were crying in victory. There were an incredible number of great plays. We just happened to make the last one."

Duke Atletics

# Kemba Walker

## (2009-2011)

UConn Athletics

## Carved in Stone

I loved watching magical performers who dazzled à la Mr. Walker. He had the fans in Storrs, Connecticut in the palm of his hand as he truly was, as I would say on ESPN, a three-S man…Super, Scintillating, and Sensational, baby!

Walker may have had the most remarkable run of any player in the history of March Madness, leading Connecticut to eleven straight victories, as the Huskies came out of nowhere to win both the Big East and NCAA tournaments.

## The Madness

The 6'1" All-America point guard learned how to perform on college basketball's biggest stage by creating his own stage when he was younger. Walker was just four years old when he walked into a laundromat on University Avenue in the Bronx. The place spilled out reggae music in the summertime. He'd go up to the first person he spied, tap their hip, and then—as soon as he got their attention—he'd bust out dancing. People instinctively gave him money after watching him flash his cute smile and perform a Jamaican dance called the "The Boogie."

Walker went on to become a creative break dancer, learning the sweeping steps in the basement of the local community center, and then enrolling in a hip hop and jazz dance class at the young age of eight, balancing his dance training with his love of basketball. When he was a rising star at Rice High in Manhattan, Walker took his talent up the road to Harlem, where his amateur dance troupe performed three times at the Showtime At the Apollo Showcase.

Walker loved to entertain people and the McDonald's All-American was a natural when he arrived at Connecticut. He was a three-year starter for the Huskies. He rose to national prominence when he averaged 26.8 points, five rebounds, and 3.8 assists a game. He was a first team All-American and the unquestioned leader of a young team that finished 9th in the Big East regular season. Walker exploded onto the national scene at the Big East tournament in Madison Square Garden.

He was unstoppable, scoring a record 130 points as the Huskies became the first team ever to win five games in five days to capture the tournament. He scored 28 points in a second-round win over Georgetown. Then,

*UConn Athletics*

he shook off Pittsburgh's 7'0" center, Aaron McGhee, and drained a game-winning jumper, as the time expired to give University of Connecticut a 76-74 victory in the quarters. Walker went off for 33 points, 12 rebounds, six assists, and five steals in an overtime win against Syracuse in the semi-finals. He then overcame fatigue to help the Huskies get by Louisville in the championship game. Walker was an easy choice for MVP during the amazing run.

The championship earned UConn an automatic bid to the NCAA tournament and a Number 3 seed in the West Region. The Huskies should have been exhausted, but Walker wouldn't allow them to let up, averaging 23.5 points, six rebounds, 5.6 assists, and 1.5 steals in a six-game March Madness run.

He scored 18 points, grabbed 8 rebounds. and had a career high 12 assists and two steals in a 19-point win over Bucknell and then had 33 points (16 in the final 10 minutes), six rebounds, five assists, and 1 steal as the Huskies defeated Cincinnati, 69-58, in the first two rounds. Walker went off for 36 points, three rebounds, six assists, and two steals as Connecticut defeated San Diego State, 74-67, in the Sweet 16, with Walker winning the personal matchup against 6'8" forward, Kawhi Leonard, taking over the game after the Aztecs rallied to take a lead with nine minutes to go.

Walker came back to earth in the regional final against Arizona, but he still managed 20 points, four rebounds, and seven assists in a 65-63 victory over the Wildcats. With the Huskies clinging to a three-point lead and one minute to play, Walker was Mr. Clutch as he drained a step back jump shot to lock up the victory.

Connecticut played Kentucky in the national semifinals at Houston in a rematch of their game at the Maui Invitational. Walker was too much for the Wildcats, scoring 18 points, grabbing six rebounds, and contributing seven assists in a 56-55 Maalox Masher. When UConn played Butler for the national championship, Walker was not about to let this opportunity slip away, playing relentlessly and scoring 16 points, as the Huskies defeated Brad Stevens' team, 53-41, in an ugly, low-scoring game.

"You can see the tears in my eyes," Walker said. "I have so much joy in me. It's unreal. It's surreal. I am so happy right now. I just remember everybody saying we couldn't do it. Each and every game, they said there's no way we could win another game. But we did anyway."

The little guy always came up big, baby!

# Glen Rice

## (1986-1989)

*Robert Kalmbach / Bentley Historical Library*

## Carved in Stone

Let's face the facts. The University of Michigan stands for greatness, academically and athletically. When I think of the Maize and Blue in college hoops, I immediately reflect on that incredible moment in 1989, when they won the national championship. The key reason for their win was the shooting ability of the solid gold PTP'er (Prime Time Player), Glen Rice.

Listen, my friends: Rice changed the dynamics of Michigan basketball during March Madness in 1989. The 6'7" senior All-American forward from Flint, Michigan, was one of the best shooters ever to play in the Big Ten. He was a three-S player in the big dance that season, averaging a record-breaking 30.7 points and shooting 57.2 percent as the Wolverines, who changed coaches just before the start of the 1989 NCAA tournament, won their first national championship.

His effort turned Steve Fisher into a hero!

Rice's 184 points in six games is a record that may never be broken.

"If that record is going to be broken, it'd have to be by a guy on a team that doesn't have three or four guys that are elite players," Rice said. "He's going to have to be the man, and probably the only man. Other than that, I don't think it'll be broken."

## The Madness

Rice is arguably the best player ever to come out of talent-rich Flint, averaging 28.6 points as a senior. He was named Mr. Basketball in the state after leading Northwestern High to a second consecutive state title.

But there was a time basketball was not part of his life. When Rice moved to Flint from Benton, Arkansas, as an eleven-year old, he didn't even own a pair of basketball sneakers to bring with him to Garfield Elementary, despite already being six-feet tall. He had to be talked into trying out for the middle school team by a childhood friend and eventual DePaul star Terence Greene.

His career took off from there. Four Michigan players from that team made it to the NBA. Fisher was elevated to full time head coach. And Rice was selected by Miami with the fourth pick overall, and teammates began calling him "G-money" (guaranteed money), because of his sweet jump shot.

Rice, who averaged 25.6 points while shooting 58 percent from the floor and 52 from three-point range during the 1989 regular season, was projected as a mid-round selection in the NBA draft by scouts when the season started. He blew up into a lottery pick as the talented Wolverines, who replaced Bill Frieder with interim coach Fisher, discovered Frieder had signed a deal to coach Arizona State the following season.

Rice still remembers the per-tournament speech the late, great Michigan Athletic Director, Bo Schembechler, made to the team. "At that time, when Bo spoke, it was like God speaking," Rice said. "The encouragement he gave me, being a leader and a Michigan man…we were not going to be denied."

After going 9-of-22 from the floor for 23 points in a first-round win over Xavier, Rice exploded for a 36-point performance on 16-of-25 shooting against South Alabama in the second round.

He was just warming up.

He stayed hot in the Sweet 16 against North Carolina, dropping 34 points on thirteen-of-nineteen shooting, before going for 32 ont thirteen-of-sixteen shooting in a 37-point win over Virginia in the Southeast Region finals.

At the Final Four in Seattle, the magic continued. Rice went for 28 against rival Flying Illini who won the Big Ten title and beat Michigan twice during the regular season, in the semifinals. Sean Higgins scored on a tip-in with 1 second to play to give the Wolverines an 83-81 victory. Rice saw the finish line and would not be denied. He put up 31 points in the championship game as Michigan defeated Seton Hall, 80-79 in overtime when guard, Rumeal Robinson, made a pair of free throws with three seconds to play.

To put Rice's scoring bonanza in context, point guard Kemba Walker scored 141 points in UConn's remarkable six-game 2011 championship run.

Rice, who made 27 field goals in 49 attempts under NCAA pressure, was an easy choice for Most Outstanding Player in the Final Four. He became the school's all-time leading scorer with 2,442 points, a record that stood for twenty-nine years before Kathelynn Flaherty broke it during the 2018 season. In his four years, RICE never shot less than 55 percent…that's a solid PTP'er!

# *Dick Vitale's*
# MOUNT RUSHMORE
## OF
# ALL BIG SHOTS

# KRIS JENKINS

# KEITH SMART

# MARIO CHALMERS

# LORENZO CHARLES

# Kris Jenkins
## (2016)

*Phil Ellsworth / ESPN Images*

### Carved in Stone

Talk about a heroic moment that will live forever! Kris Jenkins was the hero of heroes for Villanova when he made the game-winning shot that provided the 'Cats an historic moment and another national championship for their trophy case.

### The Big Shot

Jenkins was the player Villanova coach Jay Wright almost didn't sign.

When he was entering his senior year at a Washington, D.C. Catholic school, Jenkins made an unofficial trip to the Main Line with his stepbrother, point guard, and high school teammate, Nate Britt.

Wright wanted Britt, a McDonald's All-American—a player who would eventually sign with North Carolina. He also liked Jenkins, but wasn't sure the 6'6", 280-pound forward, who had a smooth stroke but also had a body that needed work in the weight room, was the right fit for Villanova's up-tempo style of play.

Wright was honest with Jenkins, telling him he'd have to change his lifestyle and diet and cut his body fat. When he did, Wright knew he had found a highly-motivated work in progress.

"When I got here, I had a little chip," Jenkins admitted. "I felt like I had to prove I could play at this level."

Jenkins lost 35 pounds and spent hours working out with strength and conditioning coach, John Shackleton, who constantly kept an eye on his diet. Jenkins went from limited minutes as a freshman and sophomore to playing a major role on a Big East regular season championship team as a junior, picking up the nickname, "Big Smoove" from Fox TV analysts. He had been on a roll throughout the 2016 Big East and NCAA tournament, winning MVP in the South Regionals after Villanova defeated Kansas in Louisville.

The foul-prone Jenkins was almost invisible for most of the last seven minutes against Britt's North Carolina team in the national championship game at Houston. The Tar Heels, who trailed by 10 points late in the game, cut into the Cats' lead and looked like they were about to force overtime after guard, Marcus Paige, hit an off-balance three to tie the score at 74-74, with 4.5 seconds to play.

Then, Jenkins changed destiny in a flick of the wrist.

After a timeout, point guard Ryan Arcidiacono raced the ball up the floor, but found himself double-teamed by forward Isaiah Hicks and guard Joel Berry. Then he heard a bark.

"Arch, Arch, Arch."

The unselfish Arcidiacono, recognizing a trailing Jenkins, shoveled the ball back to him and Jenkins stepped into the shot, letting it fly as time ran out. "I think every shot is going in," Jenkins said. "This one was no different."

The ball dropped through the net. Villanova won, 77-74, and Jenkins' teammates wrestled him to the floor as the clock showed zeros.

This was an emotional moment for Jenkins. His birth mother Felicia, who was grieving over the loss of a baby and struggling to raise a family, had just taken the Women's Basketball head coaching job at Benedict College in South Carolina. She asked Nate Britt Sr. and his wife, Melody—who she befriended at a basketball tournament—to take her son in during middle school, because she knew they could offer him a better life. The Britt family adopted Jenkins and treated him like a son. The two families remain close. After the game, there was a family reunion. Jenkins found Britt on the court and gave his step sister, Natalya a huge bear hug. Eventually, Nate Sr. and Jenkins' two mothers, Felicia and Melody, embraced. Nate Sr. had tears streaming down his face.

"We're one," Nate Sr. said. "I feel very bad for Nate and the Tar Heels because that's our son. I know how he feels. But the best team won. It was Kris' night. It's bittersweet. He's probably a little hurt, but his brother hit the shot and he'll tell you, I guarantee he'll tell you, 'I knew it was going in.'"

"This hurt," Britt admitted. "It's bragging rights, probably for the rest of our lives."

Villanova played the perfect game to defeat Georgetown, 66-64, to win the 1985 NCAA tournament. They won their second title with the perfect ending.

Jenkins thought about declaring for the draft that spring, but decided to stay in school for his senior year. The following season, when the Tar Heels made a second consecutive appearance in the NCAA tournament title game. Jenkins attended in support of his adoptive brother's team, sitting right behind the Tar Heel bench and wearing a Carolina T-shirt.

# Keith Smart
## (1987)

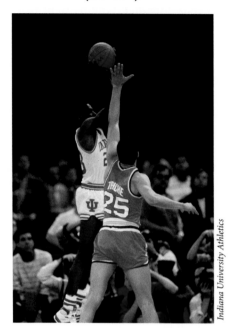

*Indiana University Athletics*

## Carved in Stone

Get Smart! It was the year the Hoosiers hit the big screen and Keith smart made a big shot! In 1987, the network cameras were focused in on Keith Smart. With five seconds to play, Smart drilled a sixteen-foot jump shot from the baseline to give Indiana a dramatic 74-73 victory over Syracuse and put an end to a riveting game that featured 18 lead changes, 10 ties, and Bob Knight's third NCAA title in eleven years.

## The Big Shot

Ten years earlier, Keith was a Boy Scout who worked Sunday afternoons as a volunteer usher at New Orleans Saints' NFL games at the Superdome. He was so far up in the stands, he needed a television just to watch the game.

Knight, a Hall of Fame inductee and the ultimate disciplinarian, had an unusual relationship with Smart. Knight preferred four-year-program prospects with a traditional Midwest work ethic. Smart was a free spirit with a junior college background.

Smart was from nearby Baton Rouge, LA, and quit his high school basketball team at mid-season during his junior year because he wasn't playing. During his senior year he broke his arm in a motorcycle accident after the third game and didn't play again.

When no one recruited him because of his size, he landed a job at a Baton Rouge McDonald's—"I flipped burgers, you know. Served 40 million a day," he said.

He also played daily at an area park, and after a year of pick-up games, one of the supervisors arranged a tryout at Garden City (Kansas) Community College.

Smart grew to 6'1", averaged 22.8 points and was being nationally recruited. Knight, feeling the talent pool in Southern Indiana had dried up, decided to think outside the box and made the decision to recruit junior college players.

Smart threw the first letter he received from Knight into the trash can. "I thought there was no way I could play for him," Smart said. "I'd always heard he beat his players, that it was like going into the Army. And I certainly didn't think he'd be interested in me."

The first time the two met, Smart was wearing gold chains and had a big city, wild haircut, with stripes around both sides leading to an arrow in the back. Both Knight and Smart made the necessary adjustments, with Smart cutting his hair, ditching the gold chains, and learning how to run Knight's complex offense.

"There is no one who ever could have dreamed up this kind of scenario for me," Smart said at the time. "I have hundreds of friends at home who still can't believe it's happening."

Knight brought in two junior college transfers to complement All-American guard Steve Alford. Smart provided quickness, and 6'10" Dean Garrett from San Francisco City College gave Knight a much-needed big man.

"No question, we wouldn't be where we are today without Smart and Garrett," Knight said. "If I had been inflexible, I never would have lasted in this business. But that doesn't mean I'm any easier on anyone. It just means I've adjusted my thinking."

Smart came up huge in the second half of that game, when he scored 15 of his 21 points in the final 12 minutes. Smart drove the length of the floor for a layup to cut Syracuse's lead to 73-72 with 30 seconds remaining. Then, after Syracuse future All-American center Derrick Coleman missed the first half of a one-on-one, Daryl Thomas grabbed the rebound with 28 seconds left and the Hoosiers held for the last shot. Most fans thought Alford would get the final shot.

But Smart got the ball to Thomas in the post with eight seconds left; he was covered, so Thomas reversed the ball back to Smart, who made Indiana University history the same year the Oscar-nominated movie *Hoosiers* hit the big screen.

"What do I remember most?" Smart said. "How quiet the arena got when the ball left my hand. And…all of a sudden…it went in."

# Mario Chalmers
## Mario's Miracle
## (2008)

*Kansas Athletics*

## Carved in Stone

Mario Chalmers never has to worry about his legacy at Kansas. He became Super Mario when it mattered most! Chalmers' game-tying three-point basket in the final moments of regulation in the 2008 national championship game, that set the stage for the Jayhawks 75-68 victory over Memphis, is shown on the overhead video board prior to introductions of Kansas basketball players before every game at Allen Field House.

## The Big Shot

There are pictures of "The Shot" hanging outside the Kansas practice facility and in bars and restaurants throughout Lawrence. There is even a mural of Mario's Miracle available for public viewing on the side of the new Two Light Luxury Apartments in Kansas City, just down the block from the Sprint Center.

Chalmers, who made his way to Kansas from Anchorage, Alaska, was a three-time state Player of the Year and a McDonald's All-American when he arrived on campus.

But the Jayhawks' 6'3" junior guard, who had won championships on every level in high school, college and the NBA with the Miami Heat, never had a bigger moment in his career than he did in the Jayhawks' 75-68 overtime victory against favored Memphis in the 2008 NCAA tournament championship game at the Alamo Dome in San Antonio.

He made the most of it, becoming Super Mario with the game on the line.

Memphis had a nine-point lead with 2:12 left in regulation, but the Tigers couldn't make free throws down the stretch—missing four of their final five attempts in the last 1:15—and Kansas had a chance to tie the game on the final possession, down three with 10 seconds to play after Memphis All-American guard, Derrick Rose, made the second of two free throws.

"You got to believe," Jayhawks' coach, Bill Self, said as he called the quick hitter from the bench.

Point guard, Sherron Collins, raced the ball up the court and handed it to Chalmers, who knocked down a wild three-point jumper with 2.1 seconds left and Kansas went on to win. It was one of the greatest shots in the history of the tournament and gave Kansas its first NCAA championship since Danny and the Miracles defeated Oklahoma in 1988.

"We knew coming into the game that their weakness was free throw shooting, so we knew that might be something to fall back on," he said. "Coach (Bill) Self just told us to keep fighting, to keep believing. That's what we did. With every shot we made, every stop we got, that just gave us more and more confidence.

"We ran the normal play we'd always run, called 'Chop,' which was a handoff for me coming off a screen, then with a back screen on the back side for Brandon Rush. I knew that was the play coach would call. We all knew that. We always knew that when it came to crunch time and we need a play, that's our go-to play. We ran that every day after practice. That's how we ended practice."

Chalmers said the shot felt good as soon as he released it. "I knew it was cash," he said. "As soon as it left my hand, I knew it was cash."

Chalmers was money from long range, making 47.6 percent of his three-point shots during the season. But none was bigger.

The Jayhawks had endured countless disappointments in the NCAA tournament and they looked as if they were headed for another until Chalmers' shot from the top of the key

"I was just looking at it with my mouth open," teammate Sasha Kaun said.

After the ball went in, Chalmers' teammates mobbed him as he returned to the bench for a timeout. At the other end, the Tigers walked off the floor, heads bowed.

"Once overtime started, we knew they were defeated," Chalmers said. "You could tell on their faces and by their body language that we sucked all the life out of them, and we took it from there."

Chalmers finished with 18 points on 5-of-13 shooting, including two-for-six from beyond the arc. He made all six free throws and had three assists and four steals. He was a natural choice for the tournament's Most Outstanding Player.

"It was just a dream come true to make that shot," he said. "As a kid, you dream about being in those moments. And you finally get here and you're successful in that moment, it's a great amount of joy. I'll always remember just how happy everyone was, not just for us as players, but for the university. That was the main thing. It was great going back and being in the parade."

Chalmers got to ride in a red Corvette for the first time that day. "It felt like everybody in the town was there," he said.

# Lorenzo Charles

## (1983)

*NC State Athletics Department*

## Carved in Stone

The Jimmy V story would not have been the same if it hadn't been for a young man converting a missed shot for an amazing victory. No one could have predicted North Carolina State (NC State) would stun heavily-favored University of Houston, with legendary future Naismith Hall of Famers Hakeem Olajuwon and Clyde Drexler, by winning the 1983 NCAA Tournament, butt that is what Cinderella stories are all about.

## The Big Shot

Sophomore forward Lorenzo Charles shocked the college basketball world when he grabbed an offensive rebound and flushed home a slam dunk at the buzzer after guard Derek Whittenburg threw up a wild thirty-foot air ball with time running out in regulation to give underdog State a 54-52 victory over the Cougars' mythical high-flying Phi Slamma Jamma fraternity at the Pit in Albuquerque, New Mexico.

That play, which led to Valvano racing around the court looking for someone to hug, has come to define the excitement of March Madness and will always symbolize the triumph of the underdog over the heavy favorite.

"It was kind of a David and Goliath thing," Charles recalled.

Charles was an unlikely hero.

The 6'7", 239-pound sophomore forward was born in Panama and grew up in a middle class Starrett City section of Brooklyn, New York. He was smart enough to secure a spot at Brooklyn Tech, a prestigious public school that specializes in math and science. Charles was recruited by St. John's, Maryland, DePaul, and Massachusetts, but Valvano couldn't make up his mind whether to recruit him after he had signed prep All-Americans, Dinky Proctor, Cozell McQueen, and Mike Warren.

Valvano finally signed him late on a recommendation from his assistant Ray Martin, but Charles, who arrived on campus as an impressible seventeen-year old kid, sat most of his first year and almost didn't make it to his sophomore season. The summer after his freshman year, he and three other athletes stole a couple of pizzas from a Domino's deliveryman on campus. Charles was arrested and faced felony charges that could have led to two years in prison. He was saved by a new first-offender diversion program that allowed him to expunge the arrest from his record, provided he reimbursed the company and did 300 hours of community service. He spent most of the pre-season washing squad cars for the North Carolina State's Department of Public Safety.

But he learned how to take life more seriously. Charles had to endure the backlash, including an incident at Duke where the Cameron Crazies showered Cameron Indoor Stadium with dozens of empty pizza boxes. He continued his community service throughout the season, visiting community centers in the Triangle to teach basketball skills and talk with kids about staying out of trouble.

On the court, Charles came into his own by the end of the season, averaging double figures and becoming a rebounding machine and an inside force to take pressure off outside shooters, Whittenburg, Terry Gannon, Sidney Lowe, and Thurl Bailey.

Lorenzo Charles saved his 15 minutes of fame for the final play of the championship game. The Pack, which had deliberately slowed down the game, forced a 52-52 tie-on a shot by Whittenburg, then got the ball back with 42 seconds remaining after Houston guard Alvin Franklin missed a free throw. State made 19 passes on the final possession and the game looked like it might go into overtime.

But then the outcome turned magical, because Charles—who had only scored one field goal in the first 39 minutes—was nowhere near where he was supposed to be to make the game-winning shot…but neither was the 7'0" Olajuwon, who briefly broke for the other end when he saw Benny Anders tip the ball out of Whittenburg's hands. The Dream couldn't recover in time when Whittenburg lofted his now-famous desperation air ball and Charles threw down an uncontested shot while he was still in mid-air.

"Most people say I was in the right place at the right time," Charles said. "Actually, I was in the wrong place at the right time. I was under the cylinder, which is exactly where you don't want to be if you are going to be a decent offensive rebounder."

Charles used the play as a springboard to become an All-ACC first team selection and an All-American two years later. He played one year in the NBA and twelve more with several international teams before retiring in 1999.

He and Valvano will always be linked in life and in death. Valvano coached at NC State until 1990 before becoming a popular ESPN broadcaster. He died in 1993 of cancer.

He is most remembered for giving an inspirational and memorable speech at the ESPYs that year, telling listeners to laugh, think, and cry each day, and saying "Don't give up. Don't ever give up." It was the inspiration for the V Foundation for cancer research.

Charles returned to Raleigh, where he worked as a bus driver for various transportation companies in the Triangle. He was driving a bus for Elite Coach of Apex when he was killed in an accident on I-40 in 2011.

Both men were 47 when they died and are buried in Oakwood Cemetery, three miles from campus.

# Dick Vitale's
# MOUNT RUSHMORE
## OF
# ALL LOCK
# HALL OF FAMERS

## JAY WRIGHT

## BILLY DONOVAN

## BRAD STEVENS

## JOHN BEILEIN

# Jay Wright

## (1995-Present)

Allen Kee / ESPN Images

## Carved in Stone

Jay Wright is starting to put up the kind of numbers that land you in Springfield, Massachusetts, home of the Naismith Basketball Hall of Fame. Jay has built one of the premier programs in college basketball, as shown by winning two championships in three seasons.

## The Naismith Nod

Wright was a young assistant at the University of Rochester when he attended his first Final Four in 1985 at Lexington, Kentucky. But he never got a chance to watch the late Rollie Massimino coach the perfect game when Villanova shocked heavily-favored Georgetown and Patrick Ewing, 66-64, at Rupp Arena that enchanted Monday night.

Wright's duties included running intramurals at Rochester and he had to return to campus Sunday night because he had a floor hockey tournament to take care of. He watched the championship game on TV with his wife and a fellow Villanova coach, Terry Garnett. Wright, who grew up in suburban Philadelphia as a huge Villanova fan, had tears in his eyes when the game ended.

Fast forward thirty-three years. Wright was hoisting his second national championship trophy in three years after the Wildcats defeated Michigan, 79-60, to win the 2018 national championship in San Antonio. All he could think about was Massimino, a fiery Italian elf who in August of 2017, succumbed to lung cancer at age 82 after a six-year battle. That's who started Wright on this journey that has led to 562 career victories and a 68.4 winning percentage. Beginning in 1987, Wright coached for five years for Massimino and has seamlessly carried on his family tradition at Villanova.

Wright's players wore an R.V.M. patch on their uniforms in memory of Massimino. "Coach Mass is here with us in spirit," Wright said. "I wish he was here to see this. He would love this team, especially Donte DiVincenzo."

DiVincenzo, the freakishly athletic 6'5" redshirt sophomore guard with the forty-inch vertical leap, was Wright's latest creation, lighting up Michigan for 31 points and five three-point goals to win the tournament's Most Outstanding Player award.

Wright was considered the hottest young coach in the country in 2001 when he left Hofstra for Villanova, after two consecutive NCAA appearances. He inherited a mediocre Big East program. It took three years to get the Cats up and running, but—beginning in 2005—he has coached them to twelve NCAA appearances in thirteen seasons and turned Villanova into one of the sport's blue bloods with his creative use of the three-point shot.

The Wildcats made a Final Four appearance in 2009, but the last four years have been special with four 30-win seasons, three Big East regular season and tournament championships, and magic moments in post-season play. Wright won his first national championship in 2016 when Kris Jenkins made a game-winning 3 as time expired to give the Cats a 77-74 victory over North Carolina in Houston. He won his second because he had a team that could spread the floor with shooters at every position and exploit the advantages that were presented both inside and out.

The Cats won all six tournament games in 2018 by an average of 17 points, making 18 three-point shots in a 95-79 national semi-final victory over Kansas. They had six players—junior point guard Jalen Brunson, the

*Phil Ellsworth / ESPN Images*

consensus national Player of the Year; DiVincenzo; a 6'9" redshirt junior forward, Eric Paschall; a 6'9" redshirt freshman, Omari Spellman; a redshirt junior guard, Phil Booth; and redshirt junior All-American forward, Mikal Bridges—who could make multiple trifectas in big game situations.

"This is the Golden State Warriors. This is a Draymond Green type of thing where your guys can shoot it, they can pass it, they can do everything," Michigan coach John Beilein said. "This is the way they play every day. This is what they do."

# Billy Donovan
## (1994-2015)

*Allen Kee / ESPN Images*

## Carved in Stone

Billy the Kid has always had a special place in my heart. From a great high school guard on Long Island, to a key in Providence's Final Four run in 1987, to cutting down the nets at Florida, and then the NBA sidelines. All I can say is…WOW!

Donovan sits at the top of his profession after accepting a five-year, $30 million offer to coach the NBA Oklahoma City Thunder in 2015, which has allowed him to work with superstar talents like Kevin Durant and Russell Westbrook.

Prior to that, he spent nineteen years building an empire at the University of Florida that included coaching the Gators to consecutive NCAA championships in 2006 and 2007, four Final Fours, multiple SEC championships, a streak of sixteen straight 20-win seasons and three SEC Coach of the Year awards.

But his rocket ship might have never lifted off if it hadn't been for his Hall of Fame college coach, Rick Pitino.

## The Naismith Nod

The fifty-two-year-old Donovan signed with Providence College out of St. Agnes High in Rockville Centre on Long Island, New York, but could not crack the starting lineup his first two years. He averaged two points as a freshman and three as a sophomore; his weight ballooned to 200 pounds.

When Pitino left his job as a New York Knicks' assistant to become the Friars' new head coach in the spring of 1985, Donovan informed him he wanted to transfer to a smaller school, possibly Fairfield or Northeastern, to get more playing time, but neither program was willing to offer him a scholarship. Pitino offered Donovan a clean slate and advised him to get himself in better shape for the upcoming season.

Donovan lost the weight and flourished in Pitino's new-age system, which stressed the three-point shot and full court pressure. By his senior year, he had picked up the nickname, "Billy the Kid," averaging 20.6 points, making first-team All-Big East, third-team All-American, and leading the sixth-seeded Friars on an unexpected run to the 1987 Final Four.

Those magical three weeks launched two careers. Donovan was drafted by the Utah Jazz in the third round of the draft, but was waived before the season started. He signed with the Wyoming Wildcatters of the Continental Basketball Association, hoping for another shot to play in the league. Pitino, who left Providence to return to the Knicks as head coach, signed him in December for the rest of the year.

Donovan was waived by the Knicks at the end of the season. He did not receive an NBA offer by the end of 1988 and realized he did not have a long-term future as a professional basketball player. In January 1989, he took a job with a Wall Street banking firm. Donovan was miserable during his brief time as a stockbroker making cold calls. After a few weeks in purgatory, he called Pitino and asked his advice on becoming a basketball coach.

Pitino was reluctant to recommend him, because Donovan had never been a vocal leader in college and he was unsure whether he had the communication skills required for the job. He told Donovan to give the financial sector more of a chance. Donovan called Pitino again in April to reaffirm his interest and Pitino, who was in the process of leaving the Knicks to become head coach at probation-racked Kentucky, agreed to bring him along as a graduate assistant to see if he had a future in the profession.

Donovan made the most of his opportunity.

A year after he arrived in Lexington, Donovan was promoted to a full-time assistant when Ralph Willard left to take a head coaching job at Western Kentucky. He played a major role as an associate head coach when Pitino led the Wildcats back to the national spotlight, taking them to a Regional final in 1992 and the Final Four in 1993. Donovan helped recruit the nucleus of Kentucky's 1996 national championship team before leaving for the head coaching job at Marshall.

He spent two years with the Thundering Herd, compiling a 35-20 record before he got his first big break. Florida Athletic

Director, Jeremy Foley, was concerned his men's basketball program, which advanced to a Final Four in 1994, was losing steam after Lon Kruger left to coach the NBA's Atlanta Hawks. Foley went looking for a young, energetic, and enthusiastic coach who could sustain success. During his search, Foley spoke with Pitino, who recommended the thirty-year-old Donovan. Foley agreed and offered Donovan a six-year contract.

Donovan inherited few talented players and suffered a two-year losing streak, but then Florida, benefiting from Donovan's relentless recruiting, caught fire, advancing to the 2000 national championship game before losing to Michigan State.

He reached the pinnacle of his success at Florida during the national championship seasons. Donovan's young team was just 10-6 in the SEC regular season, but came together in the postseason, defeating UCLA, 73-57, to win the school's first basketball title. During the championship celebration at the O'Connell Center, the Gators' entire starting five of Lee Humphrey, Joakim Noah, Al Horford, Corey Brewer, and Taureen Green announced they would return the following year and attempt to become the first team since Duke in 1991 and 1992 to win back-to-back championships.

The Gators won the SEC regular season, beating Kentucky for a sixth straight time, and won the SEC tournament, earning the Number 1 overall seed. They secured a second straight title by defeating Ohio State in a game where Pitino watched from the stands. With Florida football winning the 2007 BCS national championship, the Gators became the first school to hold both the football and basketball championships at the same time.

During Florida's national title runs, there were constant rumors Donovan might leave Florida to become head coach at Kentucky, but he calmed those fears by announcing he would never leave Florida for another college job. The NBA was a different story. In late May of 2007, the Orlando Magic offered Donovan the head coaching job, which was reportedly worth $27.5 million over five years. Donovan accepted the job and held an introductory press conference in Orlando.

A day later, he had second thoughts and returned to Florida. Orlando gave him his release with the stipulation he not accept another NBA job for five years. He stayed in Gainesville for another eight seasons, compiling a college record of 502-206 (a 71.1 winning percentage), before leaving for the Thunder.

Had he stayed in college, he would have been a strong candidate to become the 2020 Olympic coach. Donovan was unbeaten in the International Basketball Federation (FIBA) youth basketball competition. He coached two Under 18 (U18) teams to gold medals in two FIBA Americas tournaments and another U19 team to a gold medal in the 2013 World Championship in Prague.

Ironically, Donovan's and Pitino's careers have dovetailed in different directions in the past year, with Donovan continuing to grow and Pitino, who won two national championships himself, getting fired at Louisville after the program was pulled into a bribery and corruption scandal following a three-year investigation by the FBI.

"I feel sad," Donovan said. "I wouldn't be where I am today without Rick Pitino and the investment he made in me.'"

# Brad Stevens

## (2008-2013)

*Butler Athletics*

## Carved in Stone

What an incredible accomplishment: back-to-back Final Fours coaching at Butler! Brad Stevens is a basketball prodigy who has been compared to John Wooden.

## The Naismith Nod

Stevens coached at Butler for just six years from 2007-2013, but elevated the profile of the school by coaching the Bulldogs from the Horizon League to a pair of consecutive Final Fours in 2010 and 2011 as well as a national championship game against Duke in 2010, all at the young age of just 33. He eventually left to sign a seven-year, $22 million contract with the NBA Boston Celtics in 2013.

Stevens' ceiling seems unlimited. He has led the Celtics to a 2017 Atlantic Division title, four consecutive playoff appearances from 2015 through 2018, and coached the East team in the 2017 All Star game.

Stevens averaged a school-record 26.8 points at Zionsville Community High near Indianapolis. He had a strong passion for basketball but modest ability, so he decided to attend academically-oriented DePauw University in Indiana, where he became the captain of the team and was a three-time Academic All-America nominee. Stevens spent summers teaching at DePauw's summer basketball camp, but thought his career was over when he graduated with honors with a degree in economics in 1999.

He accepted a high-paying job with pharmaceutical giant Eli Lilly, but he was upset about leaving basketball. He coached at a summer camp at Butler upon graduating and was offered a job as a volunteer coach in the Butler basketball office by Thad Matta in 2000.

He ran the idea of quitting his job at Eli Lilly by his (now) wife, Tracy Wilhelmy. Tracy thought about it for just two hours before telling him to go for it.

"Now, it looks like a great idea," Stevens later remarked. "At the time, I thought it was something I really wanted to try."

Tracy went back to school to get a law degree at Case Western to support the couple if things did not work out for Brad. "We were 23 and realized this was our chance," Tracy later said. "Five years down the road, we were probably not going to be in a position to do that. The more success he had at Lilly, the harder it would be to leave."

Stevens took a job at Applebee's to support himself, but the day before pre-season training, he was elevated to director of basketball operations at a salary of $18,000. He spent fourteen hours a day for a year, logging footage of opposing teams' defensive tendencies before he was promoted to a full-time assistant coaching position for the 2001-02 season after Matta left for Xavier and was replaced by Todd Lickliter. On April 4, 2007, knowledgeable Athletic Director, Barry Collier, who was urged by the players to promote from within, hired Stevens as head coach after Lickliter left for Iowa, giving him a seven-year contract. Stevens was 30 at the time.

"Age wasn't a factor because I'd seen his ability to shine throughout the season," Collier said.

In his first year, Stevens led Butler to 30 wins and an NCAA second round appearance. In 2010, his third year as a coach, Stevens coached the Bulldogs to 33 wins and the first Final Four in school history at hometown Indianapolis. He became the second-youngest head coach behind Bob Knight of Indiana to make an NCAA national championship game, losing to Duke, 61-59, at Lucas Oil Stadium. Butler forward, Gordon Hayward, missed a desperation half-court heave at the buzzer.

*Butler Athletics*

In 2011, Stevens coached Butler to 28 wins and became the youngest coach to go to two Final Fours, leading the Bulldogs to a second consecutive national championship game before losing to Connecticut in Houston.

Stevens, who has a calming personality on the sidelines and a puzzle-solving mind, was the hottest coach in the country. He increased his personal profile when he appeared on David Letterman, threw out the first pitch at a Cubs game, and spurned multi-million dollar offers from Oregon and UCLA while signing a long-team deal worth $1 million to remain at Butler. He also increased Butler's recruiting profile, restoring the glory of playing **b**efore sellout crowds at Hinkle Field House.

Then, in 2013, after coaching Butler to a 166-42 record, a 79.2 winning percentage and five NCAA appearances, the Celtics made him an offer he couldn't refuse; so his legacy continues.

# John Beilein
## (1978-Current)

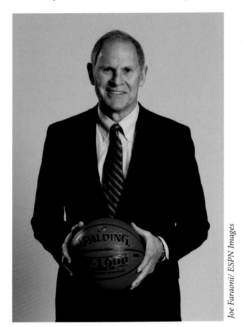

*Joe Faraoni/ ESPN Images*

## Carved in Stone

Michigan coach John Beilein has been one of the most creative coaches in college basketball for 40 years and it is about time he gets the credit he deserves after he led the Big Ten Wolverines to a second national championship game in 2018.

The sixty-five-year-old Beilein has won 799 career games and is the only active coach to achieve 20-win seasons at four different levels—junior college, NCAA Division III, Division II, and Division I, and has the most wins coaching at Michigan. But it took him a while to establish his reputation.

## The Naismith Nod

Beilein was born in Burt, New York, near Buffalo, the eighth of nine children of a mill worker and an apple farmer. His mother's cousins were the inspiration for the World War II drama, *"Saving Private Ryan."*

He played college basketball at tiny Wheeling, West Virginia College and worked his way up the coaching ladder while learning on the job. Beilein has never spent a day as an assistant coach, jumping right into the head coaching job at Newfane High School as a twenty-two-year-old making pitstops at Erie Community College, Nazareth, LeMoyne, Canisius, Richmond, and West Virginia, before getting the chance to resurrect a stagnant program at traditional Big Ten power Michigan.

Syracuse Hall of Fame coach, Jim Boeheim, still talks about making the ten-minute drive across town to the gym at LeMoyne to watch Beilein practice. Boeheim slipped in unannounced, just to watch the young Michelangelo at work.

"Some coaches, you talk about what their specialty is," Boeheim said. "John's specialty is winning."

Beilein is a coaches' coach. He has used his programs as an experimental laboratory. He has constantly been ahead of the curve, installing a spread offense with stretch fours, skilled fives, and point guards that can do a little bit of everything. His system emphasizes constant motion, passing, backdoor cuts, and 3-point shooting…and it's a nightmare to guard.

Beilein arrived at Michigan in 2007 at age 54 after coaching West Virginia to an Elite Eight, a Sweet 16, and an NIT championship in five years with unknown soldiers like center Kevin Pittsnogle and guard Mike Gansey, a transfer from St. Bonaventure's. Beilein inherited a team that was in the final year of scholarship reductions from the Ed Martin Fab Five scandal.

*Phil Ellsworth / ESPN Images*

He won 20 games his second season, defeating both UCLA and Duke in non-league play, and he took his team to the first of eight NCAA tournaments in eleven seasons. Four years later, he coached a team of undervalued players—including first team All-America point, Trey Burke, from Columbus, who was passed over by Ohio State, to the Number 1 ranking and a surprise trip to the Final Four for the first time since 1993. While the Wolverines lost to Louisville, 82-76, all five starters eventually made it to the NBA.

Michigan almost made a return trip the next season, advancing to the Elite Eight before losing to Kentucky on a buzzer-beater by Aaron Harrison. Beilein proved he has staying power by winning consecutive Big Ten championships in 2017 and 2018 and advancing to another Final Four in 2018, relying heavily on 6'11" junior forward, Moe Wagner, and 6'6" Kentucky transfer, Charles Mathews, plus a gritty defense.

Beilein is used to micromanaging his players' lives on the court. It is part of his success. But all of his hard work almost came tumbling down on a windy day in March, 2017, when the Wolverines were flying a private charter to the 2016 Big Ten championship in Washington, D.C.

As the plane barreled down the runway at Willow Creek airport at 190 miles per hour, the pilot pushed the throttle forward. The plane began the roll and the pilot eased back on the yoke. Nothing happened. There was a damaged pushrod that helped control the right elevator. If the elevator can't move, the plane can't lift off.

The pilot hit the brakes and the plane slid beyond the pavement, onto the grass, over a fence, stopping short of a stand of trees and a ravine. But he saved all 100 souls on board. They were safe.

Beilein remembers the winds had knocked out electricity at his home and he needed a flashlight to find a new suit in his closest. The players returned to their apartments to collect new clothes and toiletries. The team re-convened at 5:30 the next morning for another flight the day of the first round of the conference tournament. They proceeded to win all four games.

"I hope that, in the long run, it shakes me up a little," Beilein said. "That I have a better perspective on life. You think you're going to get to the bottom of the hill sometime on a rough toboggan ride. On that plane we had no idea what was going to happen. I don't want those things to happen to anybody, but maybe that's God sending me a message. You've got to get life right, because there's so much more in life. We all appreciate that right now."

# *Dick Vitale's*
# MOUNT RUSHMORE
## OF
# ALL MR. MARCH

## TOM IZZO

## JOHN CALIPARI

## MIKE KRYZEWSKI

## RICK PITINO

# Tom Izzo

## (1995-Present)

*Phil Ellsworth / ESPN Images*

### Carved in Stone

Tom Izzo was the perfect guy to replace his mentor, Jud Heathcote. Izzo represents the blue collar work ethic of the many people in East Lansing area. He is as good as it gets as a person as well as a coach. He has a heart of gold…trust me, I know from his generosity helping me raise money for the V Foundation for kids battling cancer.

At Michigan State, fans reverently refer to Spartans' basketball coach Tom Izzo as Mr. March because of his past success in the NCAA Tournament. Izzo led the Spartans to the 2000 NCAA tournament championship, the 2009 national championship game, seven Final Fours, eight Big Ten championships and five Big Ten Tournament championships in his 23 years as head coach. He has a record of 574-225 and a winning percentage of 71.8.

## March Magic

Izzo's journey to his 2016 induction into the Naismith Hall of Fame is the culmination of hard work that started when he was growing up in Iron Mountain in the Upper Peninsula of Michigan. At the age of twelve, he went to work in the family business, Tony Izzo and Sons, which started as a shoe repair business and expanded into carpeting and awnings. He remained there until college.

"Having to work early in my life—that was a pain in the butt then, but I wouldn't trade it for the world now," he said.

He has passed that philosophy on to his players.

Izzo met best friend and former NFL coach Steve Mariucci as a child and both attended Iron Mountain High, where they were teammates on the football, basketball, and track teams. The two went on to attend Northern Michigan University, where they were roommates. Mariucci was a three-time Division II All-American quarterback who led NMU to the 1975 national football championship. Izzo was a four-year starting guard on the basketball team who was a Division II All-American as a senior in 1977.

Both wanted to get into coaching and placed a friendly wager over who would be the first one to coach at Notre Dame.

It never happened. Mariucci found his way to the NFL, where he was the head coach of the San Francisco 49ers and then Detroit Lions from 1997 to 2005. Izzo spent seven years as a part-time assistant at Michigan State before working his way up to a full-time job on Jud Heathcote's staff in 1986 where he was eventually elevated to associate head coach 1991. After Heathcote, who coached Magic Johnson and the Spartans to a national championship in 1979, retired following the 1995 season, he recommended Izzo as his successor.

Two years later, Izzo coached Michigan State to the first of 20 consecutive NCAA tournament appearances, currently the third-longest among Division I teams. Izzo has a record of 47-19 in NCAA tournament games and in 1999 took his team to the first of three straight Final Fours, the third longest of all-time, and coached the Spartans to six Final Fours between 1999 and 2010.

Much of Izzo's success centered around his team's toughness, defense, and rebounding. He is famed for his "War" rebounding drill in which players wear football helmets and shoulder pads. Izzo made a huge dent in the state by recruiting blue-chip players who fit his style from the bleak, industrial city of Flint, Michigan.

When Izzo coached the Spartans to a national championship, he had three starters from that city—senior All-American point guard, Mateen Cleaves, late-blooming senior forward, Mo Petersen, and sophomore guard Charlie Bell. The media nicknamed his team "The Flintstones." All three, and senior forward, AJ Granger, came up huge when Michigan State defeated Billy Donovan's young Florida team, 89-76, in the championship game in Indianapolis.

Petersen, playing for his grandmother, Clara Mae Spencer, who had died the previous week, led the Spartans with 21 points and was selected Most Outstanding Player of the tournament.

Like Krzyzewski, Izzo was romanced by the Atlanta Hawks, Chicago Bulls, Cleveland Cavaliers, Orlando Magic, and New Jersey Nets for head coaching jobs in the NBA. After a brief flirtation with the Cavs in 2010, Izzo reported to the schools' Board of Trustees that he would remain at Michigan State and stated he was a "Spartan for life."

# John Calipari
## (1988-Present)

UK Athletics

## Carved in Stone

There aren't many that could handle the pressure of coaching in Big Blue Nation as winning is a must. John Calipari was the perfect hire as he brought to the table many of the coaching philosophies of Rick Pitino when he had Kentucky on top of the world.

I love teasing Cal about the days when he was at the University of Massachusetts; he would meet us in the parking lot when we arrived for an ESPN telecast to share what was happening with his program. Man, how things have changed now. At Kentucky, you have to make appointments to get a chance to see him before a game.

### *Life in the big time, baby!*

He really handles it well. At Kentucky, the Big Blue nation does not believe in rebuilding, only reloading. In that respect, Calipari has been the perfect choice to coach this elite program. Ever since he became head coach in 2010, Calipari has made the Cats a factor in March Madness.

## March Magic

Coach Cal won a national championship in 2012 and has coached the Cats to four Final Fours in 2011, 2012, 2014, 2015. He has a 273-64 record, an 80.1 winning percentage, two Elite Eights in 2010 and 2017, and a Sweet 16 in 2018. That alone would have been enough to earn Calipari induction into the Naismith Hall of Fame in 2015.

What has set Calipari apart from other elite coaches is that he has fashioned his success in the Bluegrass with the recruitment and development of 21 one-and-done players like guard, John Wall, center, Anthony Davis, and forward, Karl Anthony Towns, who were the Number 1 picks overall in the 2010, 2012, and 2015 NBA drafts, respectively. He also produced center DeMarcus Cousins who, along with Davis, was a member of the 2016 Olympic gold medal team in Rio.

Calipari has coached at University of Massachusetts (UMass), Memphis, and Kentucky. In his 22 official seasons, his record is 667-194 (.775). His record in the month of March is 107-37. His official record in the NCAA tournament is 38-12 (.760) and 15-6 in the NIT. His teams have made fifteen NCAA appearances, including 12 trips to the Sweet 16, ten Elite Eights, and six Final Fours, reaching the NCAA championship game three times.

Two of his Final Four appearances, in 1996 with UMass and 2008 with Memphis, were later vacated by the NCAA, but Calipari's name was never mentioned.

Calipari has twenty-one 20-win seasons, nine 30-win seasons and three 35-win seasons. His 2015 team won thirty-eight straight games before losing to Wisconsin in the national semi-finals. Calipari has also coached six teams to the NIT, winning the NIT championship in 2002. He is one of only four coaches in NCAA Division I history to lead three different schools to a Number 1 seed in the NCAA tournament.

The 59 year-old Calipari was born in Moon Township, in the shadow of the Pittsburgh Airport, where his father worked refueling airlines. He was a point guard who played for both UNC-Wilmington and Clarion State. He got his start in coaching as an assistant at Kansas under Ted Owens and Larry Brown, before leaving for an assistant coaching job at Pittsburgh.

Calipari got his first head coaching job at UMass in 1988 when he was just 29, inheriting a program that ranked 295 in the RPI. He coached the Minutemen to five consecutive Atlantic 10 titles and NCAA appearances from 1992 through 1996, advancing to the Sweet 16 in 1992 and the Elite Eight in 1995, before moving on to the Final Four in his final year at Amherst. His team spent part of the 1993 and 1996 seasons ranked Number 1.

Calipari was named Atlantic 10 Coach of the Year three times and won several national Coach of the Year awards in 1996 when 6'10" Marcus Camby, the Wooden Award winner, led the Minutemen to the Final Four. But their appearance was later vacated when it was discovered Camby had accepted $40,000 from a sports agent with no connection to the program. He was luring him to enter the NBA draft after his sophomore season.

Calipari transformed Mass into a dominant program during his tenure, despite having just two draft picks—Camby and forward, Lou Roe. He also helped accelerate the construction of the Mullins Center, UMass' basketball and hockey facility, and turned UMass into the state's team before moving on to the head coaching job with the NBA New Jersey Nets.

He was with the Nets for three seasons, reaching the playoffs in 1998. The Nets were considered a sleeper team in 1999, but Calipari was fired after the team got off to a 3-17 start. He joined Larry Brown as an assistant with the Philadelphia 76ers for a year and half before becoming the head coach at Memphis in 2000. He won 214 games there, reviving a stagnant program with seven consecutive 20-win seasons to earn seven consecutive postseason bids and winning 38 games to advance to the national championship game in 2008, when he was selected Naismith national Coach of the Year.

The Tigers played Kansas in the finals and had a three-point lead with 10 seconds left. It looked like they might win the title before Jayhawks' guard Mario Chalmers forced overtime with a desperation three-point jumper and Kansas went on to win, 75-68 in overtime. The Tigers had their entire season vacated by the NCAA after the Clearing House invalidated All-American guard, Derrick Rose's, SAT scores.

Calipari made his biggest jump after the 2009 season, when he accepted the Kentucky job after Cats' head coach Billy Gillespie was fired after two unsuccessful seasons at the school. Calipari signed a contract worth $34.65 million over eight years. He started his own dynasty in the Bluegrass state, winning his first national championship in 2012 with a 36-1 record.

The Cats defeated Kansas, 67-59, getting 16 points, six blocked shots, five assists, three steals and six points from 6'10" freshman, Anthony Davis, who was selected Most Outstanding Player of the tournament. Davis, a first-team All-American, averaged 15.2 points, 11.2 rebounds, and 4.6 blocks in six games, leading the Cats to their eighth NCAA championship.

# Mike Krzyzewski
## (1975-Present)

Phil Ellsworth / ESPN Images

### Carved in Stone

I firmly believe, when you ask today in the modern era, who is the best active coach in all of sports, there is one answer. My choice would be Mike Krzyzewski. His ability to consistently have Duke in the running for a national title, plus what he did internationally with the USA Olympic teams, has been simply awesome baby, with a capital A!

Duke's Hall of Fame Coach Krzyzewski has built an impressive resumé himself in the modern era, where all but one of his NCAA appearances were played in a 64-to-68 team field, as opposed to the days when only the conference champion was eligible to participate in a 24 or 32 team bracket. The winning team must win six games over three weeks to be crowned national champion.

Coach K has coached Duke to five national championships and a record twelve Final Fours during his 43-year career at Army and Duke. He has won a record 90 NCAA tournament games during that stretch.

## March Magic

Krzyzewski has won many of his historic games in March, defeating Connecticut and Kentucky in the regional finals on last-second shots by Christian Laettner in 1990 and 1992 and upsetting previously-unbeaten, top-ranked UNLV in the 1991 national semi-finals on the way to his first national championship.

The most dramatic game in the Krzyzewski March Madness era might be the Blue Devils' 95-84 comeback victory over ACC rival Maryland, in the 2001 national semi-finals in Minneapolis. The Blue Devils, who got 25 and 23 points from their two All-Americans, Shane Battier and Jay Williams, wiped out a 22-point first half deficit to defeat their troublesome ACC rivals for the third time in four games.

None of the games was easy. In the two teams first meeting that season, the Devils rallied from a 10-point deficit in the final minute to win in overtime at Cole Field House in College Park. The Terrapins spoiled Duke's Senior Day, rallying from a 10-point deficit after center Carlos Boozer fractured his right foot with 10 minutes to play to defeat the Devils, 91-80, at Cameron Indoor Stadium. In the ACC semi-finals, Duke rallied from an 11-point deficit and won, 84-82, on a tip-in by fifth-year senior forward Nate James.

This time, it looked like Maryland might bury the Devils. Maryland's star guard, Juan Dixon, scored 16 points in the first half and was the catalyst for a Terrapins' suffocating defense that was determined not to let Duke shoot threes. Krzyzewski made two adjustments at half that changed the outcome. First, he told his team to stop running plays and just play. Secondly, he switched the 6'6" James onto Dixon.

The Blue Devils came back with a furious surge, outscoring Maryland by 33 points, and 57-35 in the second half, despite the fact Battier and Williams shot a combined 13-for-31. James limited Dixon to just three points in the final 20 minutes. Boozer, who missed six games before returning for the NCAA Eastern Regional Sweet 16, also came up huge, scoring nine of his 19 points in the final five minutes as the Devils completed one of the biggest comebacks in NCAA tournament history.

Two nights later, they had enough energy left to defeat Arizona, 82-72, as Mike Dunleavy Jr. scored 21 points, making a career-high five three-pointers and Battier contributed 18 points, 11 rebounds, and six assists …to give Coach K his third national championship.

# Rick Pitino
## (1978-2018)

Louisville Athletics

## Carved in Stone

Rick Pitino was a young genius and a one-time counselor at Howard Garfinkel's Five-star camp. He built a rich tradition at four different schools—Boston University (1978-1983), Providence (1985-1987), Kentucky (1989-1997) and Louisville (2001-2017)—on his way to induction into the Naismith Hall of Fame in 2013. He also coached the NBA New York Knicks (1987-1989) and the Boston Celtics (1997-2001), before leaving coaching in 2018 with an overall college record of 629-234 and a 73.2 winning percentage.

## March Magic

The 65 year-old Pitino coached two different schools—cross-Commonwealth rivals, Kentucky and Louisville—to national championships in 1996 and 2013, although the latter was vacated by the NCAA. He is the only coach to lead three different schools—Providence, Kentucky and Louisville—to a Final Four. He is one of only four coaches in NCAA history, along with Dean Smith, Mike Krzyzewski, and Jim Boeheim—to take his school to the Final Four in four separate decades.

Pitino was born in New York City and attended Massachusetts, where he was a standout point guard, playing on the same team with Naismith Hall of Fame forward, Julius Erving, and NBA guard, Al Skinner. He graduated in 1974, spending time as an assistant at Hawaii and Syracuse before taking the head coaching job at Boston University (BU) in 1978 at the age of 26. In the two years prior to his arrival, the Terriers had won a total of seventeen games. Four years later, in 1983, they made their first NCAA appearance in 24 years.

Pitino left BU to become an assistant with the Knicks under the great Hubie Brown. He returned to the college game in 1985 to become head coach at Providence, a struggling Big East team that had gone through a dismal 11-20 season the year before he arrived. Two years later, Pitino led the Friars, with point guard, Donovan, to the Final Four.

Pitino was nomadic. He left Providence after its Final Four run to become head coach of the Knicks, then returned to college basketball in 1989 to become the coach at Kentucky. The fabled SEC program was recovering from a major recruiting scandal that cost Eddie Sutton his job and left the school on two years of NCAA probation. Pitino quickly restored Kentucky's reputation, losing on a last-second shot to Duke in overtime during the 1992 NCAA Eastern Regional finals, and then leading his second school to a Final Four in 1993.

Pitino's best team at Kentucky was his 1996 Cats, which finished 34-2 and won the NCAA championship, defeating Syracuse, 76-67, at the Meadowlands. Known as the "Untouchables," nine players from that team – Derek Anderson, Tony Delk, Walter McCarty, Ron Mercer, Nazr Mohammed, Mark Pope, Jeff Sheppard, Wayne Turner, and Antoine Walker all eventually played in the NBA. Kentucky made it back to the national championship game in 1997, losing to Arizona in overtime. The following year, he left Kentucky for the NBA Boston Celtics, and Kentucky went on to win the 1998 national championship under Tubby Smith.

He would later refer to Kentucky as "The Roman Empire of college basketball."

Who knows how many championships he would have won if he had stayed in Lexington. He was an exceptional player-development coach. It turned out, the Celtics' experiment was a failure and Pitino returned to college basketball again in 2001, this time at Kentucky's arch-rival Louisville, angering many in the Big Blue nation. Pitino had his share of success at Louisville, becoming the only coach to lead three different schools to the Final Four, when he led the Cardinals tho the Big Dance in 2005. The Cardinals advanced to three more Regional finals in 2008, 2009, and 2012 before defeating Michigan, 82-76, to win a national championship in 2013.

Pitino's life was hardly perfect off the court. The NCAA charged Pitino with failure to monitor after an NCAA investigation into an escort sex scandal. The school self-imposed a post-season ban in 2016. Then, the NCAA did the unthinkable, stripping Louisville of its title and 2012 Final Four for the involvement of a former assistant coach.

Pitino's brilliant career ended prematurely in 2017 when federal prosecutors in New York announced the school was under investigation for an alleged "pay for play" involving a recruit at Louisville. The allegations stated that an Adidas executive conspired to pay the family of a top-ranked national recruit to play for Louisville. The athlete would then represent the shoe company when he turned pro. Pitino and Athletic Director, Tom Jurich, were placed on administrative leave and eventually dismissed. To this day, Pitino denies knowing anything about the deal.

# Dick Vitale's
## MOUNT RUSHMORE
### OF
## ALL FRANK LLOYD WRIGHT COACHES

BOBBY CREMINS

JIM CALHOUN

JOHN CHANEY

LUTE OLSON

# Bobby Cremins
## (1976-2012)

*Georgia Tech Athletics*

## Carved in Stone

Trust me, I learned first-hand of the competitive spirit of Bobby Cremins, as I faced off against him in the Jimmy V golf and tennis classic on several occasions. He has the drive to win. My first memory of Cremins goes back to his days of being part of the underground railroad from New York City to Columbia, South Carolina. Frank McGuire, in the 1950s, was watching his team get taken. His answer? Get better players. Those players would come from New York, where the streets raised young people up on the game. His recruiting tactics would become known as the Underground Railroad, a team-building technique that helped his team, but not nearly as much as he helped the kids he brought in to play.

As a basketball lover, I was very familiar with Frank McGuire's team featuring Tom Rkier, Kevin Joyce, Brian Winters and, of course, their tenacious point guard, Bobby Cremins. Cremins has the Bronx flowing through his veins. The son of Irish immigrants, he is a New York story, a guy from the borough who went through various transformations in his life, going from being a teenage gangster, to basketball star, to a bellhop, to a graduate student, and finally to a successful basketball coach.

## The Architect

When Cremins was fifteen years old, he was a member of a New York street gang, the Gladiators—they were involved in car thefts, muggings, and robberies. Fortunately, Cremins found a way out through basketball, winning a scholarship to attend All Hallows High, and then Frederick Military Academy as a post graduate where South Carolina had coach, Frank McGuire. McGuire established his pipeline for New York Catholic League players migrating south and he offered Cremins a scholarship.

At first, Cremins struggled with campus life, but—eventually—he became a starting point guard for three years and the captain of South Carolina's 25-3 team. Cremins left Columbia, South Carolina, without a degree and was cut from two ABA teams before playing a year in Italy. When he returned to the states, he had no money and took a job at the Waldorf-Astoria as a bellhop. Six months of carrying luggage was enough to send Cremins back to Columbia to get a degree in marketing, which led to assistant coaching jobs, first at Point Park in Pittsburgh, and then under his former coach McGuire at South Carolina.

Cremins used that experience as a springboard to his own job. At 27, he became one of the youngest head coaches in history when he took over the head coaching position at Appalachian State. He inherited a program that had only won 22 games since joining Division I five years earlier; they were coming off a 3-23 season. Cremins had a limited knowledge of X's and O's, but he had learned how to recruit his hometown from McGuire. Six years later, he had won three Southern Conference regular-season championships and earned an automatic bid to the NCAA in 1979 after winning the conference tournament.

Cremins' success at Appalachian State gained him national attention, including catching the eye of Georgia Tech Athletic Director, Homer Rice. Tech had recently joined the ACC and Rice, who was looking to build a program that could compete with his new rivals, felt Cremins was the right man for the job, hiring him in April of 1981.

Cremins walked into a brutal situation, inheriting a program that was 4-23 overall and winless in the ACC. He won ten games his first year, thirteen his second, and then took the Jackets to the NIT in 1984—its first postseason berth in 13 years. A year later, he had assembled a team that included Mark Price, John Salley, Yvon Joseph, Tom Hammonds, Duane Ferrell, and Bruce Dalrymple, which shocked the ACC by winning a share of the regular season, then winning the ACC tournament before advancing to the Elite Eight with a record of 28-7. In 1990, Cremins' "Lethal Weapon Three" team with freshman point guard, Kenny Anderson, and wing shooters, Dennis Scott and Brian Oliver, reached the NCAA Final Four with a 28-7 record.

Cremins was named ACC Coach of the Year three times in 1983, 1985, and again in 1996, when the Yellow Jackets won the ACC regular season championship. He was honored as the Naismith National Coach of the Year during that special 1990 season.

He developed a reputation of creating an assembly line for his players to make the successful transition to the NBA, including Price, Salley, Anderson, and Stephon Marbury, and he was an assistant to Lenny Wilkens on the 1996 U.S. Olympic team that won gold in Atlanta.

Cremins was tempted to leave Georgia Tech in 1993, when he agreed to coach basketball at his alma mater, South Carolina, but changed his mind three days later to continue at Georgia Tech. With his platinum blond hair, Cremins became an iconic figure on campus and it was common for fans to show up for games at Alexander Memorial Coliseum wearing blond wigs.

Cremins announced his retirement after the 1999-2000 season with a 25-year coaching record of 424-303. He was far and away the winningest coach in Georgia Tech history and, in 2003, Georgia Tech named the basketball court at Alexander Memorial Coliseum, "Cremins Court."

Cremins turned down numerous offers to coach during his retirement. Instead, he toured the country doing motivational speeches, doing TV commentary, and working with charities like Coaches vs. Cancer and the Jimmy V Foundation. In 2006, Cremins returned to coaching at the College of Charleston, hoping to restore the program there to the mid-major power it was under coach John Kresse. He coached the team to four 20-win seasons in six years and upset a North Carolina team that was ranked Number Nine in the country in 2010.

But all stories need to have a final chapter. Cremins took a medical leave of absence in January of 2012, which lasted the duration of the season. He retired from coaching that March, citing physical exhaustion.

# Jim Calhoun

## (1973-2012)

UConn Athletics

### Carved in Stone

Man, I just marvel when I think about what Jim Calhoun achieved in Storrs, Connecticut. It was only a couple of years earlier, before being an original member of the Big East, that the Huskies were competing in the Yankee Conference. You read that right–the Yankee Conference.

There are four national championship banners hanging proudly at Gampel Pavilion.

Calhoun is the most successful college basketball coach in the history of tradition-rich (but NBA Boston Celtics-oriented) New England. He is best known for transforming the University of Connecticut from a regional to a national power, winning three national championships in 1999, 2004, and 2011, advancing to four Final Fours, winning the 1988 NIT title, 10 Big East championships and seven Big East tournament championships.

When he won his final national championship in 2011 at 68, he became the oldest coach to win a Division I men's title. He won his 800th game and finished his career with 873 victories. In 2005, he was inducted into the Naismith Hall of Fame.

## The Architect

"The thing that stands out to me is, it's one thing to take over a Duke or a Kentucky and build it and win games and championships," Syracuse Hall of Fame coach Jim Boeheim said, "but 26 years ago, Connecticut wasn't thought of in the college basketball world. He turned them into one of the top programs in the country. I think it's really, to me, the greatest building job that anyone has ever done."

The 75-year-old Calhoun made an improbable trip to the pinnacle of his profession. Born and raised in Braintree, Mass., he was a star high school athlete. After his father died of a heart attack when Calhoun was 15, though, he was left to watch over a large family that included five brothers and sisters. Calhoun received a basketball scholarship to Lowell State, but only attended school for three months, returning home to help support the family. He worked as a granite cutter, headstone engraver, scrap yard worker, shampoo factory worker, and grave digger.

After 20 months, he returned to college, this time at American International in Springfield, Mass., where he was given a basketball scholarship. Calhoun was the leading scorer and captain of a Division II playoff team. He graduated in 1968 with a degree in sociology.

Calhoun began his coaching career in high school. After coaching Dedham (Massachusettes) High to a perfect season and the Massachusetts High School state championship in 1971, he was recruited by Northeastern University to become the Huskies' head coach and oversee the transition from Division II to Division I in 1978. Calhoun coached Northeastern to four NCAA tournament appearances and in his final three seasons, the Huskies achieved automatic bids to the tournament and had a 72-19 record. He developed a reputation for producing under-recruited stars like Reggie Lewis into NBA prospects.

In 1986, Calhoun was named head coach at the University of Connecticut. In just his second year, he won 20 games and went on to defeat Ohio State to win the NIT championship in 1990. Calhoun was named national Coach of the Year two years later when the Huskies won their first Big East championship and advanced to the NCAA Elite Eight with a 29-6 record.

UConn Athletics

Calhoun won the school's first NCAA championship in 1999 when the Huskies upset favorite Duke in St. Petersburg, Florida, with Rip Hamilton leading the team to a 77-74 victory. Calhoun won another championship in 2004. The Huskies started and finished the year as the Number 1 team in the country and their two stars, Emeka Okafor and Ben Gordon, were selected Number 2 and Number 3 in the NBA draft. On April 4, 2011, Calhoun won his third national title when the Huskies defeated Butler behind the brilliant play of All-American guard, Kemba Walker.

Throughout his career, Calhoun was bothered by health problems. In 2003, he announced he had been diagnosed with prostate cancer and he took an immediate leave of absence from the team, undergoing surgery three days later to have his prostate removed. He returned six days later and was on the sidelines for his team's game against St. John's. On May 30, 2008, the school announced Calhoun was undergoing treatment for squamous cell carcinoma. The next year, Calhoun fell during a charity bike race and broke five ribs. On Feb. 3, 2012, he took a medical leave because of spinal stenosis, returning the next month after having back surgery. Finally, on August 4th of that year, he suffered a left hip fracture while bike riding.

Calhoun retired that fall, after a 26-year career.

Aside from his wins and losses, his legacy will include producing 31 NBA players, and he and wife Pat will always be known for their philanthropy. His legacy included the Pat and Jim Calhoun Cardiology Center at UConn and the annual Jim Calhoun Holiday Food Drive which has raised nearly $1 million to support food assistance agencies that serve families throughout the state.

UConn Athletics

Calhoun stayed retired until 2017 when he took a job building a new program at tiny University of St. Joseph's, a Division III school located in suburban Hartford that just began admitting men. Calhoun said he wants to become the first men's coach at the Catholic university, which has a total enrollment of 2,400 and a gym that seats about 1,200 people. I wish him continued success in his work and his health.

# John Chaney

## (1973-2006)

*Atlantic 10 Conference / Temple University*

## Carved in Stone

When people in sports talk about a fierce competitor, I simply think of John Chaney, who was as intense a competitor in the coaching fraternity as I have ever met.

John had to battle many a stumbling block, but nothing would stop him in attaining greatness. As they say, the cream always rises to the top, and he became one of the best ever to grace the sidelines in the City of Brotherly Love.

## The Architect

When the 6'3" guard, John Chaney, was a senior at Ben Franklin High School in 1951, he was selected the outstanding player in the Philadelphia Public League. Tom Gola was selected the Catholic League Player of the Year at La Salle High School. Gola, a 6'8" precursor to Magic Johnson, was recruited by everyone in the country, including Kentucky, Navy, and North Carolina State. He eventually signed to play for La Salle, located in his neighborhood of Olney. He led the Explorers to the 1954 national championship and played for the NBA Philadelphia Warriors. Chaney did not have any local offers and wound up at Bethune-Cookman in Florida, where he once scored 60 points in an NAIA tournament game. He was good enough to play in the NBA but was relegated to the old Eastern League because of the unspoken quota system that existed in the league at the time.

When Chaney got into coaching, he had to work his way up the ladder, teaching and coaching at Simon Gratz High before becoming the head coach at Cheyney State, a Division II school in suburban Philadelphia. Chaney turned Cheyney into a national small college power, posting a 232-56 record and winning a Division II national championship in 1978.

As a black coach in a barely post-civil rights era, he found it difficult to get a Division I job. Finally, in 1989, he caught a break when Temple president Peter Liacouras, intrigued by John Thompson's success at Georgetown, felt Chaney could take the Owls to another level.

When he hired Chaney, there was some backlash since Don Casey, the Owls' coach, had been a two-time Eastern Coach of the Year and was coming off a 19-win NIT season.

But Chaney eventually delivered on his promise to transform Temple into a national power. He built a reputation as a tough disciplinarian who always demanded excellence on and off the court and was well known for his 6:00 A.M. practices. He taught old-school, fundamentally-sound basketball, suffocating match-up zone defense, willingness to play anyone in tough non-conference schedules, and winning teams.

The 86-year old Chaney, who was born into poverty in the depression, fought his way to success. He won a total of 741 career games and had a 516-253 record in 24 years at Temple. His best team in 1988, which featured freshman guard and first team All-American, Mark Macon, finished 32-2 and was ranked Number One headed into the NCAA tournament. The Owls reached the Elite Eight that year, before losing to Duke.

*Atlantic 10 Conference / Temple University*

They advanced to the Elite Eight four more times in 1991, 1993, 1999, and 2001; and they made seventeen NCAA and six NIT appearances.

Chaney's career was not without controversy. He always had a competitive edge and his rage spilled over one day in 1994 when he threatened to kill then-UMass coach, John Calipari, at a post-game news conference, where Calipari was speaking at the podium. Chaney entered the conference, mid-speech, accusing Calipari of manipulating the officials because of a brief interaction Calipari had with one of the three officials after the game.

When Calipari attempted to respond to the accusation, Chaney yelled, "Shut up, goddamn it!" and proceeded to charge the stage, before being stopped by security. While being held back, Chaney shouted, "When I see you, I'm going to kick your ass!" As security restrained Chaney, he repeated himself, yelling, "I'll kill you!" and he angrily admitted telling his players to "knock your freaking players in the mouth."

Chaney received a one-game suspension for the incident. The two coaches later reconciled. Chaney praised Calipari's coaching ability and defended him in the Derrick Rose controversy at the University of Memphis.

Chaney never made it to a Final Four, but in 2001, he was elected to the Naismith Hall of Fame as a true pioneer in the game. Chaney announced his retirement from coaching in 2006 at a press conference, effective after Temple's appearance in the NIT.

# Lute Olson

## (1973-2007)

*Arizona Athletics*

## Carved in Stone

If there was ever an example of a coach that was a Frank Lloyd Wright, and deserved to have a court named after him, it was Lute Olson. When I think of Lute, I always see a smiling face at his side in his late wife, Bobbi. She was also instrumental in the success of Arizona basketball. (They were married for 47-years until her passing from ovarian cancer in 2001; he is remarried, today.) They were a dynamite *team* together and had great pride in Wildcat hoops.

The University of Arizona (UA) unveiled a statue of Hall of Fame basketball coach Olson in the spring of 2018. He was carrying the 1997 national championship trophy under one arm and waving to the crowd with the other, with a smile on his face.

In 24 seasons in Tucson, Olson put Arizona basketball on the map. He had a record of 589-184 (75.9 winning percentage) at UA. He had an overall record of 780-280 in 34 years before retiring in 2007. Olson led the Wildcats to four Final Four appearances, 23 consecutive NCAA tournaments and 11 Pac-10 titles, as well as the national championship.

When his statue was unveiled outside the McKale Center on campus, the distinguished-looking 83-year-old coach—who still has a magnificent shock of white hair—looked it over and pronounced, "They got the hair right."

## The Architect

Once a game, inevitably, Olson appears on the large video board and the sellout crowds react appropriately. "Luuute."

"It's nice that they recognize that this whole thing started when I first came here," Olson said. "I tell Kelly (his wife) that it's better than people throwing things at us."

Olson is an icon for the way he resurrected a program in this sleepy retirement community. It had suffered through its worst season in school history at 4-24 with only one Pac-10 win in 1983; and transformed it into an elite program.

Newly-hired UA athletic director, Cedric Dempsey, fired Ben Lindsey after only one season and hired Olson as his successor. UA needed a coach with a history of quickly turning around programs, which Olson had done previously at Iowa.

"I knew we had a tremendous amount of work to do," Olson said. "The program was in shambles at that point after the terrible year before."

Olson quickly woke the program up. In only his second year, the Wildcats recorded their first winning season in six years and made the first of what would become 23 consecutive NCAA tournament appearances. A year later, in 1986, Arizona won its first Pac-10 title. Then, in 1988, the Wildcats spent much of the season ranked Number 1 and made their first Final Four.

Olson was voted Pac-10 Coach of the Year seven times and coached the Wildcats to 20 straight 20-win seasons. His teams won forty-six NCAA tournament games, defeating three Number 1 seeds, Kansas, North Carolina, and Kentucky, on their 1997 national championship run. He was elected to the Naismith Hall of Fame in 2002.

One of Olson's greatest strengths was player development. He produced fifty-two NBA draft picks, including thirty-one at Arizona, and he coached nineteen All-Americans. Luuute had stars like Sean Elliott, Steve Kerr, Gilbert Arenas, Mike Bibby, Damon Stoudamire, Miles Simon, Chris Mills, Richard Jefferson, Luke Walton, and Andre Iguodala.

Olson, who was born in Mayville, North Dakota, knew he wanted to be a basketball coach from the time he was in ninth grade. He was willing to work hard to achieve his goals. When Olson accepted a scholarship to play football and basketball at tiny Augsburg College, he would finish up with athletics, then work the overnight shift at a local filling station, cleaning grease bays, restocking shelves, and waiting on customers… for four years. In the summers, he worked for Minneapolis Bottling, delivering soda and beer.

In his first coaching job at Mahnomen, Minnesota, near the Great Lakes, he coached three sports (head basketball and baseball coach and assistant in football) and taught six classes. He lined the football field on game day. Mahnomen didn't have a baseball diamond, so Olson's team had to play all their games on the road and practice on the football field. In his second year, the team won its first basketball championship in 32 years.

Olson coached high school for thirteen years at places like Two Harbors, Minnesota, and in California at Anaheim and Huntington Beach. His success translated into a job at Long Beach City College, where he spent four more years in the background, before he became head coach at Long Beach State. He was only there for one year before leaving for Iowa, but the 49ers finished 24-2 and were ranked 3rd in the AP poll behind Bill Walton's UCLA team and eventual national champion NC State. Long Beach never got to play in post season because they were serving a three-year NCAA probation for sanctions against previous coach, Jerry Tarkanian.

*Arizona Athletics*

Olson resurrected a stagnant Iowa program that had finished 10th in the Big Ten the year before he arrived, in 1974. The distinguished-looking, silver-haired Olson coached the Hawkeyes for nine years and was the winningest coach in school history with a 161-91 record. After two years of progressive improvements, he led the Hawkeyes to five consecutive NCAA tournaments from 1979-1983, the Big Ten title in 1979 and an NCAA Final Four in 1980. The Hawkeyes lost to eventual national champion Louisville, 80-72, in the 1980 national semifinals. They had the Cardinals on the ropes before guard Ronnie Lester, who scored the first 10 points of the game, suffered a season- ending knee injury eight minutes into the game. Iowa advanced to the Sweet 16 in 1983.

Then Olson surprised the Iowa faithful by leaving for an Arizona program that had just suffered the worst season in school history, winning only four games and one in the Pac-10. He said he left Iowa because life in Iowa City had become a fishbowl and he needed a change in scenery; he was off to create a dynasty in the desert.

# *Dick Vitale's*
# MOUNT RUSHMORE
## OF
# ALL DIPSY DOO DUNKAROOS

## DARRELL GRIFFITH

## DOMINIQUE WILKINS

## CLYDE DREXLER

## JEROME LANE

# Darrell Griffith

## (1976-1980)

*Louisville Athletics*

## Carved in Stone

Darrell Griffith was one of college basketball's first astronauts, a 6'4" guard who defied gravity and was appropriately known as "Dr. Dunkenstein" because of his 48-inch vertical leap when he led the Louisville Cardinals to the 1980 NCAA tournament championship.

His nickname came from George Clinton's Parliament-Funkadelic music collective of rotating musicians from two individual bands—Parliament and Funkadelic—whose distinctive funk style drew on psychedelic culture, outstanding fashion, science fiction, and surreal humor. Griffith's brother Michael came up with the idea because he was a big fan of Parliament, a band which had a song called, "Dr. Funkenstein."

## Dipsy Doodling

Griffith was a local hero at Louisville Male High School and was heavily recruited by colleges all over the country. Griffith, the only high school player invited to the 1976 Olympic trials, reportedly turned down an offer to forgo college and sign with the ABA Kentucky Colonels. He opted to attend the University of Louisville, much to the delight of Cardinals' fans.

From there, he proceeded to write his own legend, leading the Cardinals to a 105-25 record that included four NCAA appearances, two Metro Conference regular season titles, and two conference tournament championships, showcasing his astonishing leaping ability and hang time.

"Nobody could fly like Darrell could," Memphis coach Dana Kirk once said. "He could dip his wings twice in salute as he passed over the rest of us."

Griffith averaged 18.2 points, 4.6 rebounds and 2.9 assists during his career and became the first Cardinals' player to surpass 2,000 points, finishing with 2,333.

Griffith was projected as a TopFive pick in the NBA draft as a junior, but he returned to fulfill a promise he made to the locals to bring the city a first-ever NCAA championship. He worked hard to make it happen, staying in the gym until midnight in the summer, working out with a weighted vest. He would position volleyball practice stations (tall nets held up by metal poles) on the court and place baseball gloves on top of them to simulate opponents' hands.

He made his teammates work just as hard that summer, borrowing a key to the gym from coach Denny Crum and organizing marathon late night pickup games.

Griffith stepped up big-time as a senior, averaging 22.9 points and shooting 56.3 percent, an otherworldly

*Louisville Athletics*

statistic for a guard. He scored in double figures in thirty-four straight games, was a consensus first team All-American, and National Player of the Year in 1980. More importantly, he led a young Louisville team (with four sophomores in the starting lineup) to the national championship. The Doctors of Dunk went 33-3 and defeated UCLA, 59-54, in the national championship game.

Griffith scored 23 points against the Bruins, none of them dunks. He ignited a game-winning rally, hitting sophomore guard Jerry Eaves for two field goals and draining a jump shot to break a 54-54 tie with 2:21 remaining.

Griffith dedicated the game to Jerry Stenger, who was dying of cancer. The next day, the team visited Stenger, who was bedridden at home, and draped the strands of the net around his head.

Griffith was drafted by the Utah Jazz with the second pick in the first round of the 1980 draft and was selected the 1981 Rookie of the Year. He played in the league for eleven years, but he never forgot his hometown community. He lives there now; he opened a restaurant called "Griff's" on the campus of the Univeristy, built a new gymnasium, known as the Darrell Griffith Athletic Center, for the

West End School for Boys, and started a Foundation for youth in the community that holds festivities around the Kentucky Derby each year.

"When you retire, you've got to take another course in your life and you have more time to do some of the things that I'm doing," he said. "I don't do it for publicity. This stuff I do is what I'm supposed to do."

The city of Louisville has never forgotten Griffith, either. There is a five-story mural of him dunking in a Louisville jersey on the Waterson City building as part of the city's Hometown Heroes program.

*Louisville Athletics*

# Dominique Wilkins
## (1980-1982)

*UGA Sports Communications*

## Carved in Stone

T alk about a high-wire act! Dominique Wilkins was like my buddy, Nik Wallenda, an aerial act that had no equal. He was a dipsy doo, dunkaroo machine.

Prior to Dominique Wilkins' arrival at the University of Georgia in 1979, the Bulldogs' basketball program was buried near the bottom of the Southeastern Conference and had never played in post-season. The high-flying 6'8", 200-pound small forward lifted Georgia to new heights during his three years on campus. He averaged 21.6 points, grabbed 7.5 rebounds and had electrifying, swooping, windmill dunks that put him in the same rarefied air as Elgin Baylor, Connie Hawkins, and Julius Erving.

## Dipsy Doodling

Wilkins earned the famous nickname "The Human Highlight Film" for his gravity-defying play when he started for Hugh Durham. The great thing about Wilkins' dunks is he combined the power and strength of

Shawn Kemp and Karl Malone with the creativity of Michael Jordan and Erving. He had all the tools necessary to explode to the rim—a forty-seven-inch vertical leap, as well as the ability to run a 48-second quarter mile and a 22-second 220-yard dash.

He was more than just a mad dunker, though. Averaging 21.6 points, 7.5 rebounds, and shooting 53 percent from the field and 75.2 from the line from 1980-1982, he reinvented his SEC team that went 53-27 before advancing to the NIT in 1981. That year, Wilkins averaged 23.6 points, 7.5 rebounds and shot 53.3 percent. He was selected SEC Player of the Year, as well as second team All-American. Wilkins was a first team All-American the next season when the Bulldogs returned to the NIT and advanced to the semi-finals, before losing to Purdue. He made All-SEC three times.

Wilkins was the most exciting player ever to wear a Georgia basketball uniform.

Wilkins was born in the basketball hotbed of Paris, France, the son of an airman in the U.S. Air Force. He was named by his French babysitter. When he was three, the family moved back to the states, first to Dallas, and then Ft. Sill, Oklahoma, before settling in Baltimore. Wilkins learned the game on the concrete playgrounds of Sparrows Point and Patterson Park, playing against the likes of Earnest Graham, who later played at Maryland, and Skip Wise, a playground legend who played a year at Clemson before his career was cut short by drugs.

Wilkins learned quickly, "If you want to get the ball, you have to get the ball" and he became a relentless offensive rebounder.

The first time Washington, North Carolina High coach, Dave Smith, saw him play was at Bridge Recreation Center the year he was visiting his grandmother the summer before he was supposed to enter Patterson Park High. Smith was blown away by his talent and convinced Wilkins to stay in the same state as a young Michael Jordan. Wilkins and his family moved to North Carolina and Wilkins, who grew from 6'3" to 6'8" as a sophomore, led tiny Washington High to a pair of AAA state championships, averaging 29 points and 6 rebounds.

Wilkins made it into the "Faces in the Crowd" section of Sports Illustrated for a performance against a higher-classification school, when he scored 48 points, had 27 rebounds, nine dunks, and eight blocked shots. He went on to star in the McDonald's All-American game with 16 points and 12 rebounds.

Dozens of schools recruited him, but most expected Wilkins to sign with North Carolina State (NC State), following in the footsteps of the ACC's original spacewalker, David Thompson. Wilkins surprised everyone when he signed with Georgia, a school that had been considered a longshot.

UGA Sports Communications

"Our approach was you can go to NC State and be the second coming of David Thompson, or you can come to Georgia and be the one and only Dominique Wilkins," Durham said.

After Wilkins signed, the townsfolk who once revered him did not react well, breaking windows in Wilkins' grandmother's house and spilling paint on a car they felt had been purchased for him by Georgia boosters. Wilkins' mother said she purchased the car from a local car dealer who lowered the price because of Wilkins' fame. No NCAA charges were filed against Georgia.

"It was my decision," Wilkins said. "I lost a lot of friends over it."

Norm Sloan, the former NC State coach who had moved to Florida, said his only regret was not getting a chance to coach Wilkins. "You never expect to coach a player like David Thompson," Sloan said. "I almost got a chance to coach two."

The extroverted Wilkins made an immediate impact as a freshman, averaging 18.6 points and 6.5 rebounds while mesmerizing the crowd with an array of dunks, including a spectacular 180-degree slam dunk against Alabama midway through the season. The feat has since been commemorated on the Georgia campus in posters of all sizes. Later in the same game, he suffered a sprained knee. He did not play the last 13 games of the year.

Wilkins had a breakout year as a sophomore. He found it hard to forget the bitterness of recruiting and hammered Sloan's Gators for 37 points when the two teams met in January of 1981. The Dawgs went on to finish 19-12, their best record in fifty years. (It's no wonder he was the first basketball player at Georgia to have his number retired.)

After the NIT that year, Wilkins considered leaving school for the NBA at the end of a spectacular sophomore season. He was offered a four-year deal by Detroit worth $1.6 million, but he pulled out eight hours before the April 25 deadline for filing. He did leave the following season and was selected by Utah as the Number Three pick overall in the 1982 draft. The hometown Atlanta Hawks eventually secured his rights and Wilkins became their greatest player ever, making nine All-Star appearances and scoring 50 or more points on eight different occasions, before being inducted into the Naismith Hall of Fame in 2006.

# Clyde Drexler
## (1980-1983)

*University of Houston Athletics*

### Carved in Stone

The Phi Slama Jama team, composed by Guy V. Lewis, was special to me in many ways. It was the first time that I was assigned to the Final Four by Scotty Connal, the head of ESPN's remote productions. The reason it stood out to me was because I stated the Cougars could not win a national championship with a freshman point guard. Reid Gettys and many of the Houston faithful took exception to that statement.

They came very close to proving me wrong as Lorenzo Charles found a way to bring jubilation to Raleigh, North Carolina. I learned to appreciate the talents of Clyde "The Glide" Drexler.

### Dipsy Doodling

When Drexler was younger, no one knew he had wings.

The 6'7" Drexler was a self-described chubby kid from the South Park neighborhood of Houston. He was too slow, couldn't jump, and was constantly picked last—if at all—in pickup games. So, he reinvented himself, adopting a regimen of self-discipline and weight training that turned him into a high flier with a 43-inch vertical leap.

As a senior at Sterling High, Drexler was an all-state selection who experienced success playing against older NBA stars like Moses Malone and Robert Reid at Fonde Recreation Center. But he might have gone unnoticed on the recruiting scene if not for Houston signee, Michael Young, who told a University of Houston assistant, Terry Kilpatrick, that Drexler was the best player he faced all season.

Drexler signed with the Cougars and went on to earn the nickname, "Clyde the Glide." He was the unofficial president of Houston's fabled, make-believe fraternity, Phi Slama Jama, and he helped the Cougars advance to two consecutive NCAA Final Four appearances. Houston fell short, losing to North Carolina in the 1982 semi-finals and then to Jim Valvano's NC State Wolfpack, 54-52, in the 1983 finals when Lorenzo Charles scored off an air ball at the buzzer.

The nickname Phi Slama Jama, aka "Texas' tallest fraternity," was originally coined early in the season by Thomas Bonk, a columnist for the Houston Chronicle, and it caught on quickly. The players wore Phi Slama Jama in red script across their warm-up jerseys.

University of Houston Athletics

Once the games began, the Cougars played a frenetic, playground-influenced style that was diametrically opposed to the fundamentally polished, methodical style taught by purists like John Wooden, who disapproved of dunking. Guy V. Lewis not only condoned dunking, but he insisted on it because he felt it produced high percentage shots.

The space cadets who made up Phi Slamma Jamma, like Drexler, Larry "Mr. Mean" Micheaux, Hakeem "The Dream" Olajuwon, and Bennie "The Jet" Anders, had been influenced by the freewheeling style of play pioneered in the old ABA and its most famous player, Julius "Dr. J" Erving.

"Sure 15-footers are fine, but I like to dunk," Drexler once said.

Drexler—who raised eyebrows when he was with the NBA Portland Trail Blazers by dunking on an 11'1" hoop—was known as a great finisher and acrobatic dunker. He was the most versatile player ever to wear a University of Houston uniform and the only one to finish with more than 1,000 points, 900 rebounds, 300 assists, and 250 steals in his career.

Drexler averaged 15.2 points and 10.5 rebounds as a sophomore when Houston advanced to the Final Four for the first time since 1968, when Elvin Hayes was in school. He averaged 15.9 points and 8.8 rebounds the next year and was a first team All-American and the MVP of the old Southwest

Conference. He had shot 53.6 percent and 73.7 from the line for a balanced 31-3 team that advanced to the national championship game in Albuquerque.

In the national semi-finals of that tournament, Drexler scored 22 points and Phi Slama Jama defeated the descendants of Louisville's "Doctors of Dunk," 94-81, in a wild dunk fest in the second half that is still described as the most exciting eight minutes of basketball in the history of the tournament. Houston soared for thirteen dunks in that wild second half.

Drexler, who finished with 21 points and four dunks, supplied one of the most thunderous moments in that game.

Houston led 58-57.

Drexler flew down the floor with the ball.

Clyde the Glide approached the basketball hoop.

He cradled the ball in his right hand and started to slam it.

Then, he brought it back and finished with a mighty two-handed dunk.

"I wanted them to think first I was going to dunk it and if they thought I was going to dunk it, I'd pass it," he told reporters. "But I changed my mind and two-handed slammed it."

Then the earth shook. Phi Slamma Jamma threw down four straight dunks in the 4,900-foot attitude to rock the sellout crowd at the Pit and introduce them to the 21st century game.

Drexler declared for the NBA after his junior year. He was selected by Portland with the Number 14 pick overall and went on to play for the 1992 Olympic Dream Team. He has since been inducted into the Naismith Hall of Fame.

My friends, it was fun to watch Clyde the Glide!

*University of Houston Athletics*

111

# Jerome Lane
## (1985-1988)

*Pitt Athletics*

## Carved in Stone

If you want the true definition of a Dipsy Doo Dunkaroo, look no further than the elevator man, the high-riser, and Mr. Slam, Bam, Jam…Jerome Lane!

I can still hear the words, *'SEND IT IN, JEROME!'*

Jerome Lane is in this group because of his backboard-shattering dunk five minutes into the game against Providence in a 1988 Big East game at sold-out Fitzgerald Fieldhouse.

## Dipsy Doodling

Lane was a 6'3", 170-pound McDonald's All-American from LeBron James' alma mater, St. Vincent's-St. Mary's High School in Akron, Ohio. Lane grew to a powerful 6'6", 230-pounds in college and became the first player 6'6" or under, since Boo Ellis of Niagara in 1958, to lead the NCAA in rebounding with an average of 13.5 rebounds. It prompted teammate, Demetrius Gore, to rap about it in his self-produced "Pitt on the Rise" video:

*Getting all the boards*
*Like he is insane*
*Is that board crashing, brother,*
*Je-Rome Lane*

Lane's career will always be defined by one play—the moment he shattered the glass backboard with a ferocious tomahawk dunk on January 25, 1988.

The reaction from ESPN's colorful announcer, Bill Raftery, was a breathless exclamation of, "Send. It. In, Jerome!"

Those four words became part of Big East lore, immortalized on T-shirts and in highlight reels ever since.

"It just popped out," Raftery said. "There was no preconceived notion about it. I'm sure I probably heard it somewhere along the way…maybe."

Lane left the sellout crowd and the national television audience in awe on a Big Monday. The play began after a steal by Sean Miller, who had a three-on-two fast break. He could have passed the ball up the floor to Jason Mathews, streaming down the left side, but instead passed it to Lane, who was gathering steam filling the lane.

Lane caught the ball and elevated over Providence's 6'0" guard, Carlton Screen. The dunk sounded like a light bulb had popped. When Lane first landed, he had no idea the bottom part of the backboard had shattered, leaving a gaping hole in the middle of the box. The rim was left hanging by a thread until the Pittsburgh mascot grabbed it and paraded around the arena with it in his hand.

"I didn't realize anything until I looked at Demetrius Gore. His mouth was wide open. Then I saw the glass on the floor. It came down like snow."

At first there was a sense of shock in what just happened.

"Everyone paused for like, five seconds because no one understood what had just happened," opponent Mathews said.

Rafferty was just calling out, "OH! OH!"

"I was trying to get away from the glass coming down because I was right under the basket," said Matthews. "I'm no physicist, but he caught it at the right angle with the right force. Most rims are used to people pulling on them straight up and down. Not at a diagonal."

Pitt Athletics

Lane is believed to be the first college player to shatter a backboard since the introduction of breakaway rims. His explosion set off a four-minute standing ovation as the whole crowd went wild. A few fans raced onto the court to grab shards as mementos. Leo Czarnecki swept up the rest and posted them onto wooden placards with the words "a piece of the Action from Pitt basketball, 1-25-88." He distributed them as gifts to the administration and members of the national media.

"Hold on at home. Here we go again. We gotta get a cut man out here to get the glass out of Jerome's hair! This is amazing," Raftery added, as the replay footage rolled. "A good dish, but he's ready, right by the foul line. Bring it down and BRING IT HOME, JEROME!"

It was thirty-two minutes before a replacement backboard was brought out.

"SMASHING!" the scoreboard flashed at the fans.

Yes, it was. Absolutely smashing, Baby!

# *Dick Vitale's*
# MOUNT RUSHMORE
## OF
## ALL AT&T
## LONG DISTANCE

### STEVE ALFORD

### CHRIS MULLEN

### REGGIE MILLER

### STEPH CURRY

# Steve Alford

## (1984-1987)

*Indiana University Athletics*

## Carved in Stone

Steve Alford epitomizes a saying from one of my New Jersey pals, years ago: "A boy, a ball, a dream."
Alford is the prime example of an athlete who got the maximum out of his talent by developing an incredible thirst for success. He didn't just talk about it, he worked feverishly to achieve his goals. It is not lost on basketball historians that the movie "Hoosiers" came out in 1987, the same year that Indiana won the national championship.

Steve Alford was the reincarnation of the character, Jimmy Chitwood, who made the game-winning shot for tiny Hickory in the mythical Indiana state high school championship game against Muncie Central in the 1950s. He was the ultimate Hoosier hero to all those kids of all ages who grew up shooting hoops on a basket put up on the side of a barn in the rural part of that rabid basketball state.

Alford achieved his ultimate dream in college when he scored 23 points and made the pass that led to Keith Smart's last-second game-winning jump shot in Indiana's national title game victory over Syracuse in New Orleans.

It was his destiny.

## The Long-Distance Tale

Alford was a self-made player who routinely wore out six or seven nets every summer while practicing shooting. In his workouts, he would pick a spot on the floor and take ten shots. If he did not make eight, he would punish himself with finger-tip push-ups or wind sprints. Alford's hard work paid off. He went from averaging 1 point as a varsity player in ninth grade to 37.2 points as a high school senior, playing for his father, Sam, at New Castle Chrysler High. He went off for 57 in the state tournament semi-final loss to Connersville and won the state's Mr. Basketball award.

Alford attended Bob Knight's basketball camps in Bloomington since sixth grade. He committed following his junior year of high school to play for the fiery genius.

The 6'2" Alford made an immediate impact, quickly disproving skeptics who claimed he was too slow and too frail to play in the Big Ten. He bulked up from 150 pounds to 180, as a freshman, and was a perfect fit for Knight's motion offense, moving without the ball and coming off screens to make effortless 20-foot jump shots. Alford led Indiana University in scoring for all four years, averaging 19.5 points and shooting 53.3 percent for his career. He was a three-time All-Big Ten selection and a two-time All-America as a junior and senior.

"Everybody talks about his hair, his all-American image, how mothers would want him to marry their daughters," Alford's wife, Tanya, once said. "Everybody thinks he's so perfect. Well, that's an accurate image. That's exactly what he is."

Playing for Knight was demanding. The General was tough on his best players and constantly threw Alford out of practice as a freshman to improve his mental toughness. That year, Alford helped lead Indiana to a stunning upset of Michael Jordan and North Carolina in the NCAA East Region semi-finals.

Knight knew how valuable Alford was. He made Knight's 1984 U.S. Olympic team because Knight realized he needed someone who could consistently knock down jump shots if international teams went zone. During the tryouts that summer, Jordan bet Alford $100 he wouldn't last four years at Indiana.

"Tell him I owe him $100," Jordan said later.

Alford averaged 10.3 points and shot 64.4 percent for the U.S. Olympic team, playing with future Hall of Famers Jordan, Patrick Ewing, and Chris Mullin—the Americans breezed through the competition.

When Alford drove home to Indiana with his parents after winning the gold medal, there were billboards all over the state saluting him on his accomplishment. Alford was close with his father, having watched all but two of his games growing up. He wound up giving him his gold medal in a tearful ceremony at the high school to make up for the last loss of his prep career.

Knight was tough on Alford all four years. Indiana was like attending a Paris Island boot camp, but Alford was mature enough to write it off as Knight's way of motivating his players.

Alford played all but one year in the pre-three-point era or his numbers would have been much higher. As it was, he helped popularize the shot during his senior year, making 7 of 10 three pointers against the Syracuse zone in the title game, including one at the end of the half that gave Indiana a one-point lead.

At the end of his college career, Knight said, "[Alford] has gotten more out of his abilities offensively than anybody I've ever seen play college basketball. He's about as good a scorer for being strictly a jump shooter as I've ever seen. He's scored more than 2,400 points that way, and that's incredible, considering he doesn't get any tip-ins, drives or, dunks."

Historically speaking, it's even more incredible. Were the three-point line in place during his college years, that number goes up past 2,800, a feat that would still have him standing as the Hoosier's all-time leading scorer (currently Calbert Chaney with 2,438 points).

Indiana fans wanted the Pacers to draft Alford, but they took Reggie Miller instead. Alford's size and quickness caught up to him in the NBA, and he played just four years as a backup, before getting into college coaching. He is currently the head coach at UCLA.

# Chris Mullin

## (1982-1985)

*St. John's Basketball*

### Carved in Stone

**M**an, I remember those golden days in the Big East, when the Mecca of college basketball, Madison Square Garden, was rocking and rolling, baby. I loved watching the passing wizardry of Mark Jackson, who would always try to get the rock to the sweet-shooting lefty, Chris Mullin.

Mullin was the classic New York City star during the Lou Carnesecca era at St. John's.

He was a key reason that Madison Square Garden was rocking and rolling, baby! I loved seeing those Big East rivalries, like the Redmen vs. the Hoyas and the Orangemen. It was a special time with hoops hysteria.

### The Long-Distance Tale

The versatile 6'7" guard, Mullin, was born in Brooklyn, where he played Catholic Youth Organization (CYO) basketball at St. Thomas Aquinas Grammar School and attended Carnesecca's basketball camp from the time he was in the sixth grade. He played for fabled Power Memorial, the home of Kareem Abdul-Jabbar, then transferred to Xaverian High in Bay Ridge because he wanted to be closer to his neighborhood.

Mullin led Xaverian to the New York state federation championship and became a McDonald's All-American, then signed with St. John's, a large commuter Catholic university in Queens in 1981, turning down offers from both Duke and Virginia from the more established ACC. He became a star in the then-recently-formed Big East.

Mullin went on to become the Big East Player of the Year and was selected to the All-American team his last two years in 1984 and 1985. He played on the 1984 United States Olympic team that won a gold medal in Los Angeles.

He was a self-made player who used to sneak into the gym in high school, just to shoot hoops by himself. He lived at home during college but got a key to Alumni Hall from the late Katha Quinn, the school's beloved Sports Information Director. He was such a fanatic that he would stay there until Carnesecca chased him out. One time, during a huge blizzard that buried the city, he stayed in the gym for two days working on his game.

"If I'd have listened to what people projected, I'd probably have quit playing in high school, because everyone said I was too slow," he said.

The left-handed Mullin was an old-school player who drew comparisons to NBA legend Larry Bird because both players lacked speed, had a great outside shot, and had the innate ability to keep defenders off guard. Mullin used trademark jab steps and crossover dribbles to free himself up for smooth jump shots, which made him a fan favorite. He was also a symbol of home-grown talent by choosing to make a name for

St. John's Basketball

himself in his own backyard. He singled handedly revived basketball in the Big Apple. New Yorkers' interest in college basketball rose, filling Madison Square Garden as St. John's battled Georgetown and Patrick Ewing for dominance in the Big East in the early 1980s. The schools had four memorable battles during the 1985 campaign.

Mullin averaged 19.5 points, 4.1 rebounds, 3.6 assists, and 1.7 steals, in 37.4 minutes for St. John's during his storied career. He finished with 2,440 points. All that time as a gym rat turned him into the best pure shooter in the history of that storied league. Mullin shot 55 percent from the floor and 84.8 percent from the line during his career.

"Chris was one of the best shooters we ever played against," former Georgetown Hall of Fame coach, John Thompson, said. "We would grab him, hold him, try everything we could to mess up his rhythm. And Chris would still get open and get his shots. He was tough."

He was the catalyst for St. John's historic Final Four run in 1985. Mullin scored 30 points against Kentucky and 25 against North Carolina State, as the Red Storm won the NCAA West Regional before losing to powerful Georgetown in the national semi-finals in Lexington. Mullin was rewarded by being selected the winner of the

Wooden Award as national Player of the Year.

Mullin played the NBA from 1986 through 2001 and was a member of the first Olympic Dream Team in 1992. He has been inducted into the Naismith Hall of Fame as both a player and a member of the iconic Dream Team. Mullin returned to his alma mater three years ago, taking a job as head coach of St. John's, as he attempted to return the program to glory.

Nothing but nylon…Mullin used to tickle the twine.

# Reggie Miller
## (1984-1987)

## Carved in Stone

Reggie Miller is generally considered one of the best long-range shooters ever to play in the NBA. The 6'7" former UCLA star, who played his entire 18-year career with the Indiana Pacers, made the NBA All-Star team five times, led the league in free throw accuracy five times, and played for the U.S. gold medal-winning team in the 1986 Olympics. By the time he retired in 2005, he was the league's all-time leader in three-pointers made with 2,650.

## The Long-Distance Tale

The seeds for Miller's success were planted at UCLA, where he played from 1984-1987.

Miller was selected MVP for UCLA's 1985 NIT championship team as a sophomore, when he scored 18 points as the Bruins defeated Indiana, 65-62, in Madison Square Garden.

He made his biggest splash his senior year when the NCAA instituted the 3-point shot.

It didn't take long for the stand-out guard to put it to good use. Miller averaged 22.8 points for a Pac-10 championship team that played in the NCAA tournament and 69 of 247 of his field goals that year were three-pointers. He lived up to his reputation as one of the program's best clutch shooters ever on January 24, when he drained a dagger three with 10 seconds left to give UCLA a 61-59 victory over Notre Dame at Pauley Pavilion. The feat re-ignited one of the best rivalries in the sport. Miller also scored 33 points in the second half during a 99-86 win against defending national champion Louisville. He finished his career as the school's third-all-time leading scorer with 2,065 points.

There was a time when Miller didn't know if he could ever play college basketball. He was born in Riverside, California, with hip deformities, which prevented him from walking correctly. After a few years of continuously wearing braces on both legs, his leg strength grew enough to compensate.

Miller was one of five siblings from an athletic family. His brother Darrell is a former major league catcher with the Los Angeles Angels. One sister, Tammy, played volleyball at Cal State-Fullerton and another, Cheryl, was a four-time All-American at USC and the star of the 1984 U.S. gold medal-winning Olympic women's basketball team. When I had the honor and pleasure of working with her on ABC, she shared her love for her brother and his greatness many times.

Cheryl used to constantly beat Reggie in games of one-on-one prior to his professional career. According to Reggie, they quit playing when he could finally block Cheryl's shots. He claims he developed his unorthodox shooting stroke so he could get his shot off against Cheryl's constant shot-blocking.

Miller attended Riverside Polytechnic High School and signed with UCLA. As of 2009, he still held the UCLA single-season records for most league points, highest league scoring average, and most free throws. He also holds several individual game records and his Number 31 jersey was retired in the rafters of Pauley Pavilion.

He has gone on to be a star in broadcasting, too…I hope he doesn't want to take my job!

# Steph Curry
## (2007-2009)

Joe Faraoni / ESPN Images

## Carved in Stone

Stephen Curry is a fantastic example of a young guy who never, ever believed in the word "can't." He believed in himself and chased his dreams, proving all the naysayers wrong. There were critics who said he was not strong enough or big enough to be an elite college player.

As they say, the rest is history. Curry added to his resumé with his third NBA championship in four years, as the Warriors swept the Cavaliers in 2018.

Curry is arguably the best long-range shooter in the history of the NBA, as can be attested by the 402 three-pointers he drained in 2016 for the Golden State Warriors. The 6'3" guard is a two-time MVP for a team that has won two NBA championships.

## The Long-Distance Tale

There was a time when Steph Curry struggled to get a scholarship, despite the fact he is the son of former NBA star Dell Curry, another pure shooter who played sixteen years in the league. When Dell played in Charlotte, he used to bring Steph and his younger brother, Seth, to Hornets' games and have them shoot around with the players during warm-ups.

Curry played his high school ball at Charlotte Christian School, where he was named all-state and led his team to three state playoff appearances. Because of his father's storied career at Virginia Tech, Steph wanted to follow in his footsteps and play for the Hokies, but he was only offered a walk-on spot, due in part to his slender 160-pound frame. He ultimately chose Davidson College, a tiny school with only 1,657 undergrads that had aggressively recruited him since tenth grade.

Davidson coach, Bob McKillop, knew he'd found a treasure. In Curry's second game of his freshman year, he scored 32 points, grabbed nine rebounds and contributed four assists against Michigan. Curry finished the season leading the Southern Conference in scoring with 21.5 points per game. He was second in the nation among freshmen in scoring, behind only Kevin Durant of Texas, and he led the Wildcats to the NCAA tournament. Curry offered a preview of things to come when he scored 30 points in a first round loss to Maryland.

Curry became a national sensation during March madness of his sophomore year when he averaged 25.9 points, made 159 threes, and then took Davidson on a magical, feel-good NCAA tournament ride to the Midwest Region finals in 2007. The 10th-seeded Wildcats played Gonzaga in the first round and fell behind by 11 points early in the second half. Then, Curry went off for 30 of his 40 points in the half with an array of high-arching rainbow jumpers as Davidson won its first NCAA game since 1969, 82-76, in Raleigh, just 150 miles from campus. Curry put on another masterful performance against heavily-favored Georgetown in the second round. He started slowly, missing 10 of 12 shots. But then he exploded again, scoring 25 of his 30 points in the second half and shooting 8 for 10 from three-point range, as the Wildcats rallied from a seventeen-point deficit to beat the Hoyas, 74-70.

The magic continued in the Sweet 16. Davidson chartered buses to transport what seemed like the entire student body, for an eleven-hour drive to Detroit, to watch Curry score 33 points as the Wildcats defeated Wisconsin, 73-56, to advance to the Elite Eight. LeBron James was also there and paid a royal visit to the Davidson locker room afterwards to meet the kid who personally outscored the Badgers, 22-20, in the second half.

"I'm glad we could entertain him," Curry said.

Davidson came close to making the Final Four. Curry scored 25 points, but the Wildcats lost, 59-57, to eventual national champion, Kansas, in Detroit. Davidson cut the lead to 2 points on a Curry three with 25 seconds left. Steph had the ball and a chance to win the game with 20 seconds to play. But Kansas double-teamed Curry off the inbounds pass, forcing him to pass the ball to point guard Jason

Scott Clarke / ESPN Images

Richards, who led the nation in assists, but missed a potential game-winning three-point shot from 10 feet beyond the arc at the buzzer.

Despite the loss, Curry was an easy choice for MVP in the region.

"That was Steph Curry's coming out party," Richards said. "People around the basketball world knew how good Steph was, but that put him on the map, because everyone watches the NCAA tournament. We became the darlings of that year, with Steph being our guy, our leader. He took the nation by storm and ran with it."

Curry could have declared for the NBA draft but instead he decided to come back to school so he could work on his point guard skills. He averaged 28.6 points, 5.6 assists and 2.5 steals. He was the NCAA scoring leader and was a consensus first team All-American. He twice scored a career-high 44 points against Oklahoma and North Carolina State. Curry finished his career with 2,635 points, but Davidson never got a chance to duplicate its NCAA Cinderella story, losing to College of Charleston in the semi-finals of the Southern Conference tournament, lining him up to settle for a spot in the NIT.

Curry opted out of his senior year but stated he still planned to earn his degree. He was selected by Golden State with the Number 7 pick in the draft and it didn't take long for Curry to be recognized as a superstar, who is currently making $34 million dollars a year.

# *Dick Vitale's*
# MOUNT RUSHMORE
## OF
# ALL THOMAS EDISON
# POINT GUARDS

## BOBBY HURLEY

## JASON KIDD

## KENNY ANDERSON

## ISIAH THOMAS

# Bobby Hurley
## (1990-1993)

*Duke Athletics*

## Carved in Stone

I always like to share a story that I believe embodies what Bobby Hurley is all about.

One day, when Hurley was a senior, Duke was preparing to battle rival, North Carolina, in the last game of the season. I went to practice and I was absolutely blown away by his work ethic. There was a loose ball and he was diving on the floor.

I turned to Coach K and I said, "Has anyone told him he already made the team and he is an All-American." That summarizes how he got the most out of his talent and physical abilities.

## To the Point

That championship attitude all started due to the intense drive and desire of his father, Bob Hurley Sr. Bobby had a lot to live up to, considering his family.

Bob Sr., a parole officer, was arguably the best high school coach in the history of New Jersey, leading St. Anthony's of Jersey City, a tiny Catholic school with an enrollment of less than 300, to 28 state championships. The Hall of Famer had more than 1,000 wins in 39 years-despite not having a home court gymnasium. His team practiced in a Bingo Hall down the street from the school's three-story brick building. In 2010, Senior became only the third high school coach ever to be inducted in the Naismith Hall of Fame.

Bob Hurley Jr. dealt with that legacy while growing up in a rough and tumble atmosphere. He used to play tackle football with his younger brother, Danny, in the living room of their row house. That was until Bobby, pretending to be Lawrence Taylor, nailed Danny with a shot that required stitches.

Bobby used to play one-on-one against his father and Danny. As he got older, his father would give him bus fare, then send him into the parks and projects of some of the toughest parts of the city—like the Duncan Projects—to test his skills in pick-up games.

The 6'0", 165-pound Hurley learned his lessons well. He was a classic street-tough gym rat who played for four consecutive state championships and posted a 115-5 record, making the McDonald's All-American team. Hurley always wanted to play for Dean Smith at North Carolina. But Smith was more interested in Kenny Anderson of Archbishop Molloy in New York City at the time, and Hurley didn't want to wait. He jumped at the chance to sign with Mike Krzyzewski at Duke and rapidly became the Blue Devils' coach on the floor, a four-year starter who averaged 12.4 points and 7.4 assists for his career.

He played a major role, along with teammate Christian Laettner, on two national championship teams in 1991 and 1992 and he helped his squad make three trips to the Final Four. When he left, he held the NCAA record for career assists (1,076) and total assists in the NCAA tournament (145).

*Duke Athletics*

Bobby's first trip to the Final Four in 1990 was a medical disaster. He fell victim to a severe stomach flu the night before the championship game against UNLV. He was all but useless against the Runnin' Rebels, shooting 0 for 3 and committing five turnovers during 32 minutes of a 103-73 blowout loss.

"The game was the turning point in my career," Hurley said. "It showed me how hard I was going to have to work and what I needed to do to get better. I needed to become more of a complete player."

Hurley got his chance for retribution the next year against the same Rebels in the national semi-finals. The top-ranked UNLV squad was 32-0. This time, Hurley had the last laugh, playing a nearly perfect game. Hurley drained a huge three-point jumper with less than a minute to play to cut UNLV's 76-71 lead to 2 and the Blue Devils rallied for a 79-77 victory. Two nights later, Duke defeated Kansas for the first championship in the school's history.

The next season, he was even better on the sport's biggest

stage, scoring 28 points in a semi-final victory over Indiana and then helped fuel the Devils to a 71-51 victory over Chris Weber and Michigan's Fab Five in the finals. He was selected Most Outstanding Player in the Final Four.

Hurley's career ended with a loss to California in the second round of the NCAA tournament. Hurley scored 32 points but it wasn't enough. When he graduated, he had his number retired.

Hurley was selected by Sacramento with the Number Seven pick in the first round. He appeared headed for a successful NBA career.

Then, in December of 1993, he almost lost everything.

When Bobby was leaving Arco Arena in his Toyota 4Runner, he was hit as he turned in front of a station wagon without its lights on. Hurley, who wasn't wearing a seat belt, was thrown into a ditch. His trachea was torn away from his left lung. Both lungs were collapsed and several ribs were fractured.

Hurley survived, but he was never the same on the court and eventually retired. He tried managing a stable of race horses but eventually found his way back into the game as an assistant to his brother Dan at Wagner. Hurley eventually got his own head coaching job at Buffalo, before going to Arizona State in 2016, coaching the Sun Devils to the NCAA tournament two years later.

# Jason Kidd

## (1993-1994)

Scott Clarke / ESPN Images

## Carved in Stone

When I think about Jason Kidd, it immediately triggers in me the term "The Three D-man":
- o **Drawing** the defense to him
- o **Driving**
- o Finishing it off by **Dishing** the rock for a layup

Kidd was so creative and innovative with the ball in his hands and he had an incredible basketball IQ. Kidd was a magician with the basketball. A lot of people did not see him because California was not on national television very often, but Kidd is generally regarded as the best point guard to come out of the Bay Area and the player who put Cal basketball back on the map for the first time since the Pete Newell era.

## To the Point

He grew up in a middle-class Oakland neighborhood and was a prodigy who took the bus to the hard scrabble inner-city playground courts. That is where he learned the finer points of the game from future NBA Hall of Famer, Gary Payton, a neighborhood icon who was five years older and took him under his wing.

131

"Jason grew up just playing on the basketball courts," Payton recalled. "But he didn't know anything about the playgrounds, where a lot of guys are going to talk trash, challenge his manhood, and things like that. He was always in the gym where guys didn't come from the streets. As soon as he started playing that way and changing his game, he started getting a lot of heart and a lot of courage."

Kidd learned how to survive and eventually thrive by passing the ball, because he realized that was the best way to get into the pick-up games against older players.

The 6'4" physically mature Kidd never had to take a back seat once he started playing for Frank LaPorte at St. Joseph's of Alameda. He was the talk of the town in eighth grade. Kidd was a prodigy who emulated his idols Payton and Magic Johnson in high school, leading the Pilots to consecutive California state championships in 1990 and 1991, averaging 25 points, 10 assists, seven rebounds and seven steals as a senior. During that year, he won the Naismith Award as the nation's top player and was selected Player of the Year by Parade and USA Today.

Kidd could have gone anywhere, but he shocked the world when he chose to sign with Cal-Berkeley—a Pac-10 school that was coming off a 10-18 season and had not won a conference title since 1959. He made the surprise pick over better-known Arizona, Kentucky, Kansas and Ohio State.

"It was a life decision," he said. "It came down to staying home so my parents could see me play, like they did in high school."

Kidd made an immediate impact at the college level. He averaged 13 points, 7.7 assists, 4.9 rebounds, and 3.8 steals a game, shepherding the Bears through a turbulent season that included a mid-season coaching change. Kidd's 110 steals set an NCAA record for most steals by a freshman and his 220 assists were a school record. He led Cal to two wins over bitter Pac-10 rival Stanford. He was selected national Freshman of the Year and made first team All-Pac-10 while leading the Bears to the 1993 NCAA tournament. Kidd's brightest moments came in March Madness when he made game-winning shots against LSU and defending national champion, Duke, as Cal advanced to the Sweet 16.

Kidd was even better as a sophomore, averaging 16.7 points, 6.9 rebounds, 3.1 steals, and 9.1 assists, breaking his previous school record and leading the country in that statistical category. He was the first sophomore to win the PAC-10 Player of the Year and was a consensus first team All-American, becoming the first Cal player to achieve that honor since Darrell Imhoff on the 1960 national championship team. The Bears made the NCAA tournament again but were upset by Wisconsin-Green Bay, 61-57, in the first round.

Kidd, a finalist for the Wooden and Naismith awards who had his Number 5 jersey retired, declared for the NBA draft after the season and was selected by Dallas with the Number 2 pick overall. He went on to lead the NBA in assists five times and played a huge role as an unselfish leader who thought *'pass first, shoot second'* on the 2000 Olympic team. That attitude helped them strike gold in Sydney and again in the 2008 Redeem team that won a gold medal in the Beijing games. Kidd played for five different NBA teams, won a championship in 2011 with Dallas, and had 107 triple-doubles. When he retired in 2013, he finished with a career average of 8.7 assists, second all-time to John Stockton, before getting into NBA coaching.

He was an easy choice for the Naismith Hall of Fame's class of 2018.

# Kenny Anderson

## (1990-1991)

*Georgia Tech Athletics*

### Carved in Stone

When Kenny Anderson came out of Archbishop Molloy High in Queens, New York, in 1989, NBA super scout, Marty Blake, said he would be the most exciting freshman guard in college basketball in fifty years.

Anderson, who played for the late, great Jack Curran, was scouted by college coaches from the time he was in sixth grade.  He was a four-time All-New York City selection and the first player since Kareem Abdul-Jabbar to make the Parade All-American team for three consecutive years. He set a New York state record for career scoring with 2,621 points that stood for eighteen years until it was broken by Sebastian Telfair of Lincoln in 2004.

Anderson, a McDonald's All-America and the state's Mr. Basketball, was considered the best prospect in the country, ahead of Shaquille O'Neal and Jim Jackson.

## To the Point

Everyone knew Anderson would be a star in college, but the big question was where he would sign. He was recruited by fifty schools over a two-year period. Most expected him to go to North Carolina and follow in the footsteps of Molloy alum Kenny "The Jet" Smith, who was a first team All-American selection and a close family friend; or go to Syracuse, which had showcased the legendary Pearl Washington in the early days of the Big East in its massive Carrier Dome.

Anderson, who approached his high school career as a job because he knew he couldn't attend college without a scholarship, cut his final list to UNC, Syracuse, and Georgia Tech. He admitted he felt the pressure of making his decision, wishing he could cut himself in three and hand pieces out like an assist.

"I couldn't cut myself in three. I couldn't give my left arm to North Carolina, my right arm to Syracuse and my body to Georgia Tech," he said.

*Georgia Tech Athletics*

In the end, Anderson surprised everyone when he selected Georgia Tech because he wanted to bring the program back and was comfortable with coach Bobby Cremins, a Frank McGuire disciple from New York City who promised to give him the freedom he wanted to run the team. The fact that he constantly received love letters from the coaching staff, players, and administration didn't hurt!

Anderson spent the next two years building a reputation as the "Wizard of Ahhs" with Tech fans. The lightning-quick 6'2", 168-pound Anderson was a smooth, left-handed starting point guard on Tech's best team ever, combining with 6'8" wing, Dennis Scott, and 6' 4" guard, Brian Oliver, to form "Lethal Weapon Three." All three players averaged more than 20 points a game. He played with flash, but also with purpose as the Yellow Jackets advanced to their first Final Four in 1990.

"I worried about what people would think of me," Anderson said. "There are a lot of flashy point guards who have come out of New York…you know…dribble, penetrate. I'm a very likable person. I didn't want people to think I was too cocky."

Anderson was selected ACC Rookie of the Week an unprecedented ten times, a first team All-ACC choice, and the National Freshman of the Year, averaging 20.6 points, 6.5 rebounds, and 8.1 assists. He shot 51 percent and 41 percent on three-pointers and constantly outplayed some of the best point guards in the history of the league—Bobby Hurley of Duke, Chris Corchiani of NC State, and John Crotty of Virginia. Anderson made the biggest shot in Tech history in the NCAA tournament when he raced down the floor and drained a jumper at the buzzer to force overtime against Michigan State in regulation at the Southeast Regional final. Fourth-seeded Tech went on to win 81-80, in overtime, to advance to the national semi-finals against UNLV.

The Jackets surged to a 56-43 halftime lead, but Cremins pulled Anderson after he picked up a fourth personal foul and Tech lost its momentum, allowing the Rebels to rally to win, 90-81.

"To this day, he's still mad at me for taking him out," Cremins admitted.

Anderson became an even bigger star his sophomore year out of necessity, after Scott left for the pros and Oliver graduated. Anderson carried the team, averaging 25.6 points, 5.7 rebounds and 5.1 assists. He had a game for the ages when he went off for a school-record 50 points during a 135-94 victory over Loyola-Marymount in which he shot 18 for 27 and made eight three-pointers and was named a first team All-American.

Anderson promised his mother he would stay in college for two years before declaring for the draft after a season that ended with a second-round loss to Ohio State. He was selected by the Nets with the Number 2 pick overall that June and played in the league from 1991 through 2005 , but his legacy will always be linked to what he accomplished in college.

# Isiah Thomas
## (1979-1981)

*Indiana University Athletics*

## Carved in Stone

Pound for pound, inch for inch, has there been a better player than Isiah Thomas?

From the time I laid eyes on him putting on that Hoosier uniform, he was destined for greatness. He certainly lived up to all of the adjectives used in describing his talents when he came from the scholastic ranks.

Isiah was a star of stars in college and a flat-out superstar in the NBA.

## To the Point

It is hard to say which was a greater accomplishment for Thomas . . . surviving the mean streets of Chicago or surviving the boot camp run by the General, Robert Montgomery Knight.

Thomas did both, eventually escaping his gang and drug-infested ghetto, becoming the best point guard in the history of Indiana basketball, and getting recognized as the Most Outstanding Player as a sophomore in the 1981 NCAA tournament.

The 6'1" Thomas was the youngest of nine children, seven of them boys. When Thomas was growing up, his family sometimes went without food and heat. His mother held the family together, pulling out a shot gun when gang members came to her front door looking to recruit her sons and threatening to shoot them. Thomas' brothers protected him, allowing him to focus solely on basketball.

Thomas was a CYO star in fourth grade, but there was some concern he might not grow because he was just 5'6" when he enrolled at St. Joseph's of Westchester—a 90-minute commute from home—in ninth grade. Thomas promised to become a McDonald's All-American and was recruited by numerous national powers before enrolling at Indiana

The decision was more difficult than it should have been. Thomas received mail saying Knight tied his players up and beat them, reports Thomas did not believe. When Knight made a home visit, one of Thomas' brothers, who wanted Thomas to attend hometown DePaul, embarrassed him by insulting the coach and engaging him in a shouting match. Thomas signed with Indiana because he felt it would be good for him to get away from home and benefit from Knight's discipline.

The street-smart Thomas made an impact before he ever enrolled in Bloomington, starring on Knight's 1979 U.S. Pan American Games team that won a gold medal in Puerto Rico. He scored 23 points with five steals and four assists in the gold medal game. Thomas also got his first taste of Knight's disciplinary philosophy on his trip to the island.

One time, Knight got so mad at Thomas, he threatened to put him on a plane home, telling him, "You ought to go to DePaul, because you sure as hell aren't going to be an Indiana player playing like that."

The two strong-willed personalities often clashed. Prior to his freshman year, Knight became so upset with Thomas that he tossed him out of practice. According to Thomas, Knight was making a point that no player, no matter how talented, was bigger than the program.

Thomas quickly proved he could play at the highest level and became a favorite with both Knight and Indiana fans. There was Hoosier Hysteria as fans displayed bedsheets with quotations from the Book of Isaiah in the old testament "And a little child shall lead them." They nicknamed him Mr. Wonderful. Knight referred to him as "Pee Wee."

Thomas became an immediate star as a freshman, averaging 14.5 points and 5.5 assists to lead the Hoosiers to the first of two Big Ten championships and a spot in the Sweet 16. He became the first freshman in conference history to make All-Big Ten and later made the 1980 Olympic team, but never got a chance to participate because of the American Boycott of the Moscow games.

*Indiana University Athletics*

Thomas was both a scorer and a playmaker and scored more than most point guards while playing in Knight's controlled motion offense. Knight made Thomas his captain as a sophomore and gave him the freedom to run the show on the floor. Thomas emerged as one of the most polished players in the country as a sophomore. He was a first team All-American, leading the Hoosiers in both scoring with 16 points per game and assists with 5.8.

The friendship between Knight and Thomas grew. When a Purdue player took a cheap shot at Thomas during a game at Bloomington, Knight called a press conference to defend his star. Nineteen days later,

Joe Faraoni / ESPN Images

when Thomas hit an Iowa player and was ejected from the game, Knight refused to criticize him. Thomas was at his best in March, leading the Hoosiers to 25 wins, scoring a game-high 23 points as Indiana defeated North Carolina, 63-50, to win the 1981 national championship in Philadelphia.

Knight and former Indiana star, Quinn Buckner, urged Thomas to stay for a junior year, but he decided to forgo the rest of his college eligibility to declare for the 1981 draft and was selected second overall by the Detroit Pistons. Thomas played his entire career in Detroit, leading the "Bab Boys" to a pair of NBA championships in 1989 and 1990.

Interestingly, Thomas remained a huge Knight supporter and even offered him a job with the NBA Indiana Pacers when he was the head coach at that NBA franchise after Knight was dismissed by Indiana in 2000. The love-hate relationship between Thomas and Knight reportedly contributed to him to leaving early. No doubt these two intense competitors clashed. In the end, they made magical music in the world of college hoops as they were in hoops heaven in the City of Brotherly Love in 1981 when they beat North Carolina and cut down the nets.

# *Dick Vitale's*
# MOUNT RUSHMORE
## OF
# ALL HUMAN ERASERS

## DAVID ROBINSON
## ALONSO MOURNING
## ADONAL FOYLE
## EMEKA OKAFOR

# David Robinson
## (1984-1987)

*Navy Athletics*

## Carved in Stone

Marvin Webster, of Morgan State University (1971-1975), was the original "human eraser," named so for his ability to erase the possible points of his opponents through blocked shots. He set a standard for players to live up to, marking the importance of this part of the game, and adding the term to basketball language.

There is no doubt that one of my favorite players in my forty years at ESPN has been The Admiral, David Robinson, the first of my four greatest human erasers.

I had the good fortune to be the keynote speaker at an event in Atlanta, where David was the recipient of the National Player of the Year award, He was dressed in his Navy blues and it was so refreshing to see a student-athlete address the crowd and specifically talk about the impact his mom and dad made on his life. I sat in awe and I am not shocked that this genuine, solid gold PTP'er has made it big in the game of life

We are so proud that David is now a member of the Board of Directors of the V Foundation, using his legacy to help raise funds for childhood cancer and cancer research.

## Superhuman

Robinson always stood out in a crowd when he attended the U.S. Naval Academy.

How many 7'1", 250-pound Midshipmen have ever attended Annapolis?

Robinson is a special case, and the best player ever to enroll in a service academy.

The son of a retired Navy veteran, Robinson excelled in school and most sports growing up—except basketball. He was 5'9" in junior high school, where he tried out for the basketball team, but soon quit. Robinson attended Osbourn Park in Manassas, Virginia, just outside of Washington, D.C., where his father was working as an engineer. He participated in tennis, gymnastics, and baseball and was an excellent student who was more interested in music, science, and mathematics than athletics.

By his senior year in high school he was 6'6" and weighed 175 pounds but had never played organized basketball or attended any basketball camps. When the coach added him to the team as a senior, Robinson blossomed, earning all-district honors. He scored 1320 on the SAT and chose to go to the Naval Academy, where he majored in mathematics.

Robinson was 6'8" when he was admitted to the Academy, two inches above the height limit due to the heights servicemen could comfortably be to work on ships, but he received a waiver from the Superintendent of the Academy.

Robinson chose Number 50 for his jersey, after his idol, Ralph Sampson. He averaged just 7.8 points a game as a freshman, though he showed an instinct for rebounding and blocking shots.

Robinson sprouted six inches in college, building a lean, muscular physique. He began dominating college basketball as a sophomore in 1985, averaging 23.6 points and 11.6 rebounds to lead the Middies to the first of three Colonial Athletic Association titles and NCAA tournament appearances.

Robinson's imposing presence, grace, and unlikely stardom vaulted Navy into the national spotlight and his clean-cut personality and well-rounded background made him the ideal face for Navy athletics. He was the highest-profile athlete to play at Annapolis since Heisman Trophy-winning quarterback, Roger Staubach, in 1962. After his sophomore year, with the prospect of an NBA career, he toyed with the idea of transferring, which would have freed him from military service, but he chose to honor his commitment after speaking with the Superintendent.

Robinson was afraid his height might prevent him from serving at sea as an unrestricted line officer, making it impossible for him to be commissioned. As a compromise, Secretary of the Navy John Lehman allowed Robinson to train for and receive his commission as a staff officer in the Civil Engineering Corps.

*Scott Clarke / ESPN Images*

Robinson had two monster final seasons. He led the country in rebounds (13.0 per game) and blocked shots (5.91) as a junior in 1986 while averaging 22.7 points and leading Navy to the Elite Eight before the Middies lost to Duke. During a second-round win over Syracuse, Robinson dominated Orange center Rony Seikaly, posting a triple-double with 35 points, 11 rebounds, and 10 blocked shots.

Robinson, playing his first three years for Paul Evans and his final year for former Georgia interim coach, Pete Hermann, became a national sensation. As a senior, he appeared on the cover of Sports Illustrated college basketball preview issue, along a headline that read, "Top Gun!"

Robinson again led the country in blocks in 1987 with 4.5 rejections, while averaging 28.2 points and 11.8 rebounds. I called one game that season when Navy played Kentucky and Robinson went off for 45 points, 20 rebounds, and 10 blocked shots, a triple-double during a 80-69 loss at Rupp Arena. Robinson made 17 for 22 shots and made 11 of 12 free throws. When Herrmann took Robinson out of the game with fourteen seconds left, Kentucky coach Eddie Sutton and the rest of the 23,275 fans gave him a standing ovation. I stood up as well, one of only two times doing that in my entire broadcasting career.

Robinson was the consensus national Player of the Year. His final game in college was bittersweet. Robinson scored a career-high 50-points, but his team lost to Michigan in the first round of the NCAA tournament.

Robinson finished his career as the first NCAA player to record more than 2,500 points and 1,300 rebounds while shooting 61.3 percent. He holds NCAA records for most blocks in a single game (14 against UNC-Wilmington) and highest single-season blocks (20-7 in 1987-88), highest single-season block average (5.9 in 1987). The Midshipmen went 81-17 in Robinson's career.

Though Robinson faced military service, the San Antonio Spurs still selected him as the Number 1 pick overall in the 1987 NBA draft. Robinson was commissioned in the Navy Reserves and served two years. After graduation, Robinson became a civil engineering officer at the Naval Submarine Base in Kings Bay, Georgia.

Robinson joined the Spurs in 1990 and, based on his prior service as an officer, he picked up the nickname "The Admiral" which stuck with him for the rest of a highly-successful career.

Robinson is a 10-time NBA All-Star, the 1995 NBA MVP, a two-time NBA champion in 1999 and 2003, a two-time Olympic gold medal winner in 1992 and 1996, and a two-time Naismith Hall of Fame inductee (2009 as an individual winner and 2010 as a member of the Dream Team). Robinson remains the only player from the Naval Academy to play in the NBA.

# Alonzo Mourning

## (1988-1992)

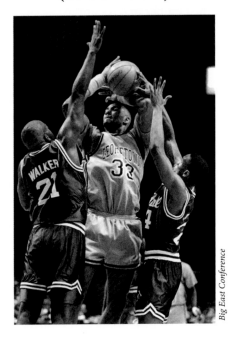

*Big East Conference*

## Carved in Stone

When I think of Alonzo Mourning, one word jumps at me immediately—CLASS. I will never forget giving a speech on the game of life at a basketball camp one summer.

After I was done, the young superstar came up to me and said, "I want to thank you so much for taking time to share these words with us."

WOW!

In a world where so many stars forget where they came from, it was great to see that a player of the caliber of Alonzo would take time to say thank you.

Man, was I impressed.

## Superhuman

I remember going to Albuquerque, New Mexico, in 1988 to call the McDonald's All-America game. I worked with the legendary Keith Jackson. I told him that the talent in that game was the greatest assembled that I had seen in 25 years.

143

One player that stood out from that group was Mourning. He was a tremendous talent with great rejection ability. He once blocked 27 shots in a high school game.

Mourning was considered the second coming of Patrick Ewing when he was a senior at Indian River High in Chesapeake, Virginia.

The 6'10", 260-pound center was the number one recruit in the country in 1988 over Billy Owens, Shawn Kemp, and Christian Laettner when he averaged 22 points, 15 rebounds and 12 blocked shots for a team that won a state championship and won fifty-one consecutive games. Mourning once blocked 22 shots in an AAU game.

There was little question about his college destination.

Mourning fell in love with Georgetown after he watched Ewing swat away North Carolina's first four shots in the 1982 national championship game. He had pictures of Ewing plastered all over his bedroom wall. He always had a competitive edge.

After Mourning signed with the Hoyas, he became the first high school player invited to try out for the U.S. Olympic team in Colorado Springs. Mourning did not make the team, but he was one of the last two players cut by John Thompson and it showed he was ready to make an immediate contribution at the highest level.

Mourning, who wore Ewing's number 33 to preserve his legacy, averaged 16.7 points, 8.6 rebounds, and 3.8 blocked shots during his four-year career. He was one of only two Georgetown players—along with Ewing— to graduate with 2,000 points and 1,000 or more rebounds and led the Hoyas to four consecutive NCAA Tournaments from 1988 through 1992.

Mourning was a third team All-American, the Big East Rookie of the Year, and Defensive Player of the Year as a freshman, and set an NCAA record with 169 blocked shots—breaking Ewing's school record with 11 blocks in only 22 minutes against St. Leo—as the 29-5 Hoyas advanced to the NCAA Final Eight.

Georgetown never reached a Final Four during Mourning's career, but he did leave his mark, playing in the same front-court as the towering 7'2", 260-pound center, Dikembe Mutombo. As a sophomore, Mourning was a second team All-American, first team All-Big East selection and co-Defensive Player of the Year with Mutombo and a third-team All-American in an injury-plagued junior season.

Then, in his senior year, he put together one of the best seasons in the history of the conference, carrying the load for a team full of role players. Mourning averaged 21.3 points, 10.7 rebounds and 5 blocks and was a consensus first team All-American. He was the first player ever to be named Big East Player of the Year, Defensive Player of the Year, and the MVP of the Big East tournament. He scored in double figures every game and grabbed double-figure rebounds in 22 games.

Mourning rocked the Big East, opening conference play with 24 points, 15 rebounds, and 8 blocks against Villanova. He scored a career-high 38 in a double overtime loss at Boston College, setting a school record in free throws, making 18 of 26 attempts. He had 26 points, 11 rebounds, and seven blocks in an upset of Villanova, then scored 76 points and grabbed 22 rebounds in three games in the conference tournament where he was named MVP, despite the Hoyas' last-minute loss to Syracuse.

Mourning's season ended prematurely when Florida State found a way to deny him the ball during a 78-68 win in the second round of the tournament. He was drafted by Charlotte with the Number 2 pick overall in the 1992 NBA draft and became a seven-time All-Star and one of the most feared centers in the league.

He and Ewing remained close after he graduated and would work out together during the summer. Mourning was diagnosed with a life-threatening kidney disorder following the 2000 Olympics in Sydney, where he helped lead the U.S. to a gold medal. He missed the 2003 season in an attempt to heal his kidneys and announced his retirement in the fall of 2003.

Mourning required a kidney transplant, and Ewing offered to donate one of his if it was needed. Mourning eventually received a left kidney from his cousin James Cooper, a U.S. Marine. Despite concerns of friends and family that a return to the NBA could prove a threat to his life, Mourning returned to the game a year later, playing a key role as the Miami Heat won the 2006 NBA title. He stayed with the Heat until his retirement in 2009. His number retired with him, and he was named to the Naismith Hall of Fame in 2014.

Since his retirement, Mourning has been at the forefront of raising funds for kidney research and has raised over $5 million through his charitable organization, "Zo's Fund for Life."

# Adonal Foyle
## (1995-1997)

Colgate Athletics

## Carved in Stone

Adonal Foyle is the closest thing to a Renaissance Man college basketball has seen since iconic former Senator Bill Bradley of Princeton and the Knicks. The 6'10", 270-pound center is known as much for his humanitarian work as he is for the NCAA shot-blocking records he set at Colgate University.

## Superhuman

Foyle never envisioned he would someday play college basketball when he was growing up in St. Vincent and the Grenadines in the Virgin Islands. He was more interested in becoming a judge, wearing a robe similar to those worn by British parliament.

But fate intervened when Foyle took up basketball, playing on iron rims that were attached to telephone pools. These "backboards" would occasionally tip over. The roads where games were played were filled with potholes and play was often halted briefly for passing cars. Flood lights kept the games going into the night.

Foyle began playing competitively at age fifteen. It was difficult to find sneakers to match his size fifteen feet and Foyle would bust through the soles, ultimately forced to use cloth and scotch tape to keep them together. He would often sprain his ankles, returning home to face his unhappy mother, who was already upset he was not spending enough time on his school work.

Education was important to the family and career opportunities on the islands were limited. Jay and Joan Mandle, two Colgate professors, discovered Foyle when they were officiating a summer tournament on Union Island. They spotted the then 16-year old Foyle playing with an older team and evaluated him as a great athlete…with limited basketball skills. But they also saw he had enormous potential and, before they left the islands, they decided to approach Foyle about coming to the United States to work on his game and his education.

They convinced Foyle's parents to make them his legal guardian and enrolled him for a sophomore year at Cardinal O'Hara High in suburban Philadelphia before arranging for him to transfer to Hamilton Central High School in a quaint village an hour from Syracuse, where he led the school to two consecutive Class D state championships. His 47 points and 26 rebounds in the 1994 state semi-finals is still the most in any classification, and he blossomed academically with the help of extra tutoring sessions.

Foyle was selected to play in the McDonald's All-American game and graduated with honors. The combination was enough to attract marquee schools like Duke, Syracuse, and Michigan. Mike Krzyzewski and Jim Boeheim visited the Mandle's home. In the end, Foyle felt a private, liberal arts local school like Colgate was the right fit.

"At the end of the day, I wanted to go to a place that would treat me as a student-athlete in every sense of the word," he said. "I wanted to have a college degree. I was certain I wasn't going back to the Caribbean without one. I wanted to be the first person in our village just to go to college."

He also liked the idea of having a coach like the late Jack Bruen, who could teach him the principles of the game and give him all the attention he needed.

Foyle was a quick study. He averaged 22.6 points, 12.7 rebounds and 5.66 blocked shots in his three years on campus. He led the Red Raiders to two Patriot League championships, was a two-time Patriot League Player of the Year, and he left school as the NCAA career leader in blocked shots with 492. He set a single-season record with an average of 6.2 blocks. Foyle recorded four career triple-doubles and had six games with 10 or more blocks.

We can quibble about the level of competition, but Foyle was good enough to be a lottery pick. He was selected by Golden State with the eighth pick in the 1997 NBA draft.

Foyle also flourished in academics. Jay Mandle, an economics professor at the school, as well as his sociology and psychology teacher, steered Foyle into an array of interesting courses, ranging from poetry to drama.

"I had amazing teachers," Foyle said. "I embraced the liberal arts. I enjoyed the journey, not only getting to know your professors, but what it brings out of you with that passion for learning."

In 1999, he graduated from Colgate magna cum laude with a degree in history.

Foyle played thirteen years in the league, but his long-term legacy will be the two foundations he started. Politically motivated, he launched Democracy Matters at Colgate in 2001. The non-partisan student organization has an active presence on eighty campuses with a goal of counteracting political apathy and encouraging college students to focus on issues of campaign finance reform. He also launched The Kerosene Lamp Foundation, which promotes education and health awareness for children in St. Vincent and the Grenadines. Since 2005, the organization has built or refurbished basketball courts in urban areas to provide safe places to play for more than 3,000 youth.

Foyle became an American citizen in 2007, after being in the United States for almost eighteen years. Today, he serves as a member of the NBA Players' Association Executive Committee.

# Emeka Okafor

## (2002-2004)

*UConn Athletics*

## Carved in Stone

When Connecticut coach Jim Calhoun first watched Emeka Okafor play in the spring of his senior year at a travel team event, he had no idea the skinny 6'9" center would someday be the best big man in school history.

## Superhuman

Okafor was the son of immigrant parents. His father, Pius, escaped Nigeria after the end of a bloody civil war that killed more than a million people in 1970. Pius continued his education, as did Okafor's mother, a nurse, who his father met and married in the U.S. The family lived in Houston, then Bartlesville, Oklahoma, and back to Texas, once more, as Pius finished his degrees and worked gas station jobs to pay the bills while raising his family.

Like his father, Okafor was studious and serious. He once came home with a B on his report card and cried over it. He was also a skilled athlete, playing soccer and baseball, running track, and swimming competitively.

When Okafor was eight, his father took him to the YMCA to learn basketball. He quickly saw Emeka had a gift for the sport. Okafor enrolled at Houston's Bellaire High, which attracted some of the city's top students.

"Basketball is a gift, but so is intelligence," Okafor said. "I don't want to waste either one of them."

Okafor played on a freshman team that won the city championship. Midway through his sophomore season, he was moved up to varsity. Okafor averaged 22 points, 16 rebounds, and 7 blocked shots as a senior for Bellaire High School in 2001, trying to pattern his game after Hakeem Olajuwon. He played on the same team as Oklahoma State star John Lucas III. Bellaire was 26-5 that season, losing in the third round of the state playoffs to Willowridge High in Sugarland with Texas standout T.J. Ford. That game was particularly notable because it featured five players who would go on to play in the NCAA Final Four: Okafor and Lucas, as well as Ford, Oklahoma State's Ivan McFarlin, and Duke's Daniel Ewing. All five of these players would eventually play at least one year in the NBA.

Okafor was a straight A student with a 4.3 GPA who wanted to go to Stanford. But the Cardinals never offered him a scholarship because the coaches there felt Okafor wasn't big enough or offensively skilled enough to play in their system. Okafor put on twenty pounds through extensive weight training and began to attract college recruiters from Rice and Vanderbilt.

UConn Athletics

Okafor eventually chose Connecticut because he liked the school's style of play and its success in the competitive Big East. When he first arrived in Storrs, he was considered a project. He had no jump shot, but he displayed a knack for blocking shots.

Okafor made vast improvements in his game under Calhoun. As a freshman, Okafor finished as the third-best shot blocker in Division I with 136 blocks. He also took thirty-five credit hours in his first two semesters.

Okafor, who grew to 6'10", 252-pounds, played in three NCAA tournaments. As a junior in 2004, Okafor transformed himself into a consensus first team All-American who won several national Player of the Year awards and was chosen National Defensive Player of the Year for a second straight season. Okafor averaged 17 points, while shooting 59.9 percent, for a Big East program that started and finished the season ranked Number 1, and won a national championship. He also grabbed 11.5 rebounds and led the country in blocked shots for a second consecutive season.

Okafor played on a team with three other future NBA players—Ben Gordon, Charlie Villanueva, and Josh Boone, but he was the big man on campus. He was the best big man I'd seen in college since Patrick Ewing and David Robinson.

Okafor suffered back problems and only scored two points during an 81-71 win over Alabama in the Elite Eight. But he came up huge in the Final Four. He scored all 18 of his points in the second half of a 79-78 victory over Duke in the national semi-finals, then had 24 points and 15 rebounds—his 24th double-double of the season—as the Huskies defeated Georgia Tech to win Calhoun's second national championship. Okafor was selected the Most Outstanding Player at the tournament.

Okafor, a two-time first team All-Academic All American, continued to take a heavy course load and graduated in three years with a 3.95 GPA and an honors degree in finance. His only B came in a course on business calculus. He finished near the top of the NCAA all-time leaders in career blocked shots with 441. He declared for the NBA draft after the season and was selected by Charlotte with the second pick overall.

"The draft was the culmination of a dream," he said.

That summer, he was selected to play for the U.S. Olympic team that finished with a bronze medal in Athens. Okafor's transition to the NBA was seamless. He won the 2005 Rookie of the Year award after averaging 15.1 points, and 10.7 rebounds. He is still playing in the NBA today.

# *Dick Vitale's*
# MOUNT RUSHMORE
## OF
# ALL WINDEX GLASS EATERS

## KARL MALONE

## HAKEEM OLAJUWON

## SHAQUILLE O'NEAL

## XAVIER McDANIEL

# Karl Malone

## (1982-1985)

Louisiana Tech Communications

### Carved in Stone

Windex glass eaters are all about getting mad rebounds. Growing up, Karl Malone had no idea he would one day turn into the best power forward in NBA history…and one of my four top glass eaters!

### Getting the Glass

Malone was one of nine children raised by a single mother in rural Summerfield, Louisiana, a town of just 200 people. He spent much of his childhood working at the family farm, chopping trees, fishing, and cleaning chicken houses.

Malone was academically ineligible to play as a freshman at Summerfield High School, but went the rest of his high school career leading the Rebels to three consecutive state championships from 1979-1981. He also played on one of the best 16-and-under travel teams of all-time in 1980, with another future Hall of Fame guard, Joe Dumars of McNeese State, as well as high-scoring forward, Hot Rod Williams of Tulane and high-flying guard, Benny Anders from Houston's Phi Slamma Jamma 1983 NCAA Final Four team.

Malone was a skinny 6'9" prospect who was recruited by Arkansas coach, Eddie Sutton, but enrolled at Louisiana Tech in Ruston, which was closer to his home. He joined the Tech basketball team in his sophomore year because his grades were too low for freshman eligibility. But he never lacked for confidence.

"I've had people doubt me all my life," he said. "Now that might come across as cocky or conceited, but when I was five-years old, I knew I was going to be the best, or one of the best. I'm not saying I'm more talented than the next guy, but I was never afraid of work. My mom instilled that in me at a young age.

Malone was so close to his mother and wouldn't report to Andy Russo's pregame meeting until he had greeted her at the door of the new Thomas Assembly Center and escorted her to her seat.

Then Malone, who picked up the nickname, "The Mailman," because he always delivered the ball to the basket, became the man. Malone was raw in college and not nearly the 250-pound physical specimen and workout fanatic he was in the NBA, but he had tremendous leaping ability and an explosive first step. He was an average free throw shooter, though with a soft shot, an assortment of low post moves, and no fear about mixing it up inside.

Malone averaged 18.7 points and 9.3 rebounds during his career, shooting 56.6 percent. He led the Bulldogs in scoring and rebounding in each of his three seasons and propelled the Bulldogs into the national spotlight,

*Louisiana Tech Communications*

leading them to their first two NCAA tournament appearances ever.

During the 1983-1984 season, Malone led Tech to a 26-7 record and the Southland Conference championship. Malone scored 24 points and grabbed 12 rebounds as Tech upset Fresno State in a first round NCAA game, then added 18 points and eight rebounds in a loss to a Houston team with Hakeem Olajuwon that advanced to the NCAA championship game against Georgetown.

The Bulldogs took another step forward in Malone's next year, finishing 29-3 and advancing to the NCAA Sweet 16. Malone contributed 27 points and 14 rebounds in a second-round win over Ohio State. Then, he posted 20 points and a game-high 16 rebounds against top-seeded Oklahoma in the regional semis before Wayman Tisdale made a last-second shot to defeat the Bulldogs in overtime.

Malone, a second team All-American and a three-time All Southland selection, was still an unfinished product, but he passed up his final year of eligibility to declare for the NBA draft and was selected by the Utah Jazz with the Number 13 pick overall.

He blossomed in the NBA, combining with point guard John Stockton to form a killer one-two punch for the Jazz during the eighteen years they played together. The rugged Malone was a member of the 1992 Dream Team that struck gold in Barcelona and the 1996 Olympic gold medal team. He was a two-time NBA MVP in 1997 and 1999, a fourteen-time NBA All Star and a record 11-time member of the All NBA first team. He played in the playoffs every season of his career, including one season with the Los Angeles Lakers. His 36,928 career points rank second all-time in NBA history (behind Kareem Abdul-Jabbar) and he holds the record for most free throws made and attempted. He is a member of the Naismith Hall of Fame and his legacy includes the Karl Malone award, given by the Hall to the top power forward in college basketball.

*Louisiana Tech Communications*

# Hakeem Olajuwon
## (1982-1984)

*University of Houston Athletics*

## Carved in Stone

In one of those magical moments that I will treasure, I remember doing the Sugar Bowl Classic in New Orleans when Hakeem Olajuwon was a freshman and playing for Guy V. Lewis and Houston. I was on an elevator at our hotel with just me and the big man. I could see on his face that he was disappointed with the way he performed.

I remember saying to him, "Just listen to your coaches, keep working hard because you possess some things that cannot be taught—size, strength and agility." I told him one day he would be special.

Did he become special? Wow, I was honored to be part of the class in Springfield when Olajuwon, Patrick Ewing, Pat Riley, Cathy Rush, Adrian Dantley were inducted into the Naismith Hall of Fame back in 2008 The 7'0" center, who was still going by the name Akeem when he played for the University of Houston, won three NBA MVPs with the Houston Rockets, two NBA championship rings, and an Olympic gold medal in 1996. He was talking about his college career during his speech when he gave yours truly a shout out.

"Dickie V. was the one who gave me the nickname "The Dream" when I played in college," he told the audience.

## Getting the Glass

"Hakeem the Dream", who grew up in Nigeria, was a charter member of the high-flying mythical fraternity, Phi Slamma Jama, known for the effortless way he dunked the ball. He was the first international star I covered for ESPN. I was in Albuquerque to see his coming-out party at the 1983 NCAA Final Four in a national semi-final game against Louisville, when the two teams staged a memorable dunking exhibition in the second half at the Pit.

Olajuwon was front and center during the Cougars victory. He scored 21 points, grabbed 22 rebounds, blocked 11 shots, and threw down 5 of 13 of Houston's slam dunks in a 94-81 victory. He was playing up in the clouds. Olajuwon went off for 20 points, 18 rebounds, and seven blocked shots in the championship game, but the Cougars lost to NC State, 54-52, on a slam dunk by Lorenzo Charles at the buzzer.

The Dream averaged 20.5 points, 20 rebounds, and 9 blocks in the Final Four and was named Most Outstanding Player, one of the few players honored from a losing team.

Olajuwon helped lead Houston to three consecutive Final Fours and two national championship games. As a senior he averaged 16.8 points, 13.5 rebounds, and 5.6 blocked shots. He led the country in rebounds, blocked shots, and field goal percentage while leading the Cougars back to the NCAA finals, where the University of Houston lost to Patrick Ewing and Georgetown in Seattle.

The Dream was a work in progress when he first arrived at Houston. He suffered from frequent back spasms, caused by growing pains and simply being out of shape. Still learning the game, he was consistently in foul trouble. From the start, though, he was a natural shot blocker. Throughout his freshman year, he worked on increasing his weight with a diet of steak and ice cream and worked one-on-one with Houston Rockets' star Moses Malone, one of the best rebounders in the history of the NBA, to improve his defense and learn the more aggressive style of American basketball.

By the time he declared for the NBA draft three years later, he was an accomplished center who had developed into one of the most athletic big men in the history of college basketball. His coordination and competitiveness made him an effective shot blocker and rebounder, who averaged 10.5 boards and 4.5 rejections during his career. His experience as a former soccer goalie in his homeland gave him a natural instinct for rebounding the ball. Unlike most American centers who played in the low post, he had the ability to shoot the ball from the perimeter.

Olajuwon was selected by Houston as the Number One pick overall in the 1984 NBA draft, ahead of Sam Bowie of Kentucky and Michael Jordan.

# Shaquille O'Neal
## (1990-1992)

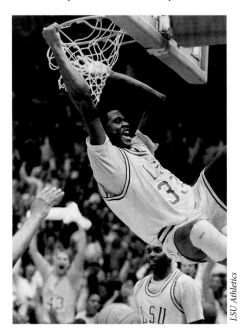

*LSU Athletics*

## Carved in Stone

There are two magical moments that jump at me when thinking about Shaquille O'Neal.

One was as a high school phenom at the McDonald's All-American game, where I had the good fortune of being behind the microphone. He ripped a rebound off the glass and dribbled the length of the court for a dunk. The place went ballistic. Needless to say, I went wild on the tube, screaming, "Are you serious, Baby!?" It became a hit on YouTube.

The other situation was when Arizona went to LSU as one of the top five teams in the nation. They had a loaded team up front with Brian Williams, Sean Rooks, Chris Mills, and Ed Stokes. I could not believe what I was watching as Shaq dominated all of them. My producer, Kim Helton, a former star in his own right at Stanford, was going nuts in the truck over what we were seeing.

I always loved calling Shaq's games at LSU. He had a big smile on his face and he loved to compete.

## Getting the Glass

I remember when Dale Brown told me about his twin towers—Shaq and Stanley Roberts. It was nice to have a pair of seven-footers inside, dominating the lane.

O'Neal was always giant-sized.

By the time he was a teenager, he had sprouted into an imposing 6'8" man-child who was hard to miss in a crowd. The first time LSU coach Brown met him, O'Neal was an Army brat living on a military base in Wildflecken, West Germany, with his father, drill sergeant Phil Harrison.

Brown was overseas, conducting a clinic for the troops, when he got a tap on the back from O'Neal, who was seeking advice.

"Coach, I can't dunk. I tire easily and I'm trying to make the team here," O'Neal said. "Can you show me some drills."

Brown offered some advice. He had one final question before he left. "How long have you been in the service, solider?" Brown asked.

"I'm not a solider," O'Neal said. "I'm fourteen years old."

It was love at first sight. Brown began recruiting O'Neal that day and his persistence paid off. O'Neal signed with the Tigers after establishing himself as a 7'1", 290-pound behemoth who averaged 32.1 points, 13.5 rebounds, and eight blocks as a senior for Robert G. Cole High in San Antonio, which finished 36-0 at the Texas state championship. His 791 rebounds is still a record for all classes that stands today.

The extroverted O'Neal, the top prospect in the class of 1989 and the MVP of the McDonald's All-American game, toyed with the competition in high school. He had a dominant college career once he got used to practicing against 7'0" heavyweight teammate Roberts.

At first, Roberts pushed O'Neal around. But in the end, O'Neal's determination won out.

*LSU Athletics*

Shaq averaged 21.6 points, 13.5 rebounds, and 4.6 blocked shots in his three years at LSU. He was a two-time consensus first team All-American, a two-time SEC Athlete of the Year, and the AP National Player of the Year as a sophomore in 1991 (when he averaged 27.6 points, 14.7 rebounds, five blocks, while shooting 62.8 percent).

O'Neal's junior statistics were just as impressive. O'Neal averaged 24.3 points, 14 rebounds, and 5.2 blocks, leading the country in the last two categories. He also snot 61.5 percent for a team that reached a ninth consecutive NCAA tournament.

Ironically, despite the fact he played with stars like two-time All-American guard Chris Jackson and Roberts as a freshman, O'Neal never played in an NCAA Final Four.

Shaq left his mark with his individual brilliance. He set a Maravich Assembly Hall scoring record as a sophomore when he poured in 53 points against Arkansas State in December

LSU Athletics

1990. He led the SEC in rebounding for three straight years. He set a conference record for most blocks in a season for three consecutive years (115 in 1990, 140 in 1991, and 157 in 1992). He set an SEC record for career blocks with 412, and he blocked five or more shots in a game in 45 of 90 career games. O'Neal set an SEC single-game record with 12 blocks against Loyola-Marymount in 1990 and blocked 11 shots against BYU in the first round of the 1992 NCAA tournament.

By the time he declared for the 1992 NBA draft, he had become a national celebrity and the man with a thousand nicknames— Diesel, The Big Aristotle, Shaq Fu, the Big Cactus, Superman, and Shaq Daddy. O'Neal was selected by Orlando with the Number One pick overall. He quickly became one of the best centers in the league. O'Neal, who played most of his pro career at 325 pounds, was the NBA Rookie of the Year and a 2000 NBA MVP. He played in fifteen All-Star games, was a 14-time NBA All Star, combined with Kobe Bryant to win three NBA championships with the Lakers in 2000, 2001, and 2002, and won another in 2006 after he was traded to Miami. He was a star on the US team that won the 1994 FIBA World championship and the gold medal in the 1996 Olympics. He was elected to the Naismith Hall of Fame in 2016.

In addition to basketball, O'Neal has released four albums, appeared in numerous films, and starred in his own reality shows, Shaq's Big Challenge and Shaq Vs. He also found time to complete his education, taking online courses to graduate in 2000 with a degree in business and earning his MBA in 2005.

O'Neal will always be fondly remembered at LSU, where a 900-pound bronze statue of him was erected in front of the LSU Tigers' Basketball Practice facility.

Now Shaq can be seen all over TV in commercials and having a great time joining Charles Barkley, Kenny Smith, and host Ernie Johnson, who deserves triple his pay for trying to control those three! They have a great blast working together.

LSU Athletics

# Xavier McDaniel

## (1981-1985)

*Wichita State Athletics*

### Carved in Stone

Wichita State coach, Gene Smithson, first heard about 6'7" forward, Xavier McDaniel, from his football coach, Willie Jeffries, who had an assistant who had lived across the street from the McDaniel family in Columbia, South Carolina.

McDaniel was a star at A.C. Flora High, where he was a teammate of Tyrone Corbin, who later played for DePaul and in the NBA. At first, Smithson thought, despite the fact Wichita was coming off a Final Eight appearance in 1981, McDaniel might be reluctant to sign because the Shockers already had two juniors and future NBA players, Antoine Carr and Cliff Levingston, playing his position.

McDaniel wasn't worried about a log jam at his position. He was confident enough in his abilities and he knew he would one day own the program. He did, becoming the first player to lead the nation in both rebounding and scoring in the same season.

*Wichita State Athletics*

## Getting the Glass

McDaniel came to school with the nickname "X Man" or simply "X." He began to shave both his head and his eyebrows to look more intimidating and he wasn't afraid of anyone. One day after a heated practice his freshman year, Carr and Levingston were riding him.

McDaniel chased them down and told them, "You two Playboy All-Americans, one day, I will have one of your jobs. They will know the X-Man was here." For his first two seasons at Wichita State, the Shockers were on NCAA probation. McDaniel had to wait a year for his turn. When Levingston left for the NBA, McDaniel became a starter and averaged 18.8 points and led the country in rebounding with an average of 14.4 a game. He did that as a power forward playing opposite Carr in 1982, a year when Patrick Ewing of Georgetown, Hakeem Olajuwon of Houston, and Ralph Sampson of Virginia were all playing. The following season, Carr left and became a first-round NBA draft pick of the Detroit Pistons. McDaniel—then a junior—raised his profile again, averaging 20.6 points and winning the first of his two Missouri Valley Conference MVP awards.

Then, in the 1984-1985 season, he provided a statistical anomaly. He became the first player in Division I history to lead the country in both rebounding and scoring, averaging 27.8 points and 14.8 rebounds and leading the Shockers to win the Valley tournament and earn an at-large bid to 1985 NCAA tournament.

"What a freak of nature," Wichita State assistant coach Randy Smithson said in a commemorative book on 100 years of basketball in the Missouri Valley written by Steve Richardson. "He would go over you, through you, and by you to get a rebound. He would rebound the ball, throw an outlet pass and get behind the defense for an alley-oop and dunk it—all on the same play. I knew one thing. The guy was tenacious. I would have to protect other players from him in practice. It was just a war. He got inside the lines and he commanded attention. He was such a competitor, he expected everybody around him to be as competitive as he would be. He was up all the time. He would rather get a rebound than a basket."

Bradley coach, Dick Versace, once made the mistake of suggesting Wichita statisticians were padding McDaniel's rebounding statistics. The next time the two teams played, McDaniel scored 34 points and grabbed 20 rebounds in the Shockers 97-96 overtime victory. This time the Bradley statisticians kept the book and during the game, McDaniel looked over at the Bradley bench.

"Is that OK," he said. "Do you know I can rebound?"

He sure could.

*Wichita State Athletics*

# Dick Vitale's

## MOUNT RUSHMORE
## OF
## ALL BOB VILA

# CHARLES BARKLEY

# DWYANE WADE

# GORDON HAYWARD

# BUDDY HIELD

# Charles Barkley
## (1982-1984)

Auburn University

## Carved in Stone

They came out of nowhere and built themselves up into stars. None so much as Charles Barkley. Every time I run into the Round Mound of Rebounding, he drops to the ground and says, "Dickie V, I want to kiss your feet. You motivated me, I knew that if that guy could make it in TV, I could too."

Man, has he made it in TV? Oh, wish I could be his agent.

Thanks for your love, Charles.

## The Build-Up

I remember being in Kansas City a few years back. I was thrilled to be on the same stage with Sir Charles as we were inducted into the College Basketball Hall of Fame.

I also remember the big bear hug he gave me that night. My ribs are still sore, baby!

Barkley was the classic late bloomer.

The 6'4 (and ¾)", 260-pound Naismith Hall of Fame forward, who is just one of four players to score over 20,000 points, grab 10,000 rebounds and contribute 4,000 assists during his 15-year professional career, was born and raised in Leeds, Alabama, near Birmingham. He attended Leeds High School. Barkley put all his energies into basketball. At first, he wasn't very good. He was only 5'7" until his junior year and he was used to getting bullied in games. But he had an innate ability to jump and learned to hit the sky after he began jumping over a three-and-a-half-foot fence hour after hour, and jumping rope while spending hours on the court.

Barkley grew to 6'1", 220 pounds as a junior and became a skilled point guard. Then, during the summer, Barkley grew to 6'4", 250 pounds and was too big to bully as a senior. He emerged as a star, averaging 19.1 points and 17.9 rebounds. He led his team to 26-3 in the Alabama state tournament. Despite his improvement, he got no attention from college scouts until the state semi-finals when he scored 26 points and outplayed the state's biggest recruit, 6'8" future Alabama standout Bobby Lee Hurt.

The late Herbert Greene, an assistant to Auburn coach Sonny Smith, was in the stands and reported seeing *"…a fat guy who's 6'3" or 6'4" and weighs 280 pounds or 290…and he can jump out of the gym. You need to see him."*

Smith was intrigued enough to go to Leeds to see Barkley in person. "The ball bounced off the board for a rebound. He jumped up and caught it and threw it to midcourt before he hit the floor," Smith said. "I said to myself, 'we've got to have this guy.' Fortunately, we ended up with him and got one of the greatest players to ever play here."

It took a while for Barkley, who played center for Auburn, to become the dominant player who led the SEC in rebounding for three years from 1981 through 1984. Smith was hard on him, and Barkley temporarily quit the team as a freshman, but his mother, desperate for her child to escape poverty, begged him to return.

Barkley did and became a star. He averaged just 14.8 points, but grabbed 9.6 rebounds and 1.7 blocks and shot 62.2 percent during his career, constantly fighting a battle with his weight. At one point, he ballooned to 300 pounds and Kentucky fans had a pizza delivered to him for a game at Rupp Arena. Sportswriters tagged him with nicknames like "Boy Gorge" and the "Round Mound of Rebound."

But nobody questioned his ability. Sir Charles, who paired a jovial personality with a physical style of play, was a popular crowd-pleaser, exciting fans with dunks and blocks that belied his overweight frame. It was not uncommon to see Barkley grab a rebound and, instead of passing, dribble the length of the floor to slam home a two-handed dunk.

*Auburn University*

Barkley was good enough to earn an invitation to the 1984 Olympic trials, but he and coach Bob Knight clashed during practices and Barkley was a late cut.

His skills weren't lost on the late Philadelphia 76ers assistant, Jack McMahon, who convinced the team to take him with the Number 5 pick in a loaded draft that had Hakeem Olajuwon, Michael Jordan, and Sam Bowie. Barkley went on to play in 11 NBA All-Star games and win two gold medals on the 1992 Olympic Dream team and the 1996 Olympic team. He was voted the NBA MVP in 1993 and was selected as one of the Top 50 players in NBA history during the league's 50th anniversary.

Auburn retired Barkley's number 34 jersey in 2001 and the school has since erected a statue to him outside Jordan-Hare Stadium, next to the school's three Heisman Trophy winners—Pat Sullivan, Bo Jackson and Cam Newton.

He has gone on to a great career in television, expressing his opinions. I would love the opportunity to call a game with him. That would be awesome baby—with a capital A!

# Dwyane Wade
## (2001-2003)

*Marquette University*

## Carved in Stone

I will never forget doing those classic Conference USA battles between Marquette and Louisville. The first time I laid eyes on Dwyane Wade, I said to myself, *This is going to be one special, big-time player.*

What really impressed and overwhelmed me was watching his mentor, Tom Crean, put him through an intense workout. When the practice session ended, I simply said to coach Crean, *"this guy's work ethic is so unique. With that combination of skills plus the passion to want to get better, there will be no holding him back."*

## The Build-Up

Wade changed the dynamics of Marquette basketball, lifting the Catholic Jesuit University in Milwaukee from mid-major status back to the national spotlight. The 6'5" junior guard exploded for a triple-double—29 points, 11 rebounds, and 11 assists—as the Golden Eagles stunned top-seed Kentucky, 83-69, in 2003 to advance to the Final Four for the first time since 1977.

It was an exclamation point on a brilliant individual season where Wade averaged 21.5 points, led the Golden Eagles to the Conference USA regular-season championship, and became the first Marquette player since Lee in 1978 to make first team All-American.

Marquette is located just ninety miles north of Chicago, but it was an eternity from where Wade grew up in the gang and drug-infested neighborhood on the South side. His mother, who gave birth to him at eighteen, became addicted, got involved in the drug trade, and spent time in prison on two separate occasions. Wade himself witnessed police—with guns drawn—raiding his home when he was only six, and he recalled finding several dead bodies in a garbage can.

When Wade was eight, one of his older sisters, Tragil, tricked him—telling him they were going to the movies—and took him instead to live with his father, a former Army sergeant, and stepmother in a nearby neighborhood. A year later, the family moved to Robbins, Illinois, where Wade turned to sports, especially basketball and football, to avoid the temptations of participating in drug and gang-related activities.

Like most kids growing up in Chicago, Wade idolized Michael Jordan and tried to pattern his game after him. Wade attended Richards High School in Oak Lawn and did not play much with the varsity basketball team, until his junior year (after he had grown four inches in the summer). He blossomed into a star and averaged 27 points and 11 rebounds as a senior, while leading his team to a 24-5 record and the Sectional Final of the Illinois State Class AA State Tournament.

Wade was lightly recruited and only had three offers (Marquette, Illinois State, and DePaul) because his board scores were below qualifying standards. While other schools backed off, Marquette's first-year coach, Tom Crean, recognizing Wade's potential, continued to push, and was the first coach to contact him in the summer recruiting period.

"I wanted to be your first call because this is how important you are to Marquette and our future," Crean told Wade.

When Crean arrived for the 2000 season, Marquette was in the midst of a protracted 22-year, post-Al McGuire slump, with almost as many losing seasons (four) as NCAA tournament victories (six).

Wade changed that. He sat out his freshman year as a Proposition 48 student (*i.e.*, his grades didn't meet the minimum standards for play eligibility). Wade sought tutoring to improve his writing skills and regain his eligibility. He immediately made his presence felt, averaging 17.8 points, 6.6 rebounds, and 3.4 assists for a team that went 26-7, achieving its best record since 1994. Although the Golden Eagles lost to Tulsa in the first round of the 2002 NCAA tournament, the Eagles became nationally relevant again.

Wade and Marquette only got better during his junior year, winning 27 games and spending the entire season in the AP Top 25. The Golden Eagles survived close calls against Holy Cross, Missouri, and Pitt to set up an Elite Eight showdown against a Number 1 seeded Kentucky team that went 16-0 in the SEC and were making their seventh regional final appearance of the last twelve seasons.

The Cats had no answers for Wade, the unheralded recruit from Chicago who got the best of Keith Bogans, the ballyhooed McDonald's All-American four-year starting guard from fabled DeMatha Catholic. Wade was selected MVP of the Midwest Region. Not only was Marquette a Cinderella story, but their victory over Kentucky resonated throughout the country and served as a springboard for its move to the Big East in 2005.

Even though the Golden Eagles lost to Kansas in the national semi-finals, they finished sixth in the final AP poll and Wade got enough visibility in the national media to declare for the 2003 NBA draft, where he became the fifth player chosen by the Miami Heat. This achievement made him the school's highest draft pick ever. No doubt, Wade will be heading to Springfield, Massachusetts, as a Hall of Famer to join the fraternity that already has former Marquette Coach, Al McGuire.

# Gordon Hayward
## (2009-2010)

*Butler Athletics*

## Carved in Stone

Imagine if the wild shot from mid-coast went in and Butler stunned the Dukies at the Final Four in Indianapolis…it almost happened, baby! The city of Indianapolis would have never been the same if it went in. That was a memorable evening as Cinderella almost found the glass slipper!

## The Build-Up

Gordon Hayward will best be remembered as the 6'8" sophomore forward from Butler who launched that half-court shot against Duke in the 2010 national championship game in Indianapolis.

The ball hit the backboard and rim, then fell off, ending the Bulldogs' run that made them one of the most beloved teams in the history of the NCAA tournament.

Hayward made a name for himself with NBA scouts that night and was selected by Utah with the ninth pick overall after he declared for the draft.

No one saw this coming when Hayward was growing up.

There was a time when it looked like he might take up another sport, all together, in tennis. Hayward's first appearance on the sports pages came when he and his twin sister, Heather, were featured in a regional edition of the Indianapolis Star after they played mixed doubles together in the Indiana State Open in 2005. Heather had played Number One on her high school team at Brownsburg, Indiana High and Gordon followed in his sister's footsteps the next year. At the time, they hoped to attend Purdue, their parents' alma mater.

Although Gordon's first love was basketball, he was only 5'11" as a ninth grader and didn't think playing basketball in college was a realistic goal. He was ready to quit the sport completely, until his mother convinced him to stick with basketball one more year.

It was a smart decision.

Everything changed for Gordon when he underwent a growth spurt, shooting up to 6'4" as a sophomore and 6'8" as a senior at Brownsburg. Hayward had grown into a power forward, but still had a guard's skill set. He averaged 18 points, 8.4 rebounds, and 3.6 assists and was named first team All-State. He led Brownsburg to the 2008 Indiana 4A state championship. In the title game, Hayward hit a game-winning layup at the buzzer to defeat Marion High, 40-39, in Indianapolis.

Hayward had three scholarship offers, one from Indiana University-Purdue University-Indianapolis (IUPUI), another from Purdue, and a third from Butler. He chose the Bulldogs because the team's 6:30 A.M. practice sessions would not interfere with his planned computer engineering major and because Heather would be able to play tennis there. When he verbally committed to Butler as a junior, he skipped travel team basketball during the following summer because he wanted to put in extra time on the tennis court, so he could contend for the state high school title his senior year. He had a 26-3 record in singles but lost in the state tournament. He could have been a contender in that sport, too, baby! But it was on the basketball courts, and not the tennis courts, where he became a memorable stand-out.

Hayward unexpectedly made an immediate impact playing for Brad Stevens his freshman year in 2009. Butler had lost four starters from a 30-win squad, but the Bulldogs went 26-5 and won the Horizon League. Hayward averaged 13.1 points and 6.5 rebounds and was named Horizon Newcomer of the Year and first team All-Conference.

_Butler Athletics_

After the season, he propelled himself into the national spotlight when he played for USA Basketball's U19 team in New Zealand, averaging 10 points and 5.7 rebounds and making the all-tournament team. Hayward was named to multiple pre-season All American teams prior to his sophomore season. He had a year to remember, finishing in the Horizon's Top Five in both scoring and rebounding with 15.2 points and 8.5 rebounds, as well as being named Horizon League Player of the Year before leading the Bulldogs to their first Final Four.

The Hayward family began hearing from agents but were not ready to counsel their son about such a big decision. So, Stevens contacted NBA scouts and general managers and discovered Hayward was projected to go in the Top 20 in the 2010 draft even before the tournament.

As his parents walked out of Lucas Oil Stadium, his mother said, "If God wanted him to go to the NBA, he would have made the shot."

His father responded with, "What else is he going to do, get Butler all the way back to the final and hit the shot?"

Gordon declared for the NBA draft, but had until May 8 to withdraw. The day before, the family announced Gordon would stay in the draft and eventually come back to school to earn his degree. He has recently been reunited with Stevens on the Boston Celtics, though an injury sidelined him for most of the 2017-2018 campaign. Hayward's former college coach, Stevens, has done a majestic job despite an injury-plagued team. The Celtic faithful can't wait to see what the coach will do as players like Hayward get healthy, again.

# Buddy Hield
## (2013-2016)

*University of Oklahoma*

## Carved in Stone

Over the years, I have been blessed to sit at courtside for some dramatic moments, but one of the greatest was on January 4, 2016, when Kansas and Oklahoma both were named number one in two respective polls. It set up a titanic battle at the famed Allen Field House. The rock, chalk, Jayhawk crowd was electric. The intensity and emotion was very similar to an NCAA tournament clash.

Buddy Hield, the sensational Sooner All-American, put on a dazzling show that even had the Jayhawks fans in awe. Fellow broadcaster, Brent Musburger, and I sat there with smiles on our faces as we wanted the game to go on and on because it was THAT GOOD!

Hield's 46 was a thing of beauty, but it fell short as Bill Self's squad escaped with a hard-fought W, 109-106 in three overtimes.

No one who grew up with Buddy could have projected Oklahoma 6'5" All-American guard Buddy Hield would win the 2016 Wooden Award and three other national Player of the Year trophies.

## The Build-Up

Hield was raised in a rough, drug-infested neighborhood in East Mile Rock, a coastal village west of Freeport in the West Grand Bahama district of the Bahamas.

He was just trying to survive.

Hield was the fifth of seven children who were raised by a single mother, Jackie Braynen, who worked three jobs cleaning other people's houses while partnering with uncles and his grandparents to hold the family together.

Hield fell in love with basketball at an early age, but needed a hoop to practice on. He created a makeshift one out of a milk crate taped to a light pole. Other times, he would take the spokes out of his bicycle tires and create a hoop that way and attach it to a pole. He used these "unique design skills" and tireless work ethic to escape poverty and give himself a chance at a new life.

Hield got his first taste of celebrity when The All-Bahamian Brand, a basketball magazine, rated him as the best eighth grader in the islands. Then he led his Jack Hayward High School team to the championship of the Providence Holiday Tournament on a buzzer beater. Next, he led his team to the Grand Bahamas High School championship as a ninth grader.

University of Oklahoma

One of the spectators who watched him play was Kyle Linsted, the coach at Sunrise Christian Academy in a suburb of Wichita, Kansas. Linsted would make an annual pilgrimage to the islands searching for kids who wanted to play in the states. He immediately offered Hield a scholarship even though he was just 6'1", 120-pounds, because he was moved by his extroverted personality and the way he interacted with fans.

"I guess you could say I got lucky," Linsted said.

Hield led Sunrise to the National Association of Christian Athletes national championship as a junior and was named MVP. His senior year, he averaged 22.7 points on 49 percent shooting in just 21 minutes per game. He ultimately chose Oklahoma over Kansas.

He was mostly a slasher as a freshman as he started about half the games. He worked on his shooting mechanics and became more of a spot-up shooter as a sophomore. Hield also was persistent with the mental part of his game.

"After every practice, he asked 'Coach, what do I need to work on? What do I need to do?" Oklahoma University coach, Lon Kruger, once said.

Hield emerged as a high volume, three-point shooter with the Sooners as a junior, averaging 17.4 points and 5.4 rebounds. He was selected Big 12 Player of the Year and was a third-team All-American as the Sooners advanced to the NCAA tournament's Sweet 16.

He considered declaring for the NBA draft, but came back because he knew he needed to work on his ball-handling, leadership, and ability to finish at the rim. He also wanted to play in a Final Four. His bet paid off!

Hield's game really took off as a senior when he averaged 25 points, 5.7 rebounds, two assists, made first team All-American, won the Wooden Award, and led the nation with 4.1 three-point goals per game. He highlighted his regular season when he went off for 46 points in the overtime loss at Kansas, tying the record for most points scored by an opponent in Allen Field House. Hield made seven of his eight three-pointers in the second half on the way to 32 points against LSU. He hit a game-winning three-pointer against Texas and scored 39 in the Big 12 Tournament against Iowa State.

Hield put on one last college masterpiece in the NCAA tournament West Region finals when he shot 13 for 20 and drained 8 of 13 three-pointers, scoring 37 points, as Oklahoma defeated Oregon, 80-68, in Anaheim...*to advance to its first Final Four since 1988*. Mission accomplished—and he did it in front of his hero, Kobe Bryant.

"Everybody who knows me knows I'm a huge Kobe Bryant fan," Hield said. "You have to perform when the Mamba is in town."

Hield will get a chance to follow in his footsteps someday. He was selected by the Sacramento Kings with the eighth pick overall in the 2016 NBA draft.

*University of Oklahoma*

# *Dick Vitale's*
## MOUNT RUSHMORE
## OF
## ALL VELCRO
## DEFENSIVE STOPPERS

STACEY AUGMON

SHANE BATTIER

TIM DUNCAN

PATRICK EWING

# Stacey Augmon
## (1988-1991)

*UNLV Athletics*

## Carved in Stone

When I would watch the Runnin' Rebels practice, during the Tark days, it was always interesting to see the superman effort of Stacey Augmon through all of their defensive drills. Tark was a big believer in pressure defense and he would rave after practice of the skills of Augmon.

Augmon earned the nickname "Plastic Man" when he played for colorful Hall of Fame coach Jerry Tarkanian on the great UNLV teams from 1988 through 1991 because of his extreme athleticism that made his elastic body look like it was made of plastic.

When I think of defense, Augmon's name comes up among the crème de la crème

## The Limiter

The athletic 6'7" forward was a super hero on a team that played in two NCAA Final Fours and an NCAA Tournament championship in 1990. Augmon was the perfect complement to 6'8", 250-pound first team All-American, Larry Johnson, a 2,000-point career scorer who was a second team All-American as a senior when he averaged 16.5 points with 275 steals and was the Rebels' most disruptive defensive force during their title run. Tarkanian discovered Augmon in Pasadena, California—his own hometown. Augmon was a talent, but wasn't recruited by either UCLA or USC, because the two PAC-10 coaches thought he would be academically ineligible.

Tarkanian, who I labeled the Father Flanagan of coaching, always loved to give second opportunities to multi-talented players who had some problems off the court. He had a special way of reaching them, because they respected his work ethic and his dedication to trying to make them realize they had potential that shouldn't be wasted. Tarkanian was under an endless investigation by the NCAA because he had gambled on kids who had some problems. He had a lot of friends from the old neighborhood like his brother, who was coaching Pasadena City Community College; and the football coach, Harvey Hyde. They lobbied Augmon on his behalf, even if it meant the recruit would have to sit out a year.

"He gave the guys that were borderline, that a lot of colleges wouldn't touch, a second chance," Augmon said. "He was like a second father to me. He was a true leader by example in my younger years. I remember, in high school, I had a reputation as a troubled kid, but coach Tark was the type of coach that believed in everyone's potential who gave everyone a second chance. I was one of those guys. I came to UNLV as a young, misled, misunderstood kid and just didn't know anything about life. Coach Tark took me under his wing, and after my five years at UNLV, I left as a young man with great values, a better person, and with a great love and understanding of the game."

Augmon quickly turned into a star at Vegas, which was considered an outlaw program by some because the players wore black sneakers, baggy shorts, and custom-made Nike uniforms. (Man, how times have changed!) Augmon won the 1988 Big West Freshman of the Year and was a member the U.S. Olympic team that summer.

*UNLV Athletics*

Augmon went on to win the 1989 Big West Player of the Year award and was named first team All-Big West in 1991.

More importantly, he won three consecutive NABC national Defensive Player of the Year awards and played a huge role in the Rebels' 90-81 victory over Georgia Tech in the 1990 national semi-finals when he scored 22 points and grabbed nine rebounds and limited deep shooting guard, Dennis Scott, who had scored 20 points in the first half and just three field goals in the second half when the Rebels took control.

Augmon had twelve points and nine rebounds when Vegas blew away Duke, 103-73, to win its first national championship, blowing the game wide open with an 18-0 run early in the second half. They became the first team to score more than 100 points in a title game.

"I was very surprised it was that easy," Augmon said. "But we were a team on a mission and we were ready to play that night."

After the game, the players put on T-shirts in tribute to Tark the Shark. "Shark Takes a Bite," the shirt read on the front with "They Just Couldn't Run with the Rebels" on the back.

Augmon went on to play in the NBA for fifteen years and coached in the league as an assistant for four years before returning to Vegas as an assistant coach in 2016. There, he will *always* be known as Mr. Rebel.

UNLV Athletics

# Shane Battier

## (1997-2001)

*Duke Athletics*

## Carved in Stone

I believe Shane Battier will be a success in any venture goes into. I've always believed Battier could even be a future President of the United States! He is that awesome, baby!

The one thing I remember, in the world of broadcasting is that you could say fifty nice things about a player or coach, but—when you say one negative thing—the phone rings off the hook. Shane was a rarity and I will never forget, prior to an ACC Goliath match-up between Duke and arch-rival North Carolina, he came up to me before the game. He said, "Dickie V, I want to thank you for all the beautiful things you've said about me during my four years at Duke." I was stunned because that does not happen very often.

## The Limiter

Duke's 6'8" forward Battier arguably had the best senior year of any player in the Mike Krzyzewski era.

In 2001, Battier was the co-ACC Player of the Year, ACC tournament MVP, consensus National Player of the Year, ACC and National Defensive Player of the Year for a third straight time, a first team Academic All-American for the second time, and the leader of a national championship team.

He made it look so easy.

But Battier had to be prodded into becoming the next Bill Bradley. When Battier arrived at Duke from Detroit Country Day School in Birmingham, Michigan, he was a McDonald's All-American and the state's Mr. Basketball as well as an excellent student. But in the early part of his career, he constantly deferred to the upperclassmen and more assertive players, content to be the glue guy who played defense and made everyone else better with his fundamentals—sometimes at the expense of his own success.

After Duke lost to Connecticut in the 1999 NCAA championship game and four players—Elton Brand, Corey Magette, William Avery, and Trajan Langdon—left early for the NBA, Duke coach Mike Krzyzewski and his assistants Quinn Snyder and Johnny Dawkins knew it was time for a change.

They told Battier, a sophomore who averaged less than five shots a game, it was time to step up his game offensively. The team needed a leader and Krzyzewski thought Battier was ready. Krzyzewski started calling him from the office.

He would say, "Hey Shane, are you ready to be an All-American next year?"

Battier would sort of laugh and answer, "Well, Coach" and, all of a sudden, *click*, Coach K would hang up.

Battier was confused.

The next day, Krzyzewski called him again.

This time he said, "Hey Shane, are you ready to average 20 points and grab 10 rebounds a game?"

Battier begain, "Well, Coach…" Click. Hung up on again.

The following day, Krzyzewski called one more time and said, "Hey, Shane, are you ready to lead us to a national championship?"

He said, "Yes, Coach, I am." He needed to believe in himself and, more importantly, visualize what he was capable of doing before he was going to be able to go on that journey.

Battier took the lesson to heart.

He averaged 17.4 points, was a second-team All-American a first team All-ACC selection, and NABC Defensive Player as a junior when the Blue Devils advanced to the Sweet 16.

Then, he took over college basketball as a senior, playing his most complete basketball during March Madness when

*Duke Athletics*

Duke Athletics

he averaged 22.5 points and 10.5 rebounds during the Blue Devils' championship run. He scored 25 points during Duke's dramatic 22-point comeback victory over ACC rival Maryland in the national semi-finals in Minneapolis. Then, he scored 18 points and grabbed 11 rebounds as the Devils defeated Arizona in the finals. Battier was an easy choice for Most Outstanding Player.

It was the perfect ending to a fairy tale season. By the time Battier finished his college career, he was one of the only players in NCAA history to finish with at least 1,500 points, 500 rebounds, 200 blocks, 200 steals and 200 assists. Battier played in 131 victories, an NCAA record and just fifteen losses. Duke went 59-5 in the ACC with Battier in the lineup, winning the ACC tournament three times.

He was the ultimate team player who believed there was always more to a game than making or missing shots.

# Tim Duncan
## (1994-1997)

*Wake Forest Athletics*

### Carved in Stone

Tim Duncan was a video game fanatic in college. He acknowledges a certain joy of playing himself on basketball video games and said, if he had a chance, he would challenge NBA champions Wilt Chamberlain and Kareem Abdul-Jabbar to a one-on-one game.

No fear, as the T-shirt he wore said.

You can make a case for Wake Forest's 6'11" center Duncan as the best four-year player since 7'3" Ralph Sampson of Virginia in the history of the Atlantic Coast Conference.

### The Limiter

Duncan was a quiet, understated superstar who dominated play in the ACC in an era when the league was in its glory years in the 1990s. Mike Krzyzewski of Duke won two consecutive national championships and Dean Smith of North Carolina won another. Duncan arrived in Winston-Salem from the U.S. Virgin Islands in 1993, right after Duke's All-America forward Christian Laettner departed.

183

Duncan was a three-time All-American, two-time ACC of the Year who was the consensus national Player of the Year as a senior in 1997. He averaged a double-double for his career, averaging 16.5 points and 12.5 rebounds. He became the 10th player in NCAA history to reach the 2,000-point, 1,500-rebound milestone, finishing with 2,117 and 1,570, respectively. He ranks second in NCAA history in career blocked shots. In 1995, following his sophomore year, Lakers' General Manager, Jerry West, suggested Duncan could be the first pick in the draft. The same applied to the 1996 and 1997 NBA drafts, but he stayed in college because he promised his mother he would earn his degree.

"Tim wins most of the statistical battles and he's set a lot of records that are going to be hard to break but it's hard to say where he stands with the greatest centers of all-time." Wake coach, Dave Odom, who coached Sampson one season and faced Patrick Ewing of Georgetown and Hakeem Olajuwon of Houston as an assistant at Virginia in the 1980s, told Sports Illustrated, "I'll say this, though. If you're looking for a fearless warrior who plays his A game every single night, you'd have a hard time finding anyone better than Timmy in every era."

Duncan taught Wake—the smallest school in the ACC—how to win at the highest level. The Demon Deacons went 97-31 during Duncan's career, making him the most successful player in school history. He led Wake to back-to-back ACC championships in 1995 and 1996, the 1995 ACC regular season title, and four appearances in the NCAA tournament, including a trip to the Sweet 16 in 1995 and the Elite Eight in 1996.

Wake ended up losing to Kentucky, 83-61, in a game where Duncan was less than 100 percent due to having the flu.

What really set Duncan apart was his defense. Long before he was a fifteen-time NBA All Defensive team selection with the San Antonio Spurs, Duncan was the only player ever selected as a three-time Defensive Player of the Year by the National Association of Basketball Coaches.

Duncan had size and wingspan and athleticism and was an imposing shot-blocking presence in the paint as Wake limited most of its competition to less than 40 percent shooting. Duncan, who rarely came out of the game, was a constant obstacle.

"It seems like every time you turn around he's staring you in the face," Missouri forward, David Grimm, once said. "I could have sworn there were four or five Tim Duncans out there."

Duncan first made his presence felt as a sophomore in 1995 when he averaged 16.8 points, 12.5 rebounds and 3.98 blocks. He neutralized North Carolina's 7'0" All-American forward, Rasheed Wallace, and teammate, Randolph Childress, who scored 37 and hit a game-winning shot during an 82-80 victory. Then, playing against Oklahoma State in the Sweet 16, he scored 12 points to go with 22 rebounds, outplaying 7'0" Bryant "Big Country" Reeves, but his team lost, 71-66.

Duncan went off for 27 points, 22 rebounds and 6 assists as a junior when Wake defeated Georgia Tech, 75-74, to win another ACC tournament championship. Duncan, who was selected MVP, missed two free throws with 18 seconds to play, but his presence caused Tech guard Steph Marbury to adjust his thinking and his shot.

Marbury, who scored 26 points, drove the right baseline and went up for a jumper, falling away as he released the ball, but his line of sight was obscured by a leaping Duncan. "When I shot the ball, I couldn't really see the rim because Tim was in the way," Marbury admitted.

The ball never reached the rim, hitting the side of the backboard and falling out of bounds with 2.3 seconds to play.

It was the Duncan nightmare effect.

Wake advanced to the 1996 Elite Eight before losing to eventual national champion Kentucky, 83-63, in a game where Duncan was less than effective because of the flu and the fact the Cats constantly double and triple teamed him.

"One of the most amazing things about him, when he started to evolve as a player, is he blocked a lot of shots from behind," Wake assistant Ernie Nestor said. "Guys would get by him, and then he'd block them from behind. He had incredible defensive patience."

Duncan, who picked up the nickname "the Big Fundamental," used the enormous skills he learned at Wake to win two NBA MVPs and five NBA championships with the Spurs.

# Patrick Ewing
## (1982-1985)

Big East Conference

### Carved in Stone

Over a decade ago now (Man, time flies when you're having fun, baby!), I came out with a book that signified the top 50 players during my first three decades at ESPN. My number one player, which was a surprise to many, was the defensive dynamo of the Georgetown Hoyas, Patrick Ewing.

I always felt that Patrick was worth fifteen points per game before the contest even started. Psychologically, he was a difference maker as opponents were aware of his presence. They were affected by his shot-blocking intimidation.

### The Limiter

Ewing never saw Bill Russell play in person and only met him twice when he was a three-time All American at Georgetown, but the 7'0", 240-pound center, who had an eight-foot wing span, found himself placed in the same category when he led John Thompson's Hoyas to three NCAA championship games and one national championship in 1984. He accomplished the feat with his intimidating defense and shot blocking from 1982-1985. Ewing, who was the ultimate road block on the Georgetown suffocating press, established the Hoyas as the best defensive team in the modern era.

Ewing's offensive statistics were modest, but he finished his career with 493 blocked shots and an average of 3.93 rejections per game his junior and senior years.

"Blocking a shot is worse than dunking on a guy," Russell said. "When you dunk on a guy, it tells him something. But it usually makes him mad. Blocking a guy's shot scares him. He may challenge you once, twice, three times. But if you get to block a couple of his shots, it gets him thinking twice where you are every time he gets ready to shoot."

Ewing made his presence felt from the time he was a freshman, swatting away the first four shots North Carolina took in the 1982 national championship game on the orders of his coach. Officials called him for goaltending on four of those rejections, but he had set the tone for a physical, rugged game that ended with the Tar Heels winning, 63-62.

"I still don't think they were goaltending," Ewing recalled.

Ewing was a giant force on the court. In his team's three Final Four runs, the Hoyas played sixteen games and held their opponents to under 50 points ten times. Even allowing for the lack of a shot clock or three-point line, most NCAA teams thrived to shoot 50 percent, but in the six games they played in the regionals in those years, the Hoyas' opponents never shot higher than 41 percent and were held below 40 percent three times.

Then, in the 1985 tournament, the Hoyas faced three consecutive great guards. They held Loyola's Alfredrick Hughes, the leading scorer in the country, to just eight points, limited Mark Price to just 3 for 16 shooting in the regional finals, and completely shut down Chris Mullin, the Big East Player of the Year, in the national semi-finals. Mullin got off only eight shots, never reached the foul line, and scored just eight points.

The one game that stands out in the Ewing era was the Hoyas' 53-40 victory over Kentucky in the 1984 national semi-finals. The Cats started two seven footers—Sam Bowie and Melvin Turpin—in a twin towers offense. Kentucky jumped out to a seven-point lead in the first half when Ewing had early foul trouble and was on the bench for the final 8:52 of the half with three personals.

Then, the world collapsed on the Cats, who had never lost a national semi-final game.

Georgetown's suffocating defense took over, overwhelming the Wildcats with a 12-point outburst at the start of the second half and keeping them scoreless for the first 9 minutes and 56 seconds. "We like to tease our enemies, making them happy and think they will blow us out," Thompson said. "Then we come back."

The key to Georgetown's success was a pressing defense that smothered Kentucky, forcing hurried shots, caused fifteen turnovers, and prompted a frustrated Joe B. Hall, Kentucky's coach, to toss his rolled-up program over his shoulder with four minutes to play. Kentucky, which made just 24.5 percent of its shots in the second half when none of its starters made a field goal, shooting 0 for 21. Ewing and forward Michael Graham personally took care of Bowie and Turpin, forcing them to shoot jump shots instead of powering their way inside for easier, high percentage shots, and never challenging Ewing for a fourth or fifth foul. The 40 points were the fewest by any team in the Final Four since 1949, when Kentucky defeated Oklahoma State, 46-36, in the championship game.

"What happened was totally beyond me," Hall said. "I've never seen a team shoot like we did today. There had to be some electronic device sending out sounds around the basket."

There are still stories that Hall, later that night, sent his manager back to the arena to measure the rims to make sure they were 10 feet high. That was the type of Hoya Paranoia Ewing instilled in opposing coaches.

# *Dick Vitale's*

## MOUNT RUSHMORE
### OF
## ALL ONE AND DONES

### KEVIN DURANT

### CARMELO ANTHONY

### ANTHONY DAVIS

### KARL-ANTHONY TOWNS

# Kevin Durant
## (2006)

## Carved in Stone

Many people in the recruiting world were feeling pretty confident that Kevin Durant would join one of his best friends, Ty Lawson, at North Carolina to play with the Tar Heels. Durant fell in love with what Rick Barnes was preaching about coming to Austin, Texas and he never regretted making that move. In fact, he loved his Longhorn stay so much that he has donated millions to upgrade their basketball facilities.

## The One

Durant might have never set foot on a college campus if the NBA commissioner, David Stern, hadn't instituted its one-and-done rule for the 2006 season, which prevented players from entering the league directly out of high school. It forced them to spend a year in college before declaring for the NBA draft.

The versatile forward from Montrose, Maryland Christian Academy, who was selected MVP of the McDonald's All-American game, decided to spend his freshman year at Texas. He chose the Longhorns over defending national champion the University of North Carolina, despite the fact that his favorite player, Vince Carter of the Toronto Raptors, and his best friend, point guard Lawson, both played at UNC.

Durant knew he had a chance to play in the NBA from the time he was eleven-years old. Texas was the first school to send Durant a recruiting letter after assistant coach Russell Springman, who is from Silver Spring, Maryland and has strong connections in the state, attended one of Durant's games when he was a freshman at National Christian. The Longhorns were also helped by the fact that Durant had an independent streak that was fostered by his mother, Wanda Pratt.

"My mom always told me, 'don't be a follower, be a leader,'" he said.

Several people Durant and his family trusted, including Lovell Pinckney, who played receiver for Texas in the 1990s, also pushed the idea of his becoming a Longhorn.

"At first, people were kind of shocked that I chose Texas over North Carolina," Durant said. "But after a few days, they got over it."

Texas coach Rick Barnes had attracted top talent to Austin before Durant, signing eight McDonald's All Americans since he arrived in 1998. But Durant was by far the best.

Durant, a gifted athlete who had polished shooting and ball-handling skills, was considered the second-best prospect in the class of 2005 behind Ohio State's 7'0" recruit, Greg Oden. He came to Texas with enormous potential.

Durant attended three different high schools, playing for high-profile Oak Hill Academy as a junior before moving to Montrose, forty-five minutes from his home in Prince George, Maryland for his senior year so his parents could monitor his grades. He averaged 23.6 points, 10.2 rebounds, three assists, three steals, and 2.6 blocked shots and had a breakout moment when he scored 31 points as Montrose gave his former school, Oak Hill, its only loss to the season.

Durant made the best use of his time. He grew two inches to 6'9" and added fifteen to twenty pounds working out with strength coach, Todd Wright, before his freshman year since arriving in early June of 2006 at a skinny 205 pounds. He worked hard to improve his defense. And then he went out and dominated the game with his 7'5" wingspan and size eighteen shoes.

Durant averaged 25.8 points, 11.1 rebounds, and 1.3 assists for the Longhorns, which finished 25-10 before being upset by New Mexico in the second round of the NCAA tournament. He was recognized as the unanimous National Player of Year, winning the Wooden Award, the Naismith College player of the Year award and all eight other widely recognized honors. Durant was the first freshman to win any of the National Player of the Year awards.

Durant declared for the 2007 draft after the season and was selected by Seattle with the second pick overall, behind Oden, who went to Portland. In retrospect, Portland's decision to pass on Durant brought back memories of the 1983 draft when the Trail Blazers passed on Michael Jordan with the second pick to select center Sam Bowie of Kentucky.

Durant has since won two NBA championships with Golden State, an NBA MVP award, the Bill Russell NBA Finals MVP award in consecutive seasons, an NBA All-Star game MVP award, four NBA scoring titles, the NBA Rookie of the Year award and two Olympic gold medals in 2012 and 2016. Durant has also been selected to seven All-NBA teams and nine NBA All-Star teams.

# Carmelo Anthony
## (2003)

Syracuse Athletics

## Carved in Stone

Dan Shulman and I were on the call for ESPN when Carmelo Anthony played his first big game in a Syracuse unicorn at the Mecca, Madison Square Garden, against John Calipari's Memphis Tigers. I remember vividly speaking with Carmelo before the game. We were talking about him being himself and playing to his potential. We talked about him not putting pressure on himself due to the expectations that so many fans had after his scholastic success.

## The One

Syracuse Hall of Fame coach, Jim Boeheim, normally does not like taking a lot of long recruiting trips during the college season. But in early January of 2001, he took the advice of assistant, Troy Weaver, and made the pilgrimage to Baltimore to watch Anthony, a 6'5" junior swingman from Towson Catholic, play.

Weaver had been sold on the kid since he first watched him play in a travel team game for the Baltimore Blues against powerhouse D.C. Assault when he was in ninth grade and Anthony scored 16 points in the first half.

Anthony had grown five inches since then and it took Boeheim just five minutes to make an assessment on Anthony. The Towson player was born in Brooklyn and grew up in the roughest part of Baltimore, where violence and drugs were a part of daily life.

"This is the best player in the country, regardless of class," Boeheim pronounced.

Syracuse dogged recruitment of Anthony paid off that spring when Anthony verbally committed to Syracuse. He transferred to Oak Hill Academy for his senior year to prop up his grades and attracted serious interest from NBA scouts after he averaged 25.2 in the Adidas Big Time tournament in Las Vegas. He had 34 points and 11 rebounds in a matchup against LeBron James during a 72-66 win over St. Vincent-St. Mary's High in Akron. Anthony was a USA Today first team All-American and played in the 2002 McDonald's All-American game.

After getting the necessary score on the ACT to become eligible, he stuck with his commitment and led Syracuse to Boeheim's lone national championship in 2003 during his only year in college.

Anthony was arguably the best young player ever to play for Syracuse in the Boeheim era. He averaged 22.2 points and 10 rebounds. He introduced himself to college basketball in the game I called on November 14, 2002–the Coaches vs. Cancer Classic at Madison Square Garden. He scored 21 of his 27 points in the first half of a 70-63 loss to John Calipari's Memphis team. The loss motivated the Orange to go on an eleven-game winning streak and set the stage for a postseason run.

*Syracuse Athletics*

Anthony led the Orange, who had a strong group of complimentary players, in every statistical category with an old-school game during the regular season and was a second-team All-American. Then he finished strong in the Final Four. Anthony scored a freshman-record 33 points on twelve-for-19 shooting and a game-high fourteen rebounds as Syracuse defeated Texas in the semi-finals. He then played his part as the Orange jumped out to an 18-point lead over Kansas in the championship game, holding on for an 81-78 victory in New Orleans.

"We had to win that game," Anthony said. "If we didn't ,nothing would have mattered.".

Anthony became only the third freshman to earn the tournament's Most Outstanding Player Award.

Afterwards, Boeheim reiterated his praise for Anthony. "He is by far the best player in college basketball. It wasn't even close. Nobody was even close to him last year in college basketball. That's the bottom line."

Anthony said he originally planned to stay at Syracuse for two or three seasons, but having led the Orange to a 30-5 record and winning the sport's ultimate prize, he chose to declare for the draft, where he was drafted by the Denver Nuggets with the third pick overall. Since entering the NBA in 2004, Anthony has been named an All Star 10 times and an All-NBA team member six times. Anthony set a New York Knicks' single-game scoring record with a career high 62 points in 2014 and is one of six players to score 24,000 points, grab 6,000 rebounds and contribute 2,500 assists, 1,000 steals and 1,000 three-point goals.

He has been a member of USA's Olympic team four times, winning a bronze medal in 2004 and three gold medals in 2008, 2012 and 2016. He is the national team's all-time leading scorer, rebounder, and leader. Last year, Anthony joined his buddies, Russell Westbrook and Paul George, in forming a trio for Billy Donovan at Oklahoma City.

# Anthony Davis
## (2012)

*UK Athletics*

## Carved in Stone

No one would have guessed 6'10" Anthony Davis would play major college basketball, let alone be the Number One pick in the 2012 NBA draft by the New Orleans Hornets, but his one-and-done sealed the deal.

## The One

Davis started his high school career at Perspective Charter School, a math and science academy in the Southside of Chicago. He was a 6'0" guard as a ninth grader who played for a losing team in the Blue Division of the Chicago Public League. The team had no gymnasium, practiced at a local church, and received little to no attention from the media.

In those high school years, Davis underwent a dramatic growth spurt, growing to 6'8". He went from being unnoticed locally after three seasons to becoming the Number One prospect in the country after he started for Mean Streets, a Nike Elite Youth Basketball League (EYBL) travel team, the spring and summer before his senior year. He dominated the NBA Top 100 camp. Syracuse spotted him early, but Davis eventually committed to play for John Calipari at Kentucky in August of 2010, over DePaul, Ohio State, and the Orange.

Davis backed up the hype by playing well in the McDonald's All-American game with 14-points, six rebounds, two steals, and four blocked shots in front of a hometown crowd at the United Center. Then, he led USA Basketball to a 92-80 victory over the World team with 16 points and 10 rebounds before breaking loose for 29 points, 11 rebounds, and 4 blocked shots in a co-MVP performance at the Jordan Brand Classic.

Calipari has developed a reputation for developing one-and-dones into lottery picks since his first year at Kentucky in 2010, when he transformed guard John Wall and center DeMarcus Cousins into NBA franchise players. Davis inherited their DNA.

"He's a 6'10" with a 7'3" wingspan…tremendous shot blocker because of his size and length," Calipari said. "He can make threes, dribble the ball, and get up and down quicker than some of our guards because of his long, loping strides."

It didn't take long for Davis to make an impact at Kentucky. He led the Wildcats to a perfect 16-0 record in the SEC regular season, finishing the year with averages of 14.2 points, 10.4 rebounds, 4.7 blocks, and a field goal percentage of 62.3 percent.

Then he took over the NCAA Final Four, posting 18 points, 14 rebounds, and five blocks against Louisville in the semi-finals and 16 rebounds, six blocks, five assists, three steals, and six points against Kansas in the title game. He became the fourth freshman to win the tournament's Most Outstanding Player award.

UK Athletics

Davis was the SEC Player of the Year, a unanimous first team All-American who dominated the national Player of the Year balloting, winning the Wooden Award and becoming the first Kentucky player to win the Naismith College Player of the Year in forty-two years. He finished with twenty double-doubles and was selected the NABC Defensive Player of the Year after blocking 189 shots.

When the season ended, Davis declared for the draft alongside the rest of the national championship starting five, including fellow freshmen, Michael Kidd-Gilchrist ,and point guard, Marquis Teague.

Before Davis ever played an NBA game, he was a late addition to Team USA and earned a gold medal at the 2012 Summer Olympics in London. Davis has since gone on to lead the NBA in blocked shots in his second year, become a five-time All Star and the youngest player to score 59 or more points in an NBA game. He was named recipient of the NBA All-Star game MVP award in 2017 after setting an All-Star game scoring record with 52 points. Davis was also named a finalist for NBA MVP for the 2017-18 campaign.

# Karl-Anthony Towns

## (2015)

*UK Athletics*

## Carved in Stone

Karl-Anthony Towns will certainly rate as one of the best one-and-done players to compete for John Calipari by the time his NBA career is concluded.

Towns was always a prodigy.

## The One

He was born in Edison, New Jersey to an African-American father, Karl Towns, Sr., and a Dominican mother, Jacqueline Cruz. Towns' father was a former player at Monmouth and coached basketball at Piscataway Technical High School, where his son practiced with the junior varsity team as a fifth grader and then beat the varsity as a 6'6"seventh grader.

The 7'0" Towns was trained to be an elite basketball prospect. He repeated seventh grade to gain an extra year of development, then proceeded to lead St. Joseph's of Metuchen to the first of three straight New Jersey state championships as a freshman in 2012. The following summer, he was selected to play for the Dominican Republic national team, coached by John Calipari of Kentucky, in 2011 and 2012 when the team finished third in the FIBA Americas championship and fourth in the FIBA World Olympic Qualifying Tournament.

The popular Towns was more than just an athlete in high school. He was an exceptional student who spent his free Saturdays prior to college volunteering with his girlfriend on behalf of Parents of Autistic Children, served on student council, made baked goods for his teachers, and found time to become an avid pianist and golfer.

Towns was touched as a sophomore when he reached out to the family a former student, a Marine, who was killed in Afghanistan. He did not know him, but he heard the Marine's sister at the funeral say her brother would have turned 25 that day. The next game, Towns scored with ease for three quarters against neighboring Perth Amboy but stopped shooting when he reached 25 points.

"I wanted to honor the boy who passed away," Towns said.

During the summer before his junior year, Towns felt the need to challenge himself. He felt he was ready for college, so he told his parents he wanted to merge his junior and senior year so he could graduate a year early and enroll at Kentucky, where he committed in 2012. He took extra classes in the summer, took online classes, and stayed up until three in morning some nights to get his course work done. He graduated with a 4.2 GPA.

Towns put an exclamation on his high school career when he was selected to the McDonald's All-American game and was named Gatorade National Player of the Year in 2014 after averaging 20.9 points, 13.4 rebounds, and 6.2 blocked shots.

Towns put up modest numbers for Kentucky during his freshman year, averaging 10.3 points and 6.7 rebounds in 21.1 minutes, as Calipari used a unique platoon system that limited the minutes of each player. He studied kinesiology in his only year in college with hopes of becoming a doctor after his basketball career, so he could build a hospital in the Dominican.

UK Athletics

Towns' future in basketball became even brighter when he came up huge in the 2015 NCAA Midwest Regional, scoring 25 points as the Cats rallied to beat Notre Dame in Cleveland to enter the Final Four with a 38-0 record. Wisconsin ruined Kentucky's dreams of a perfect season in the national semi-finals, but Towns impressed NBA scouts enough that the consensus was he was a better defensive player than Duke center Jahlil Okafor and he had an opportunity to become a better offensive player as well. Towns and six other Kentucky players declared for the draft at the end of a near-perfect season and Towns was selected by the Minnesota Timberwolves with the Number 1 pick overall.

He went on to become NBA Rookie of the Year in 2016 and blossomed into an elite scorer and rebounder by his second year, averaging 25.1 points and 12.3 rebounds. He went off for 47 points and 18 rebounds in a game against the Knicks as a 21-year old second-year player. Towns averaged 21.3 and 12.3 rebounds in 2018, leading the T-Wolves back to the playoffs.

# Dick Vitale's
# MOUNT RUSHMORE
## OF
# ALL PREP PHENOMS

## LEBRON JAMES

## KOBE BRYANT

## TRACY McGRADY

## KEVIN GARNETT

# LeBron James
## (2000-2003, 2004-Present)

LRMR Ventures

## Carved in Stone

I never thought in my lifetime that I would ever think of someone in the same league as Michael Jordan. It has happened for me. LeBron James, in my eyes, has become the greatest of all-time, as his passing and rebounding ability gives him an edge over Michael. I don't want to hear about the number of rings because basketball is a TEAM game. There is no way James has played with the cast in Cleveland that Jordan played with in Chicago. It's not apples to apples. James is the GOAT (greatest of all-time).

I remember when I was assigned to call a high school game featuring LeBron James. I wondered if we were over-hyping this young man. Well my friends, during the contest, I turned to broadcast partner Bill Walton and proclaimed that King James was even better than advertised. LeBron or Michael? Michael or LeBron? I have always been a huge Michael Jordan fan and felt he was the best I'd ever seen. But LeBron James has barged into the conversation…and I was there at the beginning, but it wasn't for the NCAA. We're talking high school, man!

## The Making of a Phenom

It happened in Cleveland, 2003. LeBron mania was coming on strong. He was big long before I met him. He was on the cover of Sports Illustrated. They were calling him "The Chosen One." I had to see for myself. When ESPN signed on to do LeBron's game against Oak Hill Academy at Cleveland State's Convocation Center in 2002, it was the first time ESPN had done a *high school* game since 1988.

I'll be honest. I was a little apprehensive about doing it the first time my boss Dan Steir called me. I didn't want to over-hype this *kid*, but ESPN was into it. They went with a cast of stars like Bill Walton and Dan Shulman to witness the coronation of the King. There were fourteen or fifteen television vehicles outside when we arrived plus 100 media guys. Scalpers were getting $100 a ticket. This was a high school game, baby!

It didn't take me long to see what they were so excited about. The powerful 6'8", 250-pound James went off for 31 points, 13 rebounds, and six assists leading Akron St. Vincent-St. Mary's to a 65-46 upset victory before a sellout crowd who showed up on a Thursday night. The TV ratings for that game were 2.0. St. Vincent-St. Mary's was big everywhere that year. They played all over the country in places like Greensboro, Los Angeles, Columbus, and Trenton. They held their home games at the University of Akron's 5,200 seat arena.

James was selected Ohio's Mr. Basketball and was named to USA Today's first-team All-American team for three straight years. He averaged 31.6 points, 9.6 rebounds, 4.6 assists, and 3.4 steals a game and scored a career-high 52 points in a game at Trenton. James was named Gatorade National Player of the Year for a second consecutive year. He participated in three post-season All Star games—the EA Sports Roundball Classic, the Jordan Classic, and the McDonald's All-American game. He lost his NCAA eligibility because you are only allowed to play in two all-star games, making it official he would enter the 2003 draft.

*Allen Kee / ESPN Images*

James was an easy choice for the Number One pick in the NBA draft, when he was selected by the Cleveland Cavaliers. Before he ever played a game, he signed a $90 million endorsement deal with Nike.

It was the culmination of a long journey for James, whose mother Gloria raised him on her own. When James was growing up, life was hard and the two moved from apartment to apartment, in the seedy neighborhoods of Akron, while Gloria struggled to find steady work. Realizing her son would be better in a more stable family environment, she allowed him to move in with the family of Frank Walker, a local youth coach, who introduced James to basketball when he was nine-years-old.

Allen Kee / ESPN Images

It didn't take long for James to leave his mark. James played travel team ball with the Northeast Ohio Shooting Stars. The team enjoyed national success and James, along with friends Stan Cotton, Dru Joyce III, and Willie McGee decided to attend the same high school, choosing St. Vincent's-St. Mary's.

James became such a dominant player by his junior year, he thought he could make the leap to the NBA and unsuccessfully petitioned for a change to the NBA draft eligibility rules, which required prospective players to have at least a high school diploma to attempt to enter the 2002 NBA draft.

It was just a matter of time before the thirty-three-year old James became the face of the NBA, winning three NBA championships and two Olympic gold medals in 2008 and 2012. His accomplishments include four NBA Most Valuable Player Awards, three NBA Final MVP Awards, two Olympic gold medals, three All-Star game MVP awards, an NBA scoring title, and the all-time NBA playoffs scoring leader. He has also made fourteen NBA All-Star appearances, twelve All-NBA first-team selections and five All Defensive first-team honors. In 2018, he made his eighth straight appearance in the NBA Finals.

James has done endorsement deals with Coca-Cola, Dunkin' Brands, McDonald's, Nike, State Farm, Beats by Dre, and Samsung. He has a minority stake in Liverpool FC in the English Premier League. In 2013, he surpassed Kobe Bryant as the top basketball player in the world with earnings of $56.5 million.

James also has his own charity foundation, the LeBron James Family Foundation, which is based in Akron. In 2015, honoring his roots, James announced a partnership with the University of Akron to provide scholarships to as many as 2,300 children beginning in 2021.

In July of 2018, LeBron signed with the Los Angeles Lakers.

# Kobe Bryant
## (1993-1996)

*Scott Clarke / ESPN Images*

## Carved in Stone

I was mesmerized sitting at courtside, calling the action at the Magic Roundball Classic in the Motor City as the best of the best high schoolers showed off their talents. I heard many comments raving about how good Kobe Bryant was. Sonny Vaccaro and many in the basketball world sung his praises. Seeing him first-hand blew me away. Kobe had great touch, superb feel for the game, and could score in a multitude of ways. We then interviewed him after the game and he even impressed me more with his magical personality and understanding of the game at such a young age. After seeing him in person, there was never any doubt that this young man was going to be a superstar without ever stepping into the NCAA.

## The Making of a Phenom

Bryant is one of the greatest players in NBA history and he has been called the greatest player of his generation. He led the Los Angeles Lakers to five NBA championships in a twenty-year career spent with the same franchise. The 6'6" guard was an eighteen-time All-Star, fifteen-time member of the All NBA team and twelve-time member of the All-Defensive team. He was the league's MVP in 2008, and a four-time All-Star game MVP. Bryant led the league in scoring twice, scoring 81 points against the Toronto Raptors in 2006, the second most points in league history behind Wilt Chamberlain's fabled 100-point game in 1962.

Bryant had career averages of 25 points, 5.2 rebounds, and 1.4 steals and was the first player in NBA history to score at least 30,000 career points and dish 6,000 career assists. He also played on two Olympic gold medal clubs for Team USA in 2008 and 2012, before retiring after the 2016 season.

But there was a time when Bryant looked like he might play a different sport altogether.

Bryant, who was born in 1978, is the son of former NBA player, Joe Bryant. His parents named him after the famous beef of Kobe, Japan, which they saw on a restaurant menu. When Bryant was six, his father retired from the NBA and moved his family to Reiti, Italy to continue playing pro basketball at the European level. Kobe became accustomed to his new lifestyle and learned how to speak fluent Italian. During summers, he would return to the United States to play in summer leagues.

Bryant started playing basketball when he was three-years old and the Lakers were his favorite team growing up. His grandfather would mail him videos of NBA games, which Bryant would study. He also learned to play soccer and his favorite team was A.C. Milan. Bryant was introduced to football of the rest of the world when he was just six-years old. He used to go to the park to play basketball and would jump into a game of soccer before hitting the courts. Bryant started out as a goalie because he had long arms and lacked the feel for handling the ball. As his skills progressed, he eventually moved to midfield.

When Joe Bryant retired as a player in 1991, the family moved back to the States. Because few players in his neighborhood were playing soccer, Bryant decided to concentrate on basketball. He still credits the game of soccer with helping his footwork on the basketball court.

Bryant earned a national reputation during a spectacular high school career at Lower Merion High School in suburban Philadelphia.

"I had invited him to scrimmage against our varsity," Lower Merion coach Greg Downer said, "and after five minutes, I turned to my assistant coaches and said, 'This guy is a pro.'"

Bryant became the first person to start on the varsity as a freshman, but the team finished with a 4-20 record. The next three years, the Aces compiled a 77-13 record, with Bryant rotating between all five positions. During his junior year in 1995, Bryant averaged 31.1 points, 10.4 rebounds, and 5.2 assists and was named Pennsylvania Prep Player of the Year. He was heavily recruited by Duke, North Carolina, Villanova, and La Salle, which hired his father as an assistant, while he played there in college.

However, when Kevin Garnett turned pro out of high school and was taken in the first round of the 1995 NBA draft, Bryant began considering doing the same thing.

Bryant made a huge splash at the Adidas ABCD camp the summer before his senior year when he earned the senior MVP award while playing alongside Lamar Odom. As a senior in high school, Philadelphia 76ers' coach John Lucas invited Bryant to work out and scrimmage with the NBA team and he played one-on-one against Jerry Stackhouse, a rookie who was the third overall pick in the 1995 draft. The next day, North Carolina's Dean Smith started recruiting him. Bryant led Lower Merion to its first PIAA state championship in 53 years, averaging 30.8 points, 12 rebounds, 6.5 assists, 4 steals and 3.8 blocked shots for a 31-3 team in 1996. He ended his high school career as Southeastern Pennsylvania's all-time leading scorer with 2,833 points, surpassing Wilt Chamberlain and 1990 National Player of the Year, Lionel Simmons from La Salle.

Bryant won the Naismith and Gatorade High School Player of the Year, was a McDonald's All-American. Bryant was a local celebrity, even taking R&B singer, Brandy, to his senior prom. Bryant had the grades to go to any college that recruited him, but ultimately, at age seventeen, he made the decision to go directly to the NBA. He was selected by Charlotte with the Number Thirteen pick overall, then traded to the Los Angeles Lakers before his rookie season, where he built his legacy with a brilliant pro career.

*Scott Clarke / ESPN Images*

# Tracy McGrady
## (1994-1997, 1998-2013)

*Scott Clarke / ESPN Images*

### Carved in Stone

I was privileged to be in Hackensack, New Jersey at Sonny Vaccaro's basketball camp when Tracy McGrady was the talk of the camp. He was dazzling, the star of stars among many PTP'ers, from the scholastic ranks there. I remember vividly being the keynote speaker at the camp, addressing the young, talented stars. I told them to make a decision about college or an immediate jump to the NBA. After Tracy dominated the camp, and his stock went up and up, everyone had the impression that he would be an immediate NBA player. McGrady may have been the ultimate sleeper, slipping in under the radar and passing up on top schools to head straight for the NBA.

### The Making of a Phenom

The 6'8" Naismith Hall of Fame forward was a local star who played three years of basketball and baseball for Auburndale High School in Floridabefore transferring to Mt. Zion Academy in Durham, North Carolina.

He was a relative unknown when he was invited to Sonny Vaccaro's Adidas ABCD camp the summer before his senior year.

McGrady was given jersey Number 175, which was reflective of his recruiting status. He then dominated the camp in Hackensack, New Jersey, that was headlined by Lamar Odom.

"When I first got there, some of my Florida guys were telling me about this kid, Lamar Odom from New York City," McGrady recalled. "That's all I was hearing, 'Man, he got game. Lamar Odom is a 6'10" guard. And I'm like, 'What? Where I'm from if you're 6'9", you're the tallest cat on the team. If you're 6'5", you're a center. And they're like, 'Man, he's a 6'10" point guard out of New York City.' And I'm like, 'I ain't never seen that before.' But my mindset was this is that door you wanted to open and you've got to take advantage of it. He was the first person I played, and I put it down. Nobody had a clue who Tracy McGrady was. Sonny Vaccaro gave me that platform, and I played against the best players in the world at that time. I left that camp the Number 1 player in the nation, 175 to Number One."

McGrady's leadership helped Mt. Zion, a small, private church-related school to the Number 2 ranking in the country. McGrady was named a McDonald's All-American, National Player of the Year by USA Today and North Carolina's Mr. Basketball. McGrady considered playing college basketball for the University of Kentucky, but he ultimately decided to enter the NBA draft after he was projected to be a lottery pick and was selected by the Toronto Raptors with the ninth pick overall.

McGrady went on to become a seven-time NBA All-Star, seven-time All NBA selection, two-time NBA scoring champion, and one-time winner of the NBA's Most Improved Player Award. He worked his way up from a limited role to star status, playing with his cousin Vince Carter, on the Raptors. He left for Orlando in 2002, where he became one of the league's most prolific scorers, averaging 32.1 points in 2003, and then surfaced in Houston where he paired with 7'5" center, Yao Ming, to help the Rockets become a perennial playoff team, before spending a year in China. McGrady went seven straight years from 2000 through 2007 where he averaged more than 24 points a game.

McGrady retired in 2013 after 16 years of pro basketball. Interestingly, McGrady doesn't think players should be able to follow in his footsteps and go right to the league out of high school. In fact, he believes the age rule should require players to attend two years of college before entering the league.

"I actually think they should implement having these guys go to school for two years," he said. "What is it now? One year? The league is so young. I think we need to build our league up. I mean, I hate to say, it, but the talent in this league is pretty down."

Tracy now gets the opportunity to share his views on the NBA on ESPN, where he is part of the coverage.

# Kevin Garnett
## (1992-1995)

*Phil Ellsworth / ESPN Images*

### Carved in Stone

My first introduction to Kevin Garnett was through Sonny Vaccaro, who played a big-time role in creating golden opportunities for college coaches to make mega-dollars signing shoe deals. Vaccaro also produces mega-camps, which feature future stars like Garnett. It was I had the chance to speak at one of his prestigious camps that I got a glimpse of this future great.

### The Making of a Phenom

Garnett's journey to NBA stardom took a slight and almost disastrous detour when he was in high school.

The versatile 6'11" forward did not play organized basketball until ninth grade at Mauldin High School in South Carolina. But he developed into a huge star in his first three years before his life changed one day the summer before his senior year in 1994.

A fight between white and black students broke out, and though in pre-trial Garnett was ruled not to be involved, the incident was scary enough for him to reassess his plans. Due to the racially-charged issue and fearful of being a target, Garnett decided to leave Maudlin High and transferred to Farragut Career Academy in Chicago for his senior year.

"I'm from the bottom," Garnett said. "I understand what it's like to not have."

Garnett led Farragut to a 28-2 record and was named National High School Player of the Year by USA Today in 1995. He also was named Mr. Basketball for the state of Illinois after averaging 25.2 points, 17.9 rebounds, 6.7 assists, and 6.5 blocks, while shooting 66.8 percent from the field.

In four years of high school, Garrett posted an impressive 2,552 points, 1,809 rebounds, and 737 blocked shots. Garnett went on to be named the Most Outstanding Player at the McDonald's All-American game after scoring 18 points, 11 rebounds, 4 assists, and 3 blocked shots. That was enough to make him feel confident about playing in the NBA and declared for the 1995 draft.

Garnett thought about attending Maryland, but his decision not to play college basketball was influenced in part by his failure to score high enough on the ACT test to meet NCAA requirements for freshman eligibility.

Phil Ellsworth / ESPN Images

Garnett wound up being selected by Minnesota with the fifth pick overall, becoming the first high school player in twenty years to turn pro. He was driven by his past in rural South Carolina to lead the T-Wolves to eight consecutive playoff appearances and win the NBA's MVP award in 2004 when Minnesota reached the Western Conference finals. Garnett won the NBA All-Star MVP in 2003 and played in fifteen All-Star games. He was named the NBA Defensive Player of the Year in 2008 and was selected nine times to All-NBA teams and 12 times to the All-Defensive team. He won a gold medal, playing for the U.S. Olympic team in the 2000 summer games in Sydney, Australia.

"I'm not the type of person to give up because something gets rough," he said. "That's a coward. That's not me."

In 2007, after twelve seasons with the T-Wolves, Garnett joined the Boston Celtics in a blockbuster trade and helped the Celtics win an NBA championship in his first year in Boston. In 2013, Garnett was part of another blockbuster trade that sent him to Brooklyn. He was traded back to Minnesota in 2015 before retiring prior to the start of the 2016 season. Garnett finished with 26,071 points, 14,662 rebounds and 5,445 assists in his career.

# Dick Vitale's

# MOUNT RUSHMORE
## OF
# ALL PASSPORT

## TIM DUNCAN

## STEVE NASH

## HAKEEM OLAJUWON

## DIKEMBE MUTOMBO

# Tim Duncan

## (1994-1997)

*Wake Forest Athletics*

## Carved in Stone

Tim Duncan was born and raised on Saint Croix, one of the main islands composing the U.S. Virgin Islands. In school, he was a bright student and dreamed of becoming an Olympic-level swimmer like his sister, Tricia. He excelled in the sport. Duncan was a rising teenage star in the 50-, 100-, 200-, and 400-meter freestyle and had a realistic hope of making the United States 1992 Olympic team.

But his life changed after Hurricane Hugo destroyed the island's only Olympic-sized swimming pool in 1990. Duncan was forced to train in the ocean and lost his enthusiasm for swimming because of his fear of sharks. Duncan was hit with another emotional blow when his mother was diagnosed with breast cancer. Before she passed, she made Duncan and his sisters promise they would earn their college degrees.

## Passport to Greatness

Duncan never swam competitively again, but took up basketball at the urging of his brother-in-law. He began playing for St. Dunstan's Episcopal High School. At first, he was just a tall, awkward kid, but by the time he was a senior, he had grown to 6'11", 250 pounds and averaged 25 points per game, attracting the interest of Wake Forest coach, Dave Odom, who was looking for a big man to complement his two stars—Randolph Childress and Rodney Rodgers.

Odom first heard about Duncan from an ex-player, Chris King, who had scrimmaged against Duncan when a group of NBA players went to the islands. According to King, Duncan, then just sixteen and with just two years of organized basketball experience, played Alonzo Mourning to a draw in a five-on-five pickup game.

Odom was concerned about the level of competition in the islands, so he made a visit to St. Croix to see for himself. Duncan had offers from Providence, Delaware, and Hartford. But Odom loved what he had seen of Duncan the summer before his senior year and signed the biggest sleeper in the history of the ACC.

Odom thought about redshirting Duncan as a freshman, but after fellow freshman center, Makhtar N'Daiye, was ruled ineligible due to NCAA rules violations and transferred to Michigan, he was forced to play him. The stoic Duncan did not score in his first college game, but he quickly became a huge factor for a 20-11 team as a freshman. He then averaged 16.2 points, 12.5 rebounds, and 4.2 blocked shots as a sophomore when he was selected All ACC as the Deacons won the ACC tournament title and made a Sweet 16 appearance.

Lakers' GM, Jerry West, suggested Duncan could be the Number 1 pick in the 1995 NBA draft after the season, but Duncan promised his mother he would earn his degree, so he went on at Wake Forest to become a two-time first team All American and a two-time ACC Player of the Year the next two years. He was also a three-time NABC Defensive Player of the Year.

He averaged 19.1 points and 12.3 rebounds as a junior, along with 3.98 blocked shots. Duncan was selected MVP as Wake won a second ACC tournament and advanced to the NCAA Sweet 16 again. Then he averaged 20.8 points, 14.7 rebounds and 3.2 assists and 3.3 blocked shots as a senior while shooting 60.6 percent from the field to win the 1997 Wooden Award as the National Player of the Year. He earned the honor even though the Deacons were eliminated by Stanford in the second round of the NCAA tournament.

Wake never got to an NCAA Final Four during the Duncan era, but he did leave his mark. Duncan became the first player in NCAA history to reach 1,500 points, 1,000 rebounds, 400 blocked shots, and 200 assists... and he kept his promise when he earned his degree in psychology. He was an easy choice as the first pick overall in the 1997 NBA draft and was selected by the San Antonio Spurs.

# Steve Nash

## (1993-1996)

*Santa Clara University Athletics*

## Carved in Stone

My first recollection of Steve Nash was back in 1993. He was a member of a Santa Clara team, seeded fifteenth in the big dance, that stunned second-seed Arizona in a major shock city. The Wildcats had Damon Stoudamire, Khalid Reeves, Chris Mills, Ed Stokes, and Reggie Geary, to name a few.

## Passport to Greatness

His story is pretty amazing when you think about it. Even though basketball was invented in Canada and the first NBA game was played in Toronto, the Great White North has not produced many pro prospects, with only twelve making the league in fifty years, until Nash arrived in the league in 1996. I firmly believe Nash's popularity played a role in the star power coming from Canada now in the collegiate and pro level.

The 6'3" point guard was a two-time NBA MVP, was selected for eight NBA All-Star games, and was eventually selected for the Naismith Hall of Fame.

But he got a late start in the sport.

Nash was born in Johannesburg, South Africa, to a Welsh mother, Jean, and an English father, John, in 1974. His family moved to Regina, Saskatchewan, when he was eighteen-months-old, ultimately settling in Victoria, British Columbia. Before the family immigrated to Canada, his father played semi-pro soccer and, while growing up, Nash often played soccer and ice hockey with his older brother, Martin.

Nash did not start playing basketball until he was twelve years old, but it didn't take long for him to fall in love. His bedroom was plastered with posters of Michael Jordan, Magic Johnson, and Isiah Thomas. In eighth grade, he told his mother thatone day he would play in the NBA and become a star.

"They were my heroes," he said. "Especially Isiah, he wasn't very tall. He played the game mostly on the floor and it made me feel I could do the same."

Nash made his name playing for St. Michael's University School, a private boarding institution. After

Scott Clarke / ESPN Images

working out with the Canadian national team and building his confidence the summer before his senior year, Nash averaged 21.3 points, 11.3 assists, and 9.1 rebounds, leading his team to the 1992 British Columbia AAA provincial championship. That year, he was named the province's Player of the Year.

Nash's high school coach Ian Hyde-Lay sent letters of inquiry and highlight reels on Nash to thirty American colleges but received limited feedback until Santa Clara coach, Dick Davey, requested video footage. After watching Nash in person, he knew he had found the ultimate sleeper.

"I was nervous as hell just hoping that no one else would see him," Davey said. "It didn't take a Nobel Prize winner to see this guy was pretty good. It was just a case of hoping that none of the big names came around."

Davey did feel Nash wasn't a finished product. "I told him he was the worst defensive player I had ever seen," Davey said.

When Davey offered Nash a scholarship, the Broncos had gone five years without an NCAA appearance. But that changed when Nash led Santa Clara to the West Coast Conference tournament title and an upset win over second-seed Arizona in the first round of the 1993 NCAA tournament, locking up the game by making six free throws in the final 30 seconds.

Two years later, Nash emerged as the conference Player of the Year after leading the WCC in scoring and assists. The Broncos returned to the tournament, losing to Mississippi State in the first round. Nash thought about turning professional, but decided against it, spending the summer after his junior year playing for the Canadian national team and working out against NBA stars Gary Payton and Jason Kidd in the Bay Area.

Nash began attracting national media attention and attention from NBA scouts as a senior. He was named WCC Player of the Year for a second straight year, the first Santa Clara player to do that since forward, Kurt Rambis. Nash averaged 20.9 points and 6.4 assists and scored 28 points as the tenth-seeded Broncos upset seventh-seeded Maryland in the NCAA tournament before losing to Kansas. Nash was selected honorable mention All-American, finished his career as Santa Clara's all-time leader in free throw percentage (86.2), and was third in career scoring with 1,689 points. He was the first Santa Clara player to have his number retired.

A month after graduating with a degree in sociology, Steve made his family and country proud when he was selected by Phoenix with the Number 15 pick overall in the NBA draft, beginning a flood of Canadian players to the league.

# Hakeem Olajuwon
## (1982-1984)

University of Houston Athletics

## Carved in Stone

I'm proud to have brought Olajuwon the nickname that stuck with him throughout his career. Hakeem "The Dream" lived up to the title from his college days through a successful career in the NBA.

## Passport to Greatness

Unlike Patrick Ewing and Ralph Sampson, two of The Dream's contemporaries in the 1980s, the University of Houston's 7'0" center—then known as Hakeem—was not groomed for greatness.

He was born in Lagos, Nigeria, the third of eight children to Salim and Abike Olajuwon, the owners of a cement business. During his youth, Olajuwon was a soccer goalie and handball player who did not play basketball until he was fifteen years old, when he entered a local tournament. He had limited knowledge of the game and there was one story making the rounds about a local coach in Nigeria asking him to dunk, then demonstrating while standing on a chair. Olajuwon then tried to stand on the chair himself. When redirected not to use a chair, Olajuwon originally could not dunk a basketball.

All of that changed quickly. Olajuwon was a natural, using the agility he learned in soccer to balance his size and strength.

Olajuwon decided to emigrate to the United States to play basketball in college. He was not highly recruited and made up a list of potential colleges. When he visited St. John's, he stepped off the plane to frigid temperatures and asked a gate agent which of the schools on his list had the warmest temperatures. Hall of Fame coach Guy Lewis was skeptical when he took Olajuwon's call, having been let down in the past by previous international players. He invited Olajuwon to work out for the coaching staff, based on a recommendation from a friend who had watched Olajuwon play.

When Olajuwon arrived at the Houston airport, no representative from the school was there to meet him. When he called the basketball office, they told him to take a taxi to campus.

They were blown away by what they saw. Olajuwon was 6'11", not 6'7" as Lewis was told, but was still raw. His name in Nigerian means "always being on top."

And he was.

After redshirting his freshman year in 1981, because he could not get clearance from the NCAA to play, Olajuwon played sparingly as a redshirt freshman in 1982 and the Cougars were eliminated in the Final Four by eventual national champion North Carolina. Olajuwon sought advice from the coaching staff about how to increase his playing time and they advised him to work out with local Houston residents and NBA All Star Moses Malone, who was then the center for the Houston Rockets and played pickup games every summer with several NBA players at the Forde Recreation Center.

Olajuwon joined the workouts and went head-to-head with Malone in several games that summer. When he returned to school that fall, he was a different player and a rising star on Houston's high-flying Phi Slama Jama team that advanced to the national championship game before losing at the buzzer to North Carolina State. Despite the loss, Olajuwon, who scored 20 points and grabbed 18 rebounds, was voted MVP of the 1983 NCAA tournament.

He was even more dominant his junior year after the other four starters left. That's when I gave him the nickname "Hakeem the Dream" on ESPN for the

*University of Houston Athletics*

effortless way he dunked the ball. Hakeem brought it up when he and I were introduced as members of the Naismith Hall of Hall in 2008. Olajuwon averaged 16.8 points and was a consensus first team All-American as a redshirt junior, leading the NCAA in field goal percentage (.675), rebounds (13.5), and blocked shots (5.6). The Cougars reached the Final Four for a third straight year, losing to Georgetown in the championship game.

"He's the best player I've ever faced," Ewing said afterwards.

NBA GMs and scouts felt the same way. Olajuwon debated whether to stay in school or declare for the NBA. At the time, the first pick was awarded by coin flip.

"I really believed that Houston was going to win the coin flip and pick the Number 1 draft choice and I really wanted to play in Houston, so I had to make a decision."

His intuition proved correct. Houston won the flip and chose Olajuwon with the first pick in the 1984 draft...a draft that also included Michael Jordan.

# Dikembe Mutombo

## (1988-1991)

*Big East Conference*

### Carved in Stone

I have visions of Dikembe Mutombo waiving his finger, telling opponents that thou shalt not enter my lane, baby! When Mutombo arrived in America from the Congo to enroll in Georgetown as part of their basketball team, he was on full academic scholarship and more on his mind than just the game.

### Passport to Greatness

The 7'2", 260-pound center was one of eight children born in Kinshasa. He spoke eight languages—and had a world view, hoping to learn about Washington D.C.'s political and international flavor. Mutombo served as an intern, once for Congress and once for the World Bank.

He originally intended to be a doctor but enrolled in the school of linguistics. Naismith Hall of Fame coach, John Thompson, searching for a replacement for the legendary Patrick Ewing, who graduated in

1985, recruited him to play basketball on a tip from U.S. Development officer Harold Hennings, who sent Thompson a videotape. Mutombo is generally regarded as one of the greatest shot blockers and defensive rim protectors in college basketball history.

When Mutombo enrolled at Georgetown in 1987, he spoke limited English and studied under the English as a Second Language program, sitting out a year to become proficient in English. Despite some notoriety at Georgetown, Mutombo was virtually unknown outside the Hilltop campus. A clerical error in Basketball Times lists the rising sophomore as only 5'10" and, as word of Mutombo's size and agility spread throughout the Big East, some opposing coaches were sure Thompson had pulled a fast one. Once he became eligible, he was raw and not very skilled. He debuted with 6'10" Alonzo Mourning, a McDonald's All-American from Chesapeake, Virginia, in 1989. Mutombo only averaged 11 minutes a game to bring his skills up to speed in the American game. Even in limited playing time, it was obvious he had potential and was almost unstoppable from close range, shooting 70.7 percent. He had 10 games where he did not miss a shot. Mutombo only averaged 3.9 points and 3.3 rebounds, but his shot-blocking skills were extraordinary. He blocked 75 shots his first year, including *twelve* in a game against St. John's that set an NCAA single-game record, when Georgetown advanced to the NCAA Sweet 16.

*Big East Conference*

Then Coach Thompson said, 'We can win with this guy."

Mutombo then recalled, "That's when I knew I could have a future in basketball."

Thompson was the perfect coach to get the most out of Mutombo—big, intimidating and blunt.

"There was a fear you had with him," Mutombo said. "If you didn't do what you were supposed to do, you got punished doing suicide drills. And you just didn't want to get him angry at you. It was like I was in the military. But those things made me a better person. The discipline I got from Coach Thompson prepared me for the battles I had to fight as an adult."

Mutombo's development continued in 1989 and 1990. He started 24 of 31 games, averaging 10.7 points and 10.5 rebounds. With increased playing time to 26 minutes per game, he put up some impressive numbers against good teams: 10 points and 10 rebounds against North Carolina in the ACC-Big East Challenge, 17 points and 15 rebounds against Pitt, 22 and 18 against Villanova. Mutombo averaged 15 points and 13 rebounds a game down the stretch, shooting 68 percent from the field.

He and Mourning became such terrorizing shot blockers, Georgetown fans created a "Rejection Row" section under the basket, adding a big silhouette of an outstretched hand to a banner for each shot blocked during a game.

Mutombo was named first team all-conference and was considered a rising star.

Despite all that power, Georgetown lost in the second round of the tournament.

With Mourning suffering with a foot injury through much of the 1991 season, Mutombo became the scoring leader for the Hoyas, expanding his game beyond the dunk. He averaged 15.2.points and shot 58 percent. His first game that year against Hawaii-Loa, Mutombo had a triple double with 32 points, 21 rebounds, and 11 blocked shots.

He had his signature performance in the Big East tournament when he scored 27 points and grabbed 13 rebounds in a quarterfinal loss to Connecticut. Mutombo made all-conference again and was an honorable mention All-America, finishing third all-time in blocked shots, an average of one every six-and-half minutes. Mutombo graduated with a degree in linguistics and diplomacy in 1991 and was selected by the Denver Nuggets with the fourth pick overall in the 1991 NBA draft. He started his pro career late at age 25, but he went on to win the NBA Defensive Player of the Year award four times. He was an eight-time All-Star and finished his career as the second most prolific shot blocker in NBA history behind only Hakeem Olajuwon. He finished his fifteen-year career with over 11,000 points and 11,000 rebounds and was inducted into the Naismith Hall of Fame in 2015.

Even with the awesome stats, he will always be best known for raising money to build a hospital in Kinshasa, the first primary-care facility built in that city of 6.7 million in forty years. In addition, he has been a leader in the international efforts against the spread of polio, AIDS, and malaria in Africa.

# *Dick Vitale's*

# MOUNT RUSHMORE
## OF
# ALL VERSATILE

## JAMES WORTHY

## GRANT HILL

## TYLER HANSBROUGH

## CALBERT CHEANEY

# James Worthy

## (1979-1982)

UNC Athletic Communications

## Carved in Stone

James Worthy was at the top of the list of can't-miss players to come out of the state of North Carolina from the time he was in ninth grade. He was a man child at Ashbrook High School in Gastonia and became a Big Man on Campus in his college days.

## From All Sides

Worthy's nickname was "Big Game James" and the 6'9", 225-pound Naismith Hall of Fame forward became a must-get for North Carolina coach, Dean Smith. The coach first saw Worthy as a seventh grader at the Carolina Basketball Academy summer camp and knew he would be a great college player.

Worthy averaged 21.5 points, 12.5 rebounds, and 5.5 assists during his senior year and led his team to the state championship game where Ashbrook lost to Sleepy Floyd and crosstown rival Gastonia before a crowd of 10,000 at the Greensboro Coliseum. He was named both a Parade Magazine and a McDonald's All-American and was selected to play in the 1979 McDonald's All-American game that featured future Naismith Hall of Famers Isiah Thomas, Dominique Wilkins, and Ralph Sampson.

Worthy made North Carolina squirm for a commitment. During his senior year, Michigan State and Kentucky jumped into the recruiting fray and Smith was concerned that their assistant, Leonard Hamilton, who was from Gastonia and knew the Worthy family well, might steal him away.

In the end, Worthy couldn't spurn his first love and wound up signing with Carolina, where he eventually played a huge role in the Tar Heels winning Smith's first national championship in 1982.

It wasn't as easy as it looked for Worthy, who missed fifteen games his freshman season after snapping his ankle late in a home loss to Maryland. Smith was always concerned the rod and screws inserted into that ankle might hamper him for the rest of his career.

Worthy lived with the pain through his sophomore season, missing every third practice and developing tendinitis in the ankle. But he never gave up and slowly regained his confidence, averaging 14.2 points, 8.5 rebounds, and shooting 50 percent to become an All-ACC selection as Carolina advanced to the 1981 national championship game before losing to Indiana.

As a junior, Worthy was the leading scorer on a team that featured one of the greatest collections of talent in college basketball history, including future NBA stars, Sam Perkins and Michael Jordan. He averaged 15.6 points, 6.3 rebounds, and shot 57.3 percent. Worthy came up huge in the biggest games. As a junior in 1981, he had 26 points in an 80-69 win over Kentucky at the Meadowlands and 26 points and 15 rebounds in a nationally-televised game against Notre Dame.

He was a consensus first-team All-American and competed for the national Player of the Year with Virginia's towering center, Ralph Sampson. He dominated the 1982 national championship game against Patrick Ewing and Georgetown. Worthy shot 13 for 17 and scored a game-high 29 points in the Tar Heels' 63-62 victory, sealing the deal when he intercepted an inadvertent pass thrown by Georgetown point guard, Fred Brown, with just seconds remaining.

Worthy was named the tournament's Most Outstanding Player, and a tip-dunk in front of Georgetown's shot-blocking Patrick Ewing, captioned "James Worthy Slams the Door on Georgetown," made the cover of Sports Illustrated.

In the wake of his success, Worthy elected to forgo his senior year and enter the NBA draft. He was selected by the Los Angeles Lakers with the Number 1 pick overall in the 1982 draft and went on to win three NBA titles and played in seven All-Star games while averaging 3.5 more points in the playoffs than the regular season. Worthy completed his degree later, via summer school. He is one of just eight North Carolina players to have their numbers retired.

# Grant Hill

## (1991-1994)

*UNC Athletic Communications*

## Carved in Stone

There was never any doubt, from the first time I laid eyes on Grant Hill, that he would be a big-time superstar. In my forty years at ESPN, the trio of Christian Laettner, Bobby Hurley, and Grant Hill was one of the greatest core units to ever play the game.

Hill is the son of American royalty. His father, Calvin, was an All-American running back at Yale and NFL star with the Dallas Cowboys. His mother, Janet, was a suitemate of Hillary Clinton at Wellesley College, worked as a special assitant to the Secretary of the Army, and went on to be a highly-successful lawyer (and eventually a Capitol Hill lobbyist) in Washington, D.C.

But, Hill, the versatile 6'8" forward, created his own celebrity status at Duke, becoming a four-year starter on two national championship teams in 1992 and 1993 and a consensus first-team All-American, the ACC Player of the Year, and the National Defensive Player of the Year in 1994. That was the year that the Blue Devils advanced to the national championship game with Hill as a senior, before they lost to Arkansas.

Hill, who played on three ACC regular-season championship teams, became the first ACC player to finish with more than 1,900 points, 700 rebounds, 400 assists, 200 steals, and 100 blocked shots before graduating, and was selected by the Detroit Pistons with the third pick overall in the NBA draft.

## From All Sides

Hill's career almost went in a different direction. Calvin Hill wanted his son to follow in his footsteps in football. But the younger Hill, a quarterback, quit the sport in ninth grade to concentrate on basketball at South Lakes High in Reston, Virginia. It was a good move as he became a McDonald's All-American.

It originally looked like Hill was all set to go to Duke's neighborhood rival. He rooted for the Tar Heels, wore Carolina gear, and was the top recruiting objective of Dean Smith. But Duke coach Mike Krzyzewski outfoxed the Tar Heels, arranging for Hill to visit Duke the week before he was supposed to visit UNC the weekend of the annual sold out Blue-White scrimmage at Cameron Indoor Stadium. The crowd knew who he was. Hill felt under the spell of Mike Krzyzewski, who had coached the Devils to two Final Fours in the previous three years. When Krzyzewski shook Hill's hand at the end of his visit and asked him to come to Duke, Hill knew the school had everything he wanted.

UNC Athletic Communications

When he chose Duke over Carolina, he shocked everyone, including his parents, his teammates, his friends…and even Smith, who came to dinner at Hill's house only to have Hill's parents tell Smith the forward was going to Carolina.

Hill made an immediate impact. He averaged 14.9 points, shot 53.2 percent, 6 rebounds, and 3.6 assists during his career. The numbers may not have been spectacular, but Hill had a history of making spectacular plays, including the one-handed dunk off an alley-oop pass from Bobby Hurley that sealed Duke's 72-65 victory in the 1991 NCAA finals. Hill also had his 70-foot inbounds pass to Christian Laettner to set up the miracle shot at the buzzer that gave the Blue Devils a 104-103 overtime victory against feisty Kentucky in the 1992 regional finals.

Add to this Hill's huge performance in the 1994 regional finals, and he is obvious Duke royalty. In that game, he held Purdue's Big Dog, Glenn Robinson—who had just scored 44 points in a Sweet 16 victory over Kansas—to just 13 points on 6 for 22 shooting in a 69-60 victory that propelled the Devils to the Final Four.

Hill was selected the NBA's co-Rookie of the Year in 1995 and was selected to the NBA All-Star game seven times in his eighteen years in the league. Sadly, a series of ankle problems derailed his career and he was never the pro player he could have been.

Hill retired in 2013 and went on to work with NBA TV and CBS, combining with Jim Nantz and Bill Raftery to call the 2015 Final Four won by the Blue Devils. No shock that Grant was elected to the Naismith Basketball Hall of Fame. He epitomizes what coaches hope their players will be once they make the transition from the basketball court to the real world. Hill is a winner in the game of life.

*UNC Athletic Communications*

# Tyler Hansbrough
## (2006-2009)

UNC Athletic Communications

## Carved in Stone

I remember vividly sitting in Roy Williams' office and seeing the coach's face light up with joy when talking about Tyler Hansbrough's many attributes that contributed to his success during the All-American player's era.

I also recall that during our sessions, he would say, "Dick, Hansbrough is a coach's dream."

## From All Sides

Hansbrough and his two brothers, Greg and Ben, have always been close. They formed a special bond when big brother, Greg, had a brain tumor removed when he was just eight-years old. Greg, despite being told he would never play organized sports, became the captain of his high school cross-country team, lettered in basketball, and had run three marathons. Ben played college basketball at Mississippi State and Notre Dame before playing in the NBA for the Pacers. He would be joined by his brother, Tyler, thanks to a great start at North Carolina.

After North Carolina won Williams' first national championship in 2009, the Tar Heels lost their top seven scorers from that team. The aftermath of one of the Tar Heels' greatest triumphs could have been a disaster if Williams hadn't signed 6'9", 250-pound center, Hansbrough, a McDonald's All-American from Poplar Bluff, Missouri, who had dominated the McDonald's All-American game, the Jordan Brand Classic, and the Nike Hoop Summit. In the Summit, he scored 31 points in Team USA's 106-98 victory over a slew of international stars.

Hansbrough is the most decorated player in the history of the University of North Carolina. He was the first player in ACC history to be named first-team All-ACC four consecutive seasons, was a four-time consensus first-team All-American, and swept all six National Player of the Year awards as a junior in 2008. He came back in 2009 to help the Tar Heels defeat Michigan State to win Williams' second national championship as a senior.

Hansbrough, who was given the nickname "Psycho T" as a freshman at North Carolina for his relentless practice habits, set school records for career scoring with 2,872 points (a mark that will likely never be broken), and career rebounds with 1,219.

Hansbrough made an immediate impact at Carolina. He was a first-team All-American and All-ACC selection and then became the ACC Rookie of the Year and National Freshman of the Year in 2006, when he led the Tar Heels in scoring, rebounding, shooting percentage, and steals. He averaged 18.9 points and enjoyed his best game as a freshman on February 15, 2006, when he scored 40 points against Georgia Tech. Carolina won 23 games in a rebuilding year, and Williams was named ACC coach of the Year over his team including Hansbrough as the Tar Heels advanced to the NCAA Tournament Round of 32.

Hansbrough was a consensus first-team All-American and a unanimous All-ACC selection for a second straight year as a sophomore. That year, he led the ACC in scoring with an average of 18.4 points, as the Tar Heels won the ACC regular season and conference tournament, won 31 games, and advanced to the Elite Eight. The Tar Heels lost to Georgetown in overtime. On March 4, 2007, Hansbrough had 26 points and 17 rebounds before suffering an injury in the closing seconds of the Tar Heels' 86-72 victory over Duke. They clinched the top seed in the ACC tournament. With 14.5 seconds left in the game, Hansbrough leapt for a layup. After the ball left his hand, he was struck in the face by Gerald Henderson's right elbow, which broke his nose. Henderson was ejected from the game. Hansbrough went on to play with a nose guard/face mask throughout post-season play before taking it off in the second half of a NCAA second-round win over Michigan State.

As a junior in 2008, Hansbrough's best year averaged 22.6 points and 10.5 rebounds. He was the consensus National Player of the Year when the Tar Heels won 36 games, captured the ACC regular season and tournament championships (again), and advanced to the NCAA semi-finals before losing to eventual-champion, Kansas. He tied an ACC record with double figures in 39 games.

He never thought about leaving early for the NBA draft after questions arose about his ability to play the post at his size. Instead, he returned to lead the Tar Heels to a national championship, averaging 20.6 points and scoring 18 points apiece in North Carolina's Final Four wins against Villanova and Michigan State. Hansbrough was selected by the Indiana Pacers with the Number 13 pick overall in the 2009 draft and he played seven years in the league.

# Calbert Chaeney
## (1989-1993)

*Indiana University Athletics*

## Carved in Stone

Calbert Cheaney is the classic product of the Bob Knight school of coaching at Indiana.

The 6'7", 209-pound forward was a good player at William Henry Harrison High School in Evansville, Indiana, but—after he broke his foot midway through his senior year and missed postseason—he became a virtual unknown on Indiana University's (IU) top-ranked class of 1989 that included Lawrence Funderburke, Chris Lawson, Pat Graham, and Chris Reynolds.

## From All Sides

Knight, who scouted Cheaney in a high school game as a junior when he shot just 6 for 32 and his team lost badly, initially didn't think Cheaney was good enough to play in the Big Ten. He had to be convinced by his assistants to kickstart his recruiting of Cheaney again that summer.

Cheaney wasn't sure if he was good enough, either. He made a verbal commitment to play for Evansville before his senior year, then changed his mind. His signing created some tension between Knight and then-University of Evansville coach, Jim Crews, who was a key backup on IU's iconic, unbeaten 1976 team. Cheaney diplomatically claimed that he decided to go to IU because he wanted to get away from home.

"I wanted to play away from home, but not too far," he said. "It ended up working out pretty good."

Four years later, the willowy left-hander with the near-perfect stroke, insatiable work ethic, and strong mid-range game that was perfect for Knight's motion offense, swept all 12 National Player of the Year awards. He led his team to Big Ten championships in 1991 and 1993, 105 victories—the most of any IU player—and the 1992 Final Four as a junior. They lost to eventual champion Duke, 81-78. It was a physical game where five Hoosier players fouled out.

Cheaney's greatest strength was his consistency. He was a three-time All-American and a four-time IU MVP, leading the Hoosiers in scoring for all four years, scoring 30 or more points 13 times and averaging 19.8 points for his career. He finished with 2,613 points, becoming the all-time leading scorer in school and in Big Ten history—a record that still stands. When Cheaney broke the record against Northwestern at Assembly Hall his senior year, Knight went against tradition and stopped the game so the IU faithful could recognize his accomplishment.

During his last three years at Indiana, the Hoosiers spent all but two of the 53 poll weeks ranked in the Top 10. The Hoosiers might have won a national championship in 1993 if 6'10" sophomore forward, Alan Henderson, hadn't torn his ACL in practice in late February. He wasn't the same player when he tried to come back in the postseason.

As it was, Cheaney averaged 22.4 points as a senior and led the Hoosiers to a 31-4 record, a pre-season NIT championship, two wins over NCAA runner-up Michigan, and a first place 18-0 record in the Big Ten. Indiana was ranked Number 1 most of the season before Kansas took advantage of Henderson's injury to defeat the Hoosiers, 83-77, in the regional finals.

Cheaney was eventually taken by the Washington Wizards with the sixth pick overall in the 1993 NBA draft. He played thirteen years in the league.

# *Dick Vitale's*
# MOUNT RUSHMORE
## OF
# ALL LITTLE BIG MEN
## ON CAMPUS

ALLEN IVERSON

TYRONE BOGUES

SHABAZZ NAPIER

TREY BURKE

# Allen Iverson

## (1994-1996)

*Phil Ellsworth / ESPN Images*

### Carved in Stone

Georgetown had some big men on campus over the years: Patrick Ewing, Alonzo Mourning, Dikembe Mutombo. The Hoyas also had a guard who was GIANT…once the rock was in his hands, Mr. Allen Iverson.

Iverson may only be six-feet tall, but he was an unstoppable force in the NBA and an easy choice for induction into the Naismith Hall of Fame class of 2016, after leading the league in scoring three times. He finished his career with a scoring average of 26.7 points per game over fourteen years and a playoff career scoring average of 29.7 points.

## Not So Little

It's hard to believe there was a time when Iverson didn't know whether he would ever play college basketball.

Iverson attended Bethel High in Hampton, Virginia, where he was the state's Player of the Year in football and basketball during his junior year. He led his team to the Division II Virginia state championship in both sports as a quarterback and a point guard.

On February 14th, 1993, Iverson and several of his friends found themselves in serious trouble, though, following a shouting match that involved racial taunts on both sides. It escalated into huge and physical fight with several patrons at a local bowling alley. Iverson and three of his friends were arrested. Iverson, who was just seventeen at the time, was convicted as an adult with a felony charge. Iverson and his supporters maintained their innocence, claiming they left the alley as soon as the trouble began, but he had a long road ahead.

"For me to be in a bowling alley where everyone in the whole place knows who I am and be cracking people upside the head and think nothing is going to happen?" he said. "That's crazy."

Iverson was found guilty anyway, and given a fifteen-year prison sentence, with ten years suspended. After spending four months at Newport News City Farm, a correctional facility, he was granted clemency by Virginia Governor, Douglas Wilder. The Virginia Court of Appeals overturned the conviction in 1995 for insufficient evidence. The time spent behind bars brought out an inner strength in Iverson who knew he could not show any weakness with the older inmates.

Once he was released, Iverson was forced to complete his senior year of high school at Richard Milburn School for at-risk students, instead of competing in sports at Bethel. His mother Ann called John Thompson of Georgetown and asked him to take a chance on her son and Thompson offered him a scholarship after meeting with him personally.

"I felt it was the right thing to do, to give this young man a chance," Thompson said. "And Allen wasn't a problem for me. We had to talk about a lot of things—but he wasn't a problem. We worked together."

Iverson could be wild, but he made impossible shots and seemingly impossible plays that defied basketball logic and the fundamentals of the game.

"With someone like Allen, who is a prodigy, you can't change his style," Thompson said. "I knew I had to make a decision. Accept that style or send him on his way."

Thompson opted to live with both sides of Iverson's personality.

Iverson spent two years at Georgetown, setting the school record for career scoring average with 22.9 points per game and winning the league's Defensive Player of the Year both seasons. Iverson was named Big East Rookie of the Year as a freshman in 1995 when he led the Hoyas to the NCAA Sweet 16, the school's first trip that deep into the tournament in five years, before they lost to North Carolina.

As a sophomore, he averaged twenty-five points and led Georgetown to the 1996 Big East championship and the NCAA Elite Eight, where they lost to Massachusetts. He was named a first team All-American and then declared for the 1996 draft. Iverson, who was the first player in the Thompson era to leave Georgetown early for the NBA, was selected by the 76ers as the first pick overall.

He left part of his heart on the Hill Top.

# Tyrone Bogues

## (1983-1987)

*Wake Forest Athletics*

## Carved in Stone

If there was ever a poster child who would be the great inspiration to many for not letting your size dictate your destiny, it would go to Muggsy Bogues.

Think about it, what are the odds of a five-foot-three-inch athlete playing with the greatest performers on the world court of the NBA? Those incredible odds meant zilch to Bogues as he proved all the critics wrong. Not only did he play in the NBA, he starred in the league for over a decade.

I loved seeing Bogues on the court. Little in size, big in stature.

## Not So Little

Bogues has been battling the odds ever since he can remember. The 5'3", 140-pound point guard, who has the distinction of being the shortest player ever to play in the NBA, found a way to become a star at every level.

Bogues was born in Baltimore, Maryland, and grew up in the Lafayette Court housing projects, raised by his mother. When he was little, he loved playing basketball—but the other kids didn't take him seriously on the court because of his size. He was never chosen for pick-up games on the playground.

"I was 'Little Ty,'" he recalled. "I always got this negative feedback from the game. But I always knew I could play." So, he and his friends found milk crates, cut the bottom out to make baskets and tied them to each end of the fence. "We had our own milk crate basketball pickup game," he said. "It was a good time because we could jump off the fence and dunk the ball. You had to be creative to play and I wanted to play."

Bogues picked up the nickname "Muggsy" because he was a scrapper on the court. He started to wedge his way into the games because he was an aggressive defender.

"I was a little kid that was out there just trying to create havoc, trying to disrupt a lot of things," he said.

Bogues picked up a reputation in his neighborhood that carried over into Dunbar High School, where he was coached by Bob Wade, who went on to coach at the University of Maryland. He was a starter for a team that included future NBA players Reggie Williams, Reggie Lewis, and David Wingate. The Poets went 29-1 his junior year and were 31-0 his senior year in 1982, when they were ranked the Number 1 team in the country by USA Today.

Some skeptics thought Bogues had reached a glass ceiling, but Wake Forest wasn't among them, offering Bogues a full scholarship. He went on to play four years from 1983 through 1987 and got his chance to shine in a nationally-televised game against North Carolina. He established himself in the ACC with a 20-point, 10-assist performance against the Tar Heels.

Bogues averaged 11.3 points, 8.4 assists, and 3.1 steals per game as a junior. That summer, he played for the U.S. national team in the 1986 FIBA World Championships on a team that won a gold medal. As a senior, Bogues made first team All-ACC selection after averaging 14.8 points, 9.5 assists, 3.8 assists, and 2.4 steals a game. When his college career ended, he was the ACC career leader in steals and assists.

Bogues was selected by the Washington Bullets with the Number 12 pick overall in the talent-deep 1987 draft. In his rookie year, he was a teammate of Manute Bol, who stood 7'7" and the two were the tallest and shortest players in NBA history at that time, with a 28-inch difference between them. Bogues and Bol appear on three magazine covers together.

Despite his size, Bogues managed to block 39 shots throughout his fourteen-year NBA career, including one on 7'0" Patrick Ewing in 1993 when Ewing was pulling the ball back to go up for a shot and Bogues stripped him. Bogues reportedly had a 44-inch vertical leap, but his hands were too small to hold on the ball and dunk one-handed. It has been claimed Bogues once successfully dunked during pregame practice in December of 1990…but that was never confirmed.

Bogues played for four different NBA teams, but he is best known for his ten seasons with the Charlotte Hornets from 1989 through 1998, where he became one of the most popular players in the league, playing with Alonzo Mourning and Larry Johnson for a perennial playoff contender. He is the Hornets' career leader in assists (5,557), steals (1,067), and assists per 48 minutes (13.5). He also led in minutes played.

He has an official apparel line that includes a T-shirt that says, "Who says you're too small to Ball?"

# Shabazz Napier

## (2010-2014)

*UConn Athletics*

### Carved in Stone

Shabazz Napier pulled one of the great miracles in college basketball. Many of the "experts," including yours truly, didn't think they had a chance of even going to the Sweet 16, then winning a national title. Talk about a hero, baby! Napier was the star of Connecticut's most unexpected national championship.

### Not So Little

The Huskies' 6'0" first team All-American point guard, who was born in Roxbury, Massachusetts, and grew up in the Mission Hill Projects, was selected Most Outstanding Player in the 2014 Final Four. He scored a game-high 22 points, grabbed 6 rebounds, and played lockdown defense as the seventh-seed Huskies defeated Kentucky, 60-54, in the national championship game in Arlington, Texas.

He used his time in the spotlight to advocate for the rights of student athletes in an era where 79,000 fans paid an average of $500 to watch the Final Four games from dizzying heights at AT&T Stadium. CBS pays about $800 million a year for the right to show the NCAA tournament on TV, but one of its star players doesn't always have enough money to eat.

"We do have hungry nights that we don't have enough money to get any food," he said. "Sometime money is needed. I don't think you should stretch it out to hundreds of thousands of dollars for playing, because a lot of times guys don't know how to handle themselves with money. I feel like a student-athlete (sometimes has) hungry nights where (he's) not able to eat, but still (has) to play up to (his) capabilities."

Napier summoned up enough energy to become the only Connecticut player to finish his career with at least 1,500 points, 500 rebounds, 500 assists, and 250 steals during a four-year career. Napier finished fourth on the UConn scoring list with 1,959 points. Along with teammates Niels Giffey and Tyler Olander, they are the only Division I men's players in history to have won national championships as both freshman and seniors.

Napier almost missed reaching the finish line. He grew up without a father in a poor city surrounded by drugs and violence. Napier didn't always take his academics seriously in high school. If it hadn't been for Will Blalock, who went on to play for Iowa State, Steve Hailey, who played for Boston College; and a group of older friends who looked after him since he was little, he might have never escaped the tough environment.

Blalock and Hailey, two of the best guards in the region, took Napier under their wing. When Napier's

*UConn Athletics*

mother, Carmen Velazquez, was struggling financially, Napier lived with Blalock's family for three summers until Blalock left for Iowa State when Napier was twelve.

Napier started high school at Charlestown but—after three years—he wasn't on track to graduate. He enrolled at Lawrence Academy in 2008, accepting a scholarship to the $50,000 prep school located forty miles north of the city. Napier reclassified as a junior and his grades improved. He led Lawrence to an unbeaten 29-0 season and the New England prep school Class C title his senior year. He had 23 points, 8 assists, and 8 steals against a St. Mark's team that sent players to Duke, Georgetown, Arizona, and Iowa.

Connecticut Hall of Fame coach, Jim Calhoun, noticed and Napier signed with the Huskies, making the Big East All-Freshman team in 2011 when Huskies won the national championship.

When Calhoun, who was a Frank Lloyd Wright in building the program, left because of health reasons after Napier's sophomore year, the guard considered transferring because the program was going through difficult times. The Huskies were preparing for their first season in the American Athletic Conference because the Big East was in the process of being an all-basketball league, and Connecticut had major interests in promoting its football program. The Huskies tried but couldn't get into the Atlantic Coast Conference. Most damaging was that the NCAA's post-season ban in 2013 for eligibility sanctions triggered the departure of five key players to the NBA or other schools.

Napier stuck it out and played for former Connecticut star and elevated assistant coach, Kevin Ollie, averaging 17.1 points, 4.6 assists, 4.1 rebounds, and 2.0 steals, while making first team All-Big East. Napier combined with Ryan Boatwright to become one of the best backcourts in the country…but they had nowhere to go in March.

Then, after a one-year absence from the tournament, they won it all. "You're looking at the hungry Huskies," Shabazz told CBS in the post-game. "Ladies and gentlemen, this is what happens when you ban us."

Napier's career began as a freshman backup to the incomparable Kemba Walker the year Connecticut won Jim Calhoun's third NCAA title. He grew into one of Connecticut's all-time greats, becoming the American's first-ever Player of the Year after he averaged 18 points, 5.9 rebounds, 4.9 assists, and 1.8 steals.

As good as Napier was, the Huskies were not the dominant team in the AAC in 2014, finishing fourth in the regular season and losing to Louisville by 10 in the AAC tournament final. Napier predicted after that game they would cut down the nets in Texas.

 "I looked into his eyes and I really believed him," Giffey said.

The Huskies marched past St. Joseph's, Villanova, Iowa State, Michigan State, Florida, and finally Kentucky to fulfill that promise. The Huskies never trailed in the game as Napier hit clutch field goals anytime Kentucky got close. The young Wildcats pulled within a point on three occasions, including one last time with 8:13 remaining in the name. But Napier drilled a three-point jumper to stop the bleeding.

Calhoun predicted that Shabazz would soon be talked about in the same breath as Ray Allen, Rip Hamilton, Ben Gordon, Emeka Okafor, and Kemba Walker. He wasn't wrong. Shabazz Napier earned his spot in the hearts of UConn fans everywhere.

Napier is now a member of the Brooklyn Nets.

# Trey Burke
## (2011-2013)

Scott Clarke / ESPN Images

Carved In Stone

I don't think people appreciate how vital Trey Burke was to the Michigan Wolverines. He was so special on the court, and I really enjoyed calling some of his games. Like most aspiring basketball players growing up in Columbus, Burke dreamed of playing for the hometown team, Ohio State. He was trained to be a natural fit for the Buckeyes…so much for those plans, baby!

Not So Little

From the youngest age, Burke was being trained for the big leagues.

• By the age of five, Burke's local youth league changed the rules so he would not keep stealing the ball from the other team. He was not allowed over mid-court when the other team had the ball.

• At the age of nine, Burke's father, Benji, made him do everything with his left hand, including brushing his teeth and eating dinner, helping to develop his ambidexterity.

• He had a personal trainer from the time he was in ninth grade.

Burke played for the prestigious All-Ohio Red travel team before attending Northland High School. He was the starting point guard along with forward, Jared Sullinger, his best friend and a Top 5 prospect nationally. They were on a ranked team that won the state championship his sophomore year. He made 5-of-6 free throws in overtime as Northland defeated Dublin Scioto, 54-53, in the title game.

His career record at Northland was an incredible 95-5, including 23-1 as a junior, when his team was ranked Number 1 by USA Today for most of the season (before being upset by Lincoln in the state semifinals). Still, he never got a sniff from Buckeyes' coach, Thad Matta, or his staff…because he was only 5'9", 135 pounds.

The Buckeyes were more interested in Aaron Craft from nearby Findlay, Ohio, who was a year older than Burke and got to participate on the same age group team as the 6'9" Sullinger. The Buckeyes signed four members of the Ohio All-Red Under 17 team and another point guard, Shannon Scott, from Georgia, leaving Burke as the odd man out and forcing him to find success across state lines.

Burke followed in Sullinger's footsteps and was selected as Ohio's Mr. Basketball his senior year at Northland, his school that finished runner-up in the state tournament. Michigan coach, John Beilein, was willing to overlook his slow-growing body once he liked his quickness and saw him score and make magical passes in travel ball. Burke committed to the Big Ten rival Wolverines the summer before his senior season.

Beilein, one of the best evaluators in the game, got just what he was looking for. The high-strung Burke, who had grown to 6'0", 173-pounds and hated to lose, got a chance to play immediately after Darrius Morris left early for the NBA. He was selected co-Big Ten Freshman of the Year in 2012 when the Wolverines won a taste of their first Big Ten championship since 1985-1986 season by advancing to the NCAA tournament. Burke led the team in scoring, assists, steals, and blocked shots.

When Burke saw there was a shallow group of point guards entering the draft, he declared for evaluation, but then decided to return to campus for his sophomore year in hopes of becoming a first-round pick. He increased his weight to 190 pounds and his vertical leap by three inches, exploding onto the national scene as the best point guard in the country. Burke averaged 18.6 points, 6.9 assists, and 3.3 rebounds, with a 3.9 turnover-assist ratio for his young Michigan team with three freshman starters. Michigan won its first sixteen games of the year. The Wolverines zoomed to Number 1 in the polls at the end of January and won another share of the Big Ten regular championship. Burke then made a miracle 30-foot three -pointer to force overtime in a Sweet 16 win over Kansas as the fourth-seeded Wolverines eventually advanced to the national championship game against Louisville.

Scott Clarke / ESPN Images

Despite picking up two early fouls, Burke scored 24 points against the Cardinals in the finals, but it wasn't enough. Michigan fell, 82-76, when Louisville backup forward, Luke Hancock, scored 22 points.

"A lot of people didn't expect us to get this far," Burke said. "A lot of people didn't expect us to get past the second round. We fought. We fought to this point, but Louisville was the better team today."

Burke was rewarded for his efforts. He was the Big Ten Player of the Year, a consensus first team All-American, and he won every possible National Player of the Year award—the Wooden, the Naismith, and the Robertson—in addition to the Bob Cousy Award and while setting a school record for assists.

My friends, Burke could flat-out play!

In the NBA, it has been a rocky road for Burke. He showed some of his outstanding skills at the end of his first season with the New York Knicks as he had several monster games and, since Trey is young, he might still achieve success at the big-time level.

*Dick Vitale's*

# MOUNT RUSHMORE
## OF
## ALL MARCO POLO

### WALTER BERRY

### LARRY JOHNSON

### HANK GATHERS

### BO KIMBLE

# Walter Berry

## (1984-1986)

*St. John's Basketball*

### Carved in Stone

Long before Shaquille O'Neil referred to Boston Celtics star, Paul Pierce, as "The Truth," that nickname was owned by St. John 's All-America forward Walter Berry. Sometimes a solid transfer player (Marco Polo) turns out to be a name forever associated with a successful franchise.

### Moving Around On and Off the Court

Berry took his place as one of the great players in the history of St. John's during the two years he spent on the Queens campus. As a sophomore in 1985, he helped lead the Johnnies to the lone Final Four of the Lou Carnesecca era. The next year, without teammate Chris Mullin, the 6' 7" forward from Manhattan dominated college basketball. He averaged 23 points, 11 rebounds, scored a school-record 828 points, and was selected as consensus National Player of the Year for a team that advanced to the NCAA Elite Eight.

The left-handed Berry was the classic St. John's player. He grew up on the playgrounds of the city and established a reputation for himself at three different high schools in the boroughs—DeWitt Clinton, Morris, and the now-closed Ben Franklin High School. Because of his constant transfers and the fact that he fell behind academically when he had to help his mother look for a place to live after fire gutted their apartment, circumstances eventually ruined his chances to become eligible.

The NCAA Council ruled Berry was ineligible to play for St. John's because he did not graduate with his class at Franklin in 1982 and had not earned his degree by taking the graduate equivalency test. Instead Berry took a 24-credit alternative program while he sat a year at St. John's. The program was not recognized by the NCAA.

Berry filed suit through his lawyer in federal court in Brooklyn, asking the courts to rule him eligible. Judge Charles P. Sifton rejected the request for an injunction and set a trial date for October 3rd, a week after the end of late registration at St. John's. Berry wound up enrolling at San Jacinto Junior College in Texas, hoping to graduate in a year from the two-year college and return for the 1984-85 season. San Jacinto gave him his 24 credits, but the school requires sixty-four credits for a student to graduate, meaning Berry would have to earn forty credits during first semester, second semester, and summer school.

Berry accomplished that awesome job while playing for demanding Ronnie Arrow, who constantly pushed him to be great. Berry lived up to his expectations on the court and was named a consensus first team All-American and national Junior College Player of the Year after averaging 28.9 points and 14 rebounds.

After a year, he completed his requirements and was overwhelmed by marquee programs like North Carolina and Duke from the ACC.

"But there was no question I was going home," he said.

Berry was almost unstoppable in the Big East with an assortment of inside moves and shots from unique angles. He finished fast breaks with enormous efficiency and perfected the floater long before it became popular. His finest moment came in the finals of the Big East tournament when St. John's defeated Syracuse, 70-69. Berry blocked a driving layup by his friend, the late Syracuse iconic guard, Pearl Washington. Ron Rowan hit a jumper to give St. John's a one-point lead with just 8 seconds to play. Washington, who scored 27 points the night before in a semi-final win over Georgetown, went the length of the floor, was headed to the rim, and ducked under a defender to release a shot. Berry blocked him from behind and time ran out. Washington never saw him.

The Block has become part of Big East folklore, "It gets bigger and bigger over time," Berry said. "Like those fish stories."

After two impactful seasons at St. John's, Berry declared for the NBA draft following his junior year and was drafted by Portland with the Number 14 pick. He was subsequently traded to the San Antonio Spurs, where he averaged 17.6 points and 5.6 rebounds as a rookie. Berry played just three years before slipping out of the league and finished his playing career over a fourteen-year period in Italy and Greece.

There were rumors at the time that Berry couldn't get along with his NBA coaches at three different stops, but he was making $300,000 in the league. Napoli offered him millions. Simple math, my friend!

In 2010, Berry returned to St. John's for an encore, collecting his degree in Liberal Studies and completing a journey that started twenty-seven years prior through the College of Progressive Studies.

# Larry Johnson
## (1989-1991)

UNLV Athletics

### Carved in Stone

Larry Johnson owned college basketball for two years when he played for Jerry Tarkanian at the University of Nevada Las Vegas (UNLV). The 6'7", 250-pound forward was a raging bull and a two-time first team All-American on the most talented team in the country. He led the Runnin' Rebels to two Final Fours. UNLV earned a national championship in 1990 when he scored 22 points and grabbed 11 rebounds as his team blew out Duke, 103-73, in Denver.

### Moving Around On and Off the Court

Johnson, a junior college transfer who averaged 22 points and 11 rebounds and shot 64 percent for his career. He was selected the winner of both the Wooden and Naismith Awards as the National Player of the Year in 1991.

"He was the most complete player I ever coached," Tarkanian claimed.

Johnson was the ultimate nightmare matchup for defenders, combining strength with a feathery jump shot that drew defenders away from the basket. He was steeled by growing up in a drug-, violence-, and crime-infested Dixon Housing Project in South Dallas. He might have been headed for serious trouble had his mother not signed him up for Police Athletic League activities. The twelve-year-old didn't want anything to do with the police and he hated taking the bus to the recreation center, but—once there—Johnson, who was 6' 2", 190-pounds in seventh grade, started to excel in boxing. He could have been the next Evander Holyfield until he got hooked on basketball the next year.

As Johnson's body and his game grew, he was considered the best prep prospect in the country his senior year at Dallas' Skyline High School. He decided to stay home and gave an oral commitment to Southern Methodist, but a foul-up in his SAT scores made him ineligible for a scholarship. Johnson failed to obtain the necessary 800 score the first time he took the test. He hit the magic number the second time. But SMU officials, who were queasy after the football team was sanctioned by the NCAA with the death penalty, wanted him to take it a third time.

Johnson refused on principle and enrolled at Odessa, Texas Junior College, a school that had never recruited him. He attended Odessa because a friend of his from the neighborhood, Tony Jackson, was going there. Johnson dominated junior college for two years in 1988 and 1989, averaging 22.3 points as a freshman and 29 points as a sophomore. He became the first and only player to win the national Junior College Athletic Association Division I Player of the Year both years he played.

Some analysts felt Johnson could have been a first-round selection in the 1989 NBA draft had he declared, but he opted to sign with UNLV.

"If I had gone to SMU, I would have scored some points, made some dunks, but I wouldn't have won a championship," he said.

Johnson walked into a highly-successful program that was constantly monitored by NCAA investigators because Tarkanian was always taking chances on players no other schools would touch.

"Coach cared about them," Johnson said. "He wanted to help them. He wanted us to make something of our lives and get to another level. Not just in basketball, but in life. We were some renegades and we had that swagger," Johnson recalled. "We played with our shirt tails out and baggy shorts down to our knees."

UNLV Athletics

UNLV was the hip-hop nation's first team. But the Rebels were also fundamentally sound and highly motivated when they beat Duke in 1990.

"We had the mentality of 'us against the world,'" Johnson said. "We never got good press—when we played Duke, it was good versus evil. We were the bad guys of college basketball. And, honestly, we loved it at the time."

Johnson could have been a lottery pick if he had left following his junior year. "I knew I needed to come back," he said. "I wasn't interested in going to the NBA and sitting. I wanted to play and be competitive."

Johnson had one more incentive to return. He wanted to prove himself academically by making the Dean's List as a senior.

"That was one of my greatest accomplishments," he said. "That was for my mom. I told her I wasn't going to sleepwalk through school. I was going to be successful. I was going to make it."

Johnson almost didn't get a chance to defend his title. Their postseason was mired by charges of recruiting violations and misconduct and an agreement was reached by the university and the NCAA to allow for them to play in the tournament in 1992. The exception was followed by a suspension from post-season play the next year.

*UNLV Athletics*

The Rebels responded with a perfect 27-0 season with an average scoring margin of 26.7 points a game. As they entered the Final Four, they were on the verge of becoming the first college team to go unbeaten since Indiana in 1976. When they played the same Duke team in the semis, the Running Rebels had three future first-round picks—Johnson, Greg Anthony, and Stacy Augmon.

Johnson was a beast, averaging 22.1 points and 10.5 rebounds as a senior and shooting 64 percent for his career. But his final game as a college player didn't go as planned. The Blue Devils staged a remarkable second half comeback, sealing victory when Johnson's long three-pointer bounced off the rim ahead of the buzzer, ending a 45-game winning streak.

Johnson went on to become the first pick in the 1991 draft when he was selected by Charlotte and signed a long-term contract worth $84 million.

"There's no way I'm the Number 1 pick if Tark didn't coach me," he said. "We used to practice defense for two hours and forty-five minutes and then spend fifteen minutes on offense. He would tell us, 'You've been scoring all your life. Now we need to stop somebody.'"

# Hank Gathers
## (1987-1990)

*LMU Athletics*

### Carved in Stone

Hank Gathers' story is filled with tremendous accomplishment and heartbreaking sadness. Gathers grew up in the crime-riddled Raymond Rosen projects of North Philadelphia. After he and Bo Kimble led Dobbins Technical High to the Philadelphia Public League Championship in 1985, they both signed to play for University of Southern California (USC), along with high school All-American, Tommy Lewis, and Rich Grande. The euphoria lasted for a year before Stan Morrison and his top assistant, David Spencer, were fired following a 11-17 season.

The players threatened to transfer unless they had a say in the next coaching staff. That didn't happen. USC hired George Raveling, who gave the players a deadline to respond as to whether they would remain on the team. When they didn't respond, he revoked their scholarships.

Gathers and Kimble transferred together from USC to nearby Loyola-Marymount in Los Angeles, which was coached by a former Philadelphian, Paul Westhead. After sitting out for a year, their careers took off.

## Moving Around On and Off the Court

The 6' 7", 210-pound Gathers quickly found the national spotlight. He led a 28-5 team in scoring with 22.5 points and grabbed 8.7 rebounds as a sophomore in 1987 in Westhead's up-tempo offense that emphasized shooting within ten seconds of gaining possession. He was selected to the first team All-West Coast Conference team. The next year, his game took off when Gathers became the second player in Division I to lead in scoring and rebounding in the same season, averaging 32.7 points and 13.7 rebounds. Gathers was named WCC Player of the Year and won the WCC tournament MVP for a second straight time. On December 30, 1988, he scored a career-high 49 points along with 26 rebounds in a 130-125 victory over Nevada.

Gathers' teams led the NCAA in scoring in 1988 (110.3 points per game), 1989 (112.5), and 1990 (122.4). The Lions hold the record for four of the five highest scoring games in Division I history, including a record 181-150 win over U.S. International on January 31, 1989.

Gathers was a candidate for National Player of the Year when the 1990 season began and he had been projected as an NBA lottery pick. He was Loyola's strongest inside player because he seldom shot from beyond ten feet, using his power and quickness for follow-up baskets and scoring on fast breaks.

"I don't care much about the points," he said. "In fact, I should lead the nation in scoring because of my rebounding. Anyone can score 30 points a night if that's what he's concentrating on, but rebounding is special because it is all about desire and toughness."

*LMU Athletics*

Gathers averaged 29 points and 10.8 rebounds as a senior.

Ironically, it was his heart that was his tragic weakness. Gathers thought he was Superman and often bragged he was the strongest man in the world.

Sadly, he was wrong.

On December 9, 1989, Gathers collapsed at a home game against University of California Santa Barbara. He was diagnosed with an exercise-induced abnormal heartbeat and doctors prescribed a beta blocker, Inderal. After missing three games, Gathers felt the medication adversely affected his play for weeks after returning. His dosage was cut back. His play recovered in a nationally-televised game against Louisiana State University (LSU) in February 1990 when he scored 48 points and grabbed 13 rebounds, while being guarded by two seven-footers, Shaquille O'Neal and Stanley Roberts in a 148-141 overtime loss. O'Neal blocked Gathers' first five shots. Then Big Hank went off. The Lions won seven of their next eight games, with Gathers grabbing 30 rebounds against St. Mary's.

As the WCC tournament approached, Gathers did not show up for repeated appointments to test if the medication was still supressing the abnormal heartbeat. It was suspected Gathers was not taking any dosage on game days. On Sunday, March 4, in Los Angeles, he collapsed with 13:34 left in the first half of a conference tournament game against Portland after throwing down a dunk. He popped up momentarily and collapsed again. Medical personnel and family members who traveled from Philadelphia, including Gathers' mother, rushed onto the floor. He was carried outside the gym on a stretcher and shocked by a defibrillator. Gathers sat again briefly, then he stopped breathing. He was pronounced dead at a nearby hospital at 6:55 p.m. He was only 23 years old.

Minutes after Gathers was taken to the hospital, the WCC suspended the game, canceled the tournament, and awarded the conference's automatic bid to Loyola due to its regular-season title. The Gathers' family filed a $32.5 million suit for negligence. Loyola settled out of court for $1.4 million while the cardiologist who treated Gathers settled for $1 million.

It wasn't about the money. A promising career was snuffed out and college basketball coaches and players everywhere wept. Thanks for the memories, Gathers.

# Bo Kimble
## (1987-1990)

LMU Athletics

## Carved in Stone

Bo Kimble took the same path as the late Hank Gathers to Loyola-Marymount, transferring to the University following their freshman year at USC in 1986. The Lions 6'4" guard averaged 35.3 points, leading the country in scoring as a senior in 1990 when both he and Gathers were consensus second team All-Americans. The Lions averaged 122.8 points a game in Paul Westhead's up-tempo offense that culminated in a trip to the NCAA Final Eight. But it is what he did after Gathers' tragic death in the West Coast Conference tournament that will always live in the memory of college basketball fans across the country who believe in Cinderella stories.

## Moving Around On and Off the Court

Kimble and Gathers were both tight when they attended Dobbins Technical School in Philadelphia, but they were equally stubborn. Both were destined for stardom and constantly challenged one another to be great, even if it meant almost coming to blows in pickup games.

They were close enough to stick together throughout college. On the day Gathers collapsed and died during a WCC tournament game in Los Angeles, Kimble could be seen comforting Gather's mother Lucille, as medical personnel treated her son. He played that role through the rest of the emotional post-season.

"People are always asking me about living in Hank's shadow," Kimble said. "I have my own identity. I was leading the nation in scoring before Hank died. The year before, I missed 18 games with injuries and Hank led the nation in scoring. Collectively, we were stronger together than individually. I'm proud to be associated with him and people ought to realize we not only lost a great player, we lost a great person."

Because the league canceled the rest of the tournament, the Lions, who won the WCC regular-season title, were awarded the automatic bid to the NCAA tournament. Once the players and coaches navigated the emotional roadblocks and returned from Gathers' funeral in Philadelphia, they became America's team when March Madness began.

They all turned to and depended on Kimble for inspirational leadership.

The Lions, an 11th seed, weren't expected to do much, but they surprised everyone, rolling through three straight games to become the first team from the school to advance to the West Regional final. Loyola defeated New Mexico State in the first round, Michigan in the second, and Alabama in the Sweet 16, before finally losing to eventual national champion UNLV, 131-101, in the West Region finals despite 42 points from Kimble.

The guard will always be remembered hitting four consecutive awkward left-handed free throws. When he went to the line throughout the tournament, it was to honor Gathers, a right-handed shooter who began to shoot free throws left-handed after a slump.

"I made sure I let everyone know," Kimble recalled, "that making the shot wasn't important. Taking the shot was. It was a tribute to Hank, who had so much trouble with free throws, he started shooting them left-handed. Other players were writing his number "44" on their sneakers. Me, I wanted to honor the effort he put in to try to be a better free-throw shooter, even if it meant trying them left-handed."

It was though Kimble's success preserved the memories of Gathers and extended his legacy. "I think if we had Hank, we could have won it all," Kimble claimed.

LMU Athletics

*LMU Athletics*

Kimble was selected by the Knicks with the eighth pick overall in the 1990 draft. He has since co-founded Forty-Four for Life Foundation, a non-profit agency dedicated to spreading awareness of heart disease, the number one killer in America.

# *Dick Vitale's*
## MOUNT RUSHMORE
## OF
## ALL
## BUILDING BLOCKS

### WAYMAN TISDALE

### SEAN ELLIOTT

### MARK AGUIRRE

### JOHNNY DAWKINS

# Wayman Tisdale
## (1982-1985)

*University of Oklahoma*

## Carved in Stone

Why was Wayman Tisdale so special to me? I think back to a night in April of 2011. I was the recipient of the first Tisdale Humanitarian award. I shared the spotlight that night with Ohio State's Jared Sullinger (the Diaper Dandy of the year) and it was a memorable evening. Oh man, when they called me about the award, I was really touched. When I would see Wayman, he would come over and have the most incredible smile on his face. Never met an athlete who had such a smile. Now that he's gone, he still puts smiles on people's faces as people are helped at a health clinic named in his honor.

## Building a Legend

The late Wayman Tisdale's first love was music. When he was younger, his father, the late Reverend Louis Tisdale, who served as the pastor of the Tulsa First Baptist Church for more than twenty years, bought each of his sons Mickey Mouse guitars with the hope that one of them would take an interest. Wayman, his youngest, became intrigued with listening to the bass players at his church and taught himself how to play the guitar and bass.

Tisdale had no interest in basketball when he was younger. When older brothers, Weldon and William, played pickup games, he usually quit before they were finished, retreating to the family sandbox. Tisdale, who sang in the church choir, might have been happy with a spot in the high school band until he experienced a 24-inch growth spurt in junior high that left him towering over his classmates. That's crazy, man! That's when he first learned how to dunk.

By the time he was a senior at Tulsa's Booker T. Washington High School in 1982, Tisdale was 6'9" and one of the most recruited players in the country. When Oklahoma coach, Billy Tubbs, was recruiting the left-handed Tisdale, he came up with the winning sales pitch by offering to push back practice Sunday, so Tisdale could play bass guitar at morning services.

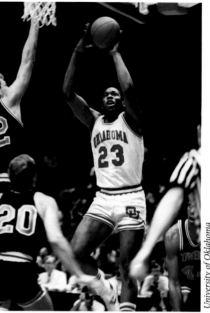

University of Oklahoma

Tisdale quickly became the face of the Oklahoma University (OU) basketball program that had traditionally been overshadowed by football. He was the first Big Eight player to make first-team All-American in each of the three years he spent in college. He led the Big Eight in scoring three times, averaging 24.5, 27.0 and 25.2 points, and he set a school record with 61 points against Texas-San Antonio in 1984. He scored 2,661 points in his career and led the Sooners to conference titles as a sophomore and junior. He averaged 25.6 points and 10.1 rebounds and shot 57.8 percent for his career. Tisdale also was selected to play for Bob Knight's U.S. Olympic team that won a gold medal in the 1984 Olympics after his sophomore year.

Tisdale's greatest accomplishment in college may have been lifting the Sooners to a 31-6 season as a junior when they advanced to the NCAA tournament Regional finals, their deepest run since 1947. They came within 2 points from preventing Memphis' advance to the Final Four.

Tisdale set the stage for Tubbs to make a successful run at the 1988 Final Four.

Tisdale was so beloved by OU fans that they erected three billboards near the Norman, Oklahoma, campus, urging him to stay for his senior year. Tisdale eventually declared for the draft and was selected by Indiana with the second pick overall. Tisdale played in the NBA for years before retiring to begin a successful career in music. He formed his own group, the Fifth Quarter Band, and released numerous albums that made it to the Top 10 on the music charts.

His most memorable was "Rebound" dealt with his personal fight, not on the basketball court, but in the medical courts as he fought against cancer. Tisdale was diagnosed with bone cancer after he fell in his Los Angeles home in the spring of 2007. His leg was amputated the following spring. Shortly after the operation, he was fitted for a prosthesis and went on a twenty-one-day national tour.

University of Oklahoma

Tragically, Tisdale died on May 15, 2009 at St. John's Medical Center in Tulsa, where his wife had taken him when he had trouble breathing. He died after his esophagus ruptured following radiation treatment for his cancer. A week later, 4,000 mourners attended Tisdale's memorial service at the Bank of Oklahoma (BOK) Center in Tulsa. That June, the University of Oklahoma-Tulsa announced that a health clinic in north Tulsa would be named in his honor.

I will always have fond memories of that warm smile and that night I was honored. His name meant so much to me I continue to raise funds to battle the dreaded disease which took Wayman's life. Tisdale's friend, country music singer, Toby Keith, shared the loss we all felt when he sang at Wayman's funeral:

> "I'm gonna miss that smile
> I'm gonna miss you my friend
> Even though it hurts the way it ended up
> I'd do it all again
> So play it sweet in heaven
> 'Cause That's right where you want to be
> I'm not cryin' cause I feel so sorry for you
> I'm cryin' for me"

# Sean Elliott

## (1985-1989)

*Arizona Athletics*

### Carved in Stone

When Sean Elliott was a star at Tucson's Cholla High School, the University of Arizona was drowning in the Pac-10 with a 4-24 record and 1-17. Elliott spent most Saturdays watching North Carolina and other ACC powers on TV, hoping for a chance to play for a nationally-ranked program. Arizona was off the radar, even though his mother, Odiemae, was a graduate of the university.

He remembers Arizona playing Oregon in the McKale Center, a game the Ducks won, 86-84, before an announced crowd of 6,027.

"I got seats and worked myself down to the second row because there was no one at the game," he said. "It was an open-gym type of game. There were 1,000 people there, tops. At that point it was like a community college game. You could hear guys talking to each other on the court."

All of that changed when Lute Olson left Iowa to take over as the new coach, and he began building a dynasty in the desert. Olson's rebuilding started slowly. Midway through his second year, the Wildcats were 3-12. But Arizona finished the season strong, winning six of their last eight games and beating Oregon State, USC, and Oregon.

Olson realized how good the young 6'8" star Elliott was after watching him work out against his players in summer pick-up games at the Bear Down Gym. He eventually convinced Elliott, a hometown hero who averaged 31.3 points for a 24-3 team and was a McDonald's All-American, to take a chance on him—to stay in town and play for the Wildcats.

## Building a Legend

"When he came to town, Coach kept telling people, 'Get your tickets, we're going to win,'" Elliott said. "People were ho-hum, but he was right. Coach Olson played an exciting style and that sold me."

The extroverted Elliott had a storybook career and a Magic Johnson-like influence on the program. He became a two-time All-American and a two-time Pac-10 Player of the Year who broke Kareem Abdul-Jabbar's conference scoring record for the Wildcats. Elliott won 105 games during his four-year career, but nothing topped Elliott's junior season.

The Wildcats, who had made the NCAA tournament in three previous seasons, entered the year with high expectations. Olson had built his rotation around Elliott. There was Steve Kerr, back on the floor after missing what would have been his senior season in 1987 with a knee injury; Craig McMillan, Olson's first blue-chip prospect, was a steady veteran presence; center, Tom Tolbert, a junior college transfer; and Anthony Cook, who

gave the Cats some bulk in the paint. Backup guard, Kenny Lofton, would go on to play major league baseball, Jud Buechler would win three NBA titles with the Bulls, and Harvey Mason would win three Grammys as a music producer.

The Wildcats produced a 35-3 record, reached Number 1 in the AP poll in December and won the Pac-10.

"They were the toast of Tucson, the big men on campus." Elloitt said with a smile. "People would clap when we walked into classrooms. It was pretty insane. They were more excited than we were. It's almost like we went through this whole process together. The players, the city, community. We were adored, but I don't think people looked at us liked we were superstars. We were them."

The Wildcats only got better, winning the Pac-10 tournament at the McKale Center, earning a Number 1 seed in the NCAA tournament, and then breezing to 40- and 29-point wins over Cornell and Seton Hall. They defeated Iowa by 20 points in the Sweet 16 and then beat North Carolina, 70-62, in the Elite Eight to advance to the school's first Final Four.

The run stopped when Arizona lost to Oklahoma, 86-78, in the national semi-finals. Elliott scored 31 points and grabbed 11 rebounds, but he also had six turnovers and four fouls. Arizona struggled trying to contain Oklahoma's two big men—Harvey Grant and Stacey King—who combined to score 42 points and went on to play in the NBA. The Sooners took Kerr out of the game, limiting him to 2 for 13 from the field and the Cats turned the ball over 15 times.

Arizona's special season convinced Elliott he should declare for the NBA draft, but he changed his mind because he wanted to play for the United States in the 1988 Olympics in South Korea. Then John Thompson cut him because he didn't think Elliott was aggressive enough defensively to fit into his Georgetown-like system.

Elliott returned for a final season as one of the best players in the country. He averaged 22.3 points and 7.2 rebounds, but the Wildcats never got a chance to make another run at the national championship, losing to UNLV in the Sweet 16. Elliott sobbed in the locker room, distraught despite the fact he scored 22 points and grabbed 14 rebounds.

Shortly thereafter, Elliott won the Wooden Award, given to the National Player of the Year. He finished his four-year career averaging 19.2 points and six rebounds, with a school-record 2,555 points. Elliott was a model of consistency, scoring double figures in 108 consecutive games and 128 of 133 career contests.

Elliott was selected by the San Antonio Spurs with the third pick overall in the 1999 draft and went on to play twelve years in the NBA with the Spurs, including a 1999 NBA championship. He also overcame a debilitating kidney disease and received a kidney transplant from his brother, Noel. He tried to come back in 2000, but retired the following year.

He never forgot his time at Arizona. When the Wildcats arrived home from Kansas City, the team rode in convertibles from the airport to campus where they were greeted by a huge cheering crowd at Arizona Stadium.

"It was lined with people the whole way," Elliott said. "We got to the stadium and there were 20,000 people there. It was astounding."

And so was he, baby!

*Arizona Athletics*

# Mark Aguirre
## (1978-1981)

DePaul Athletics

## Carved in Stone

The first game I ever did on ESPN was December 5, 1979, when DePaul played host to Wisconsin. It was the first big-time college game on what was then a brand new network. It is a day I have etched in my mind and it will be there forever. I had been recently fired by the Pistons on November 8, 1979. I did not know what the next chapter would bring. It blows my mind that, forty years later, I am still talking college hoops on the network. DePaul and Wisconsin will always be etched on my personal Mt. Rushmore of basketball!

## Building a Legend

Before Aguirre signed to play for DePaul, the state of Blue Demon basketball and Chicago's professional sports, in general, was grim. The burly 6'6", 232-pound forward from Westinghouse High in the tough Chicago Public League, who was known as "The Muffin Man," turned out to be a local hero in the pre-Michael Jordan era. Aguirre emerged as an unstoppable force offensively, who made stories of DePaul almost dropping the sport in the early 1970s a distant memory.

Aguirre was nearly born on a train. His mother, Mary, was only sixteen years old and living in Arkansas when she became pregnant. In her ninth month, she rode north to Chicago, where some family lived, thinking she would give this baby to her sister, Daisy, who wanted a child and was better prepared to raise it. When she arrived in Chicago, she was in labor. Her family rushed her from the station to the hospital.

Aguirre shuttled between his aunt's house and his mother's place. His father figures were uncles and cousins in a neighborhood filled with boarded-up houses, old churches, and gangs that would chase him when he was younger for his meager twenty-five cents of trolley money.

Aguirre remembers the days when he and a friend, Isiah Thomas, used to sneak into Chicago Stadium to watch the Bulls play. He had no idea back then he would be a pro someday.

"I was raised by Chicago, man," Aguirre recalled at a Chicago Legends event. "I got raised by the lady next door…by the bus driver, Al, who rolled into Westinghouse every day…by different guys on the street who did questionable things but made me stay out of trouble."

Aguirre became a huge star in the talent-filled Public League.

"A lot of big schools called, but I was picking a coach," Aguirre said. "Ray Meyer was the first guy who was concerned with how I perceived different things. We could talk about black-white issues. I loved him for that."

Meyer's son, Joey, a DePaul assistant, recruited Aguirre, attending two-thirds of his games his last two years in high school.

"But I have no delusions," Joey once said. "He came because of coach."

Aguirre can still remember Ray climbing five flights of stairs at Westinghouse and walking down the hall to watch him play. Aguirre helped Meyer put DePaul basketball back on the map for the first time since George Mikan played there in the 1940s. He'd led the Blue Demons to records of 26-6, 26-2, and 27-3 in his three years on the urban campus. He had one of the best years of any player in any sport, averaging 24 points and leading DePaul to a third-place finish in the 1979 NCAA tournament. That was overshadowed by the Larry Bird versus Magic Johnson final game which captivated basketball fans all over the nation!

DePaul was the most popular team in the city in those days. "The Bulls didn't get the front page," Aguirre said. "We got the front page."

Aguirre was even better the next two regular seasons, putting the Demons on top of the AP poll before they had unexpected losses to UCLA and St. Joseph's in the first round of the NCAA tournament. Aguirre was a consensus All-American in both of those seasons, winning the Naismith Award as the nation's top player as a sophomore. Who knows what might have happened if he didn't leave to become the Number 1 pick in the 1982 draft when he was selected by Dallas after his junior year.

As it was, Aguirre ranks first on DePaul's all-time scoring list with 2,189 points in 89 games with a 24.5 point per game average. He is also first, second, and third for single season point totals, including 26.8 points as a junior, when he developed a reputation as the best half-court scorer in college basketball.

Aguirre was as explosive as any medium-sized wide body before Charles Barkley. He had 47 points against Maine as a junior, 45 against Loyola-Chicago as a sophomore and 41 against the Ramblers as a junior. Sadly, most of his regular-season games didn't make it to national television and he is often defined by what he did in the postseason.

But no one can take away what he did for DePaul.

# Johnny Dawkins
## (1982-1986)

*Duke Athletics*

## Carved in Stone

Johnny Dawkins really represented a term I love to use. He was a Prime Time Player—Solid Gold! What made him special was the way he carried himself in the biggest game of all, the game of life. Johnny represented all the qualities coaches dream of and would love from their student-athletes.

Dawkins still has a picture of the 1986 Duke team in his office at Central Florida. It holds sentimental value to him because that was the group that put a stamp on the Mike Krzyzewski era by advancing to the 1986 NCAA tournament championship game before losing to Louisville. Dawkins was the driving force behind that 37-3 team, a two-time consensus All-American who was the Naismith National Player of the Year his senior season.

The skinny 6'3", 165-pound left-handed guard was also the most important recruit and best player to ever play for Krzyzewski, who was in the beginning stages of building a foundation for this perennial ACC power. The Dukies went on to win five national championships.

### Building a Legend

Dawkins was the National Player of the Year when he played for Mackin High School in the Washington, D.C. Catholic League, in 1982. And Duke was desperate for a big-name recruit. Krzyzewski was coming off a 10-17 season. Coach K and his staff had recruited and finished second the previous year with Chris Mullin, Bill Wennington, Uwe Blab and Jim Miller. Mullin and Wennington decided to stay close to home and sign with St. John's. The 7' 0" Blab signed at Indiana and Miller went to Virginia.

Krzyzewski was already taking heat from the boosters for his failure to land enough blue-chip prospects to compete with neighboring North Carolina and NC State in the ACC. Dawkins was a McDonald's All American who came from a middle-class neighborhood in northern Washington, D.C. He was being pursued by Georgetown, Notre Dame, and Maryland—all established powers.

Krzyzewski made Dawkins a priority. He went to several of Dawkins' games and assistant Bob Dwyer flew up to watch every game since Dawkins was a 10th grader. Dawkins was impressed by Duke's commitment and he took a chance.

He was the biggest star of a talented recruiting class that also included my buddy at ESPN, Jay Bilas, who was a tenacious rebounder, the multi-talented, Mark Alarie, and versatile, David Henderson. Duke won just eleven games his freshman year, but Dawkins took control of the team, starting all 28 games and scoring in double figures in all but one of them as he racked up 31 points against Maryland, a Duke freshman record. Dawkins averaged 18.1 points and was chosen second-team All-ACC.

The next year, with the addition of point guard, Tommy Amaker, the program took off. That group played in three straight NCAA tournaments. Dawkins led Duke to a 24-10 record, scoring in double figures in all 34 games and averaging a team-high 19.4 points as a sophomore. He shot 83.1 percent from the line and made first team All-ACC. He also was an alternate for the U.S. national team that played in the 1984 Olympic games in Los Angeles.

*Duke Athletics*

Dawkins always seemed to save his best performances for local rival North Carolina. During his junior year, he tortured the Tar Heels with a season-high 34 points, seven assists, eight rebounds, and no turnovers as the Blue Devils defeated UNC, 93-77, winning for the first time in twenty years at Carmichael Arena. He averaged 18.5 points and was named first team All-ACC and first team All-American.

Dawkins saved his top work for his senior year, when the Blue Devils won the preseason NIT, the ACC regular season title, and the ACC tournament before advancing to the school's first Final Four since 1977. Dawkins was the MVP of the ACC tournament, scoring 60 points and two critical free throws, as the Devils dusted off Georgia Tech, 68-67, in the finals. He went wild in the postseason, averaging 23.7 points in the NCAAs, bailing Duke out in the tournament opener against Mississippi Valley State, scoring 16 points in five minutes as the Devils rallied for an 85-75 win. He was the MVP of the East Region after scoring 29 points during a 71-50 victory over Navy in the Final Eight and scored 24 points against Louisville in the championship game.

Dawkins was a first team All-American again and finished his career as the team's all-time leading scorer with 2,556 points, which stood until 2006, when JJ Redick surpassed it. His number 24 jersey was later retired.

# *Dick Vitale's*
# MOUNT RUSHMORE
# OF
# PLAYERS WE WISH WE
# HAD SEEN MORE OF

## LEN BIAS

## BEN WILSON

## JASON WILIAMS

## CHRIS STREET

# Len Bias
## (1983-1986)

*Maryland Basketball*

## Carved in Stone

L en Bias used to wear a gold "Superman" necklace when he played for Maryland.

The 6'8", 220-pound All-American forward looked like a superhero during most of his four-year career when he played for Lefty Driesell at Maryland. Bias was a two-time ACC Player of the Year in 1985 and 1986. Twice, he led the conference in scoring and he finished his career as Maryland's all-time leading scorer with 2,149 points. More than once, he was called a Michael Jordan-type of player by other coaches in the league.

Tragically, he never played in an NBA game.

## Leaving the Court

In the early morning of June 19, 1986, two days after being selected by the Boston Celtics with the second pick in the NBA draft, Bias was dead after attending a private party in the Washington Hall dormitory on the Maryland campus. The autopsy showed he had ingested a lethal dose of cocaine. He was twenty-two.

His death shocked the college basketball world. "This is perhaps the saddest day in the history of the University of Maryland," chancellor John Slaughter said.

Bias had a huge impact on ACC basketball. In the wake of his death, Driesell was forced to resign and AD Dick Dull stepped down. When it was discovered Bias was twenty-one credits shy of graduation after four years of eligibility, the school instituted stricter guidelines for athletes.

Bias had been pudgy in high school, but he never lacked determination. At Northwestern High, he spent hours in the gym, bulking up his body, and more time selling popcorn at Cole Field House. He studied Maryland stars Albert King and Buck Williams and became an adept inside and outside threat once he learned how to handle the ball from teammate Keith Gatlin after his freshman year.

Bias had freakish athleticism. He once jumped so high for a dunk, he landed on top of the shoulders of North Carolina's 7' 0" center, Brad Daugherty. He lifted his team high, too, scoring 26 points in a 74-62 victory over Duke in the 1984 ACC tournament to give the Terrapins their first championship in thirty years. By his junior year, when he was surrounded by lesser talent, he was constantly double and triple teamed, but he still managed to lead the league in scoring with 18.9 points. He was named a second-team All-American.

In 1986, as a senior, he led the ACC in scoring, averaging 23.2 points a game. He scored 41 points against Duke's Final Four team. He also participated in a fabled game against North Carolina at Chapel Hill where he helped the Terps stun the Tar Heels in overtime with 35 points, giving the UNC its first loss at the Smith Center. Late in overtime, Bias stole the inbounds pass and converted it into a dunk, then blocked a shot by UNC guard Kenny Smith as he drove down the lane.

"If Bias is not the player of the world," Driesell said afterwards, "then people just don't know basketball."

The Maryland team that year started the season 10-11, but Bias led the Terrapins back to the NCAA tournament for a fourth consecutive time. Maryland defeated Pepperdine in the first round and then lost to UNLV, despite a superhuman performance by Bias, who poured in 31 points, scoring 19 of the Terrapins' final 21 points and carrying them within a point before they faded in the final minute.

Despite the loss, Bias looked like he was headed for greatness. He met with Celtics' officials the day following the draft and signed a $1.6 million endorsement deal with Reebok. The great Larry Bird promised to come down to training camp and work with him

Then, less than twenty-four hours later, it was over and we were all left to guess how great Bias could have been at the next level.

# Ben Wilson

## (1982-1985)

*ESPN 30 For 30*

## Carved in Stone

Benji Wilson was supposed to be the next big thing in college basketball after the 6'8" forward led Simeon High School to the City and Illinois AA State championship for the first time as a junior in 1983.

He was widely considered the best prospect in the country after becoming the first Chicago player ever to win the MVP at the high-profile Athletes for a Better Education basketball camp at Princeton the summer before his senior year.

Unfortunately, he became just another victim of the gun violence that still today ravages that Midwest city. He was shot twice during a confrontation with a student at a nearby high school. He died the next morning from the injuries he sustained from the shooting.

## Leaving the Court

Wilson grew up on the South side of Chicago with five brothers and took up basketball at an early age, practicing as early at 8:00 A.M. every day. At first, neighbors weren't happy with his practice routine, but his brothers marveled at his ball-handling. As his talent developed, friends and family made it a point to protect Wilson from trouble as he got older. When he entered Simeon, the nationwide crack epidemic was running rampant and some of the people closest to Wilson, including his older brother Curtis Glenn, became addicted. Chicago's violent crime rate was very high in his neighborhood, too.

When Wilson entered Simeon, he looked like he would become a guard, but everything changed his sophomore year. He grew seven inches in three months from 6'0" to 6'7", but still was able to maintain the grace and ball-handling skills of a shorter player.

His junior year, Simeon became a force in the Chicago Public League, and Wilson thrived playing for Bob Hambric, who described him as "Magic Johnson with a jump shot." Simeon won the city and progressed to the state tournament, where he had his best game in the semi-finals, scoring 21 points with 4 rebounds and five assists in a 67-58 victory over Aurora West before defeating Number 1-ranked Evanston in the finals.

Wilson raised eyebrows with his play in Princeton that summer and narrowed his list of schools to DePaul, Illinois, and Indiana.

That fall, Simeon was preparing to defend its state championship. The season was set to tip-off in Rockford at the Boylan Tournament on November 21st. The day before, Wilson was having issues with his girlfriend, Jetun Rush, with whom he had a son, and he eft school at lunch time to talk with her. Meanwhile, Calumet High School student, Billy Moore, was outside Simeon's campus with a handgun to avenge his cousin, who had allegedly been robbed of $10 by a Simeon student. After finding out the conflict had been resolved, Moore and a friend, Omar Dixon, decided to stay nearby and the two followed Moore's friend Erica Murphy to a nearby luncheonette.

Moore and Dixon were standing outside the luncheonette when Wilson and Rush came up the street behind them, arguing. Wilson bumped into Moore, who called to Wilson to watch where he was going. The two exchanged words and the incident escalated out of control. Moore pulled out his gun and Wilson dared him to shoot.

He did…firing two shots.

The first bullet struck Wilson in his groin and the second hit him in the heart. Either shot alone could have been fatal. Moore and Dixon then fled. Within minutes, word of the shooting reached Simeon's campus and a crowd gathered. Emergency services were called at 12:37 P.M. and paramedics finally arrived almost two hours later. The prognosis was not good as Wilson lost a lot of blood before he could get to a small community hospital that was not prepared for trauma cases like shootings. The team remained sequestered in the teacher's lounge for the rest of the day while Wilson, whose aorta was damaged by the second shot, was fighting for his life.

It was a fight he lost at 6:00 A.M. the next morning. Wilson died of his wounds, thirteen hours before the opening game of the season. His teammates played in his honor that night, defeating Evanston, 73-50. Moore and Dixon were eventually arrested and charged as adults. Moore received a forty-year sentence while Dixon received thirty years.

The event shocked the city, state, and nation. It emotionally destroyed the Simeon family. Over 8,000 people came to see his casket at the school. The team did not win that season and the nation questioned why so many children were being killed in senseless shootings…something we still don't know today.

Wilson's son, Brandon, who was only ten weeks old when his father died, became a scholarship high school player who went on to play at Maryland-Eastern Shore, wearing his father's Number 25 jersey as did Wilson's friend and teammate, Nick Anderson, who played for Illinois and the NBA. Juwan Howard played wearing the number at Michigan and NBA star guard, Derrick Rose, who graduated from Simeon in 2007, also wore the number when the team won back-to-back state championships in 2006 and 2007. The world will never know what that number could have accomplished on Wilson.

# Jason Williams

## (2000-2002)

ESPN Images

## Carved in Stone

I will never forget being at Madison Square Garden (MSG) and seeing, for the first time, this highly-acclaimed diaper dandy, Jason Williams. Duke was going to face Stanford and, in the second game, Connecticut went against Iowa. Everyone was anticipating a Connecticut-Duke final; instead they met in the consolation. It was shock city and that was the first time ESPN broadcasted a consolation game.

## Leaving the Court

After a tough MSG debut, Williams was destined to become a huge star from the first time he stepped onto the court at Cameron Indoor Stadium. Duke's 6'3" All American guard was the second coming of Johnny Dawkins, leading the Blue Devils to a national championship as a sophomore in 2001. He started every game during his three-year career and was the 2002 National Player of the Year.

Williams came with all the right credentials. Williams grew up in Metuchen, New Jersey, and attended St. Joseph's of Metuchen, the same school that produced 7' 0" Karl Anthony Towns of Kentucky a decade later. He was a McDonald's All-American and the winner of the Morgan Wooten Award as the top high school player in the country. He had strength, quickness, was a great athlete capable of taking over games, and made more big shots than any player in the history of Duke basketball…not named Christian Laettner.

Williams was forced to play immediately because the program had lost Elton Brand, Corey Maggette, William Avery, and Trajan Langdon to the NBA after the Devils advanced to the NCAA championship game in 1999.

Williams delivered from the start, averaging 14.5 points, 4.2 rebounds, 6.5 assists and 2.4 steals, winning the MVP of the ACC tournament after scoring 23 points in the finals against Maryland. As a sophomore, Williams blossomed into a great scorer, averaging 21.6 points and was a consensus All-American during Duke's championship season. He highlighted Duke's run that year when he scored 8 points in the final 54 seconds and 23 of Duke's final 31 in regulation as the Devils wiped out a 12-point deficit to defeat Maryland, 98-86, in overtime at Cole Field House. He then scored 23 when Duke rallied from 22 down to defeat the same Terrapins, 95-84, in the national semi-finals.

Williams averaged 21.3 points again as a junior when he became a two-time consensus All American and won both the Wooden and Naismith national Player of the Year awards, but the Devils were upset 75-74 by Indiana in final seconds of the Sweet 16, preventing a repeat.

Williams graduated in just three years and was the Number 2 pick overall by the Chicago Bulls. He started 75 games, averaged 9.5 points and 4.7 assists, and had stardom written all over him, but he only got to play one season in the NBA.

On June 12, 2002, Williams, riding his Yamaha motorcycle, crashed at an intersection in Chicago's Lincoln Park. His injuries included a severed main nerve in his leg, a fractured pelvis, and three dislocated ligaments in his left knee. Doctors grafted a vein from another part of his body and used it as an artery in his left leg. He nearly had to have his leg amputated.

While tragic for his career, Williams had been riding without a helmet or a licensed motorcycle and he violated the terms of his Bulls' contract. When it became evident that he could not return, they cut him, but still paid him $3 million dollars. After extensive rehab, Williams tried to make a comeback with the Nets, but was cut after a month. Then he tried the D-league with no success. Now Jason, known as Jay, has become a college basketball standout on College Gameday and during many studio appearances as he has found his niche and developed himself into a solid broadcaster at ESPN. Man, it would have been nice to see him in a few more games, but I'm glad he hasn't left the court completely.

# Chris Street

## (1990-1993)

University of Iowa Athletic Communications

### Carved in Stone

Chris Street will always be a beloved Hawkeye hero, a kid from a small town in Iowa who was a high school three-sport star. He developed into a 6' 8" NBA prospect at Iowa before his life was cut short when his car was hit by a snowplow on a winter night during his junior year in 1993.

### Leaving the Court

Street was born on Groundhog Day—February 2, 1972, and grew up with his parents, Mike and Patty, and younger sisters, Sarah and Betsy, in the small town of Humeston in southern Iowa.

Street was a good athlete growing up. He loved the outdoors and spent time hunting and fishing with his family. But his father had no idea how good he was until he moved the family to Indianola after Chris' freshman year at Mormon Trail High School.

Street became a first-team all-state quarterback on the football team and an all-conference baseball player, but his real love was basketball. He earned a starting position as a sophomore and was named first-team All-State as a junior and senior after leading his team to three consecutive state tournaments. Before his junior season, Street verbally committed to play basketball for Tom Davis at Iowa, making the earliest commitment ever to the program. Street worked his way into the starting lineup as a freshman and finished third in the Big Ten in rebounding as a sophomore, when he was voted All-Conference honorable mention. During Street's junior year, Street averaged 14.5 points and 9.5 rebounds in the first fifteen games of the season. In his final game, he scored 14 points, grabbed eight rebounds and extended his school record of consecutive made free throws to 34 in a 65-56 loss to Duke.

Three days later, everything changed.

*University of Iowa Athletic Communications*

*University of Iowa Athletic Communications*

January 19, 1993, started off like a normal winter day in the state, with cold temperatures and snowy weather. The popular twenty-year-old Street left a team dinner at the Highlander Inn Hotel in Iowa City with his girlfriend, Kim Vinton, heading for his night class. His car was struck broadside by a snow plow coming off Interstate 80. He was killed instantly. His girlfriend survived and was treated for a punctured lung and separated shoulder. The Hawkeyes' game the next night against Northwestern was postponed.

Street's tragic death left the state in mourning. The Iowa House of Representatives observed his death and honored him with a moment of silence.

"To me, I think Chris represented the intensity of life, the openness of the Midwest," former Iowa coach Davis said. "Chris represented all that is good about the Midwest and the state of Iowa. He was open, caring, honest, loving, and lived life to the fullest every day. He was one of the greatest Hawkeyes of all-time."

Most memories fade. But Chris Street's remain. His legacy is renewed every year though the Chris Street Foundation, the Chris Street Memorial Scholarship given to one player every year, and the Chris Street Award—the highest award given to players who show the qualities of spirit, enthusiasm, and intensity.

Street's family made sure their son was buried in his gold Iowa uniform and warm up jacket. His Number 40 jersey was forever retired by the school. No other number has been retired since. On February 25, 2018, Iowa guard Jordan Bohannon purposely missed a free throw against Northwestern that would have broken Street's record, instead tying it at 34.

After the game Bohannon told reporters, "That's not my record to have. That record deserves to stay in his name."

Street is buried in the IOOF Cemetery in Indianola, behind a monument that reads, "Son, Brother, Grandson, Friend, Cousin, Nephew, Hero."

*University of Iowa Athletic Communications*

# *Dick Vitale's*
## MOUNT RUSHMORE
### OF
## ALL TRAVELING MEN

BILL SELF

RICK BARNES

LEFTY DRIESELL

ORLANDO "TUBBY" SMITH

# Bill Self
## (1993-Present)

*Kansas Athletics*

### Carved in Stone

Man, was I wrong. That's right, give me a turnover, baby! I remember sharing the conversation with Bill Self at Illinois. We talked about the possibility of replacing Roy Williams at Kansas. Talk about entering a tough situation! Replacing Williams was difficult because he put together an incredible record with rock, chalk, Jayhawk.

I thought it would be hard to continue that success rate that Williams posted. Self has done that…and more. The rest is history.

### A Winner On Any Court

Winning fourteen straight Big 12 titles in succession is unbelievable. I equate it to the Joe DiMaggio 56-game hit streak. I cannot envision any school in the power conferences pulling off what he has done in Big 12 action.

Self, an Eddie Sutton disciple who played for Oklahoma State, is best known for his body of work at Kansas, where he has a 447-96 record from 2003 through 2018. He won a national championship in 2008, coached the Jayhawks to three Final Fours in 2008, 2012, and 2018, five Elite Eights, fifteen NCAA tournament appearances, fourteen consecutive Big 12 regular season championships and eight Big 12 tournament titles.

He has an overall record of 654-201 and his teams have almost been unbeatable at Allen Field House with a 202-11 record. The now-fifty-five-year old Self was selected national Coach of the Year three times (in 2009, 2012, and 2016), was a six-time Big 12 Coach of the Year, and was inducted into the Naismith Hall of Fame in 2016. During his time at Kansas, he recruited several McDonald's All-Americans, including Mario Chalmers, Andrew Wiggins, and Josh Jackson, who were all high-profile NBA first round picks.

After rebuilding Oral Roberts, Self was hired by crosstown rival Tulsa and spent three seasons from 1998-2000, with the Golden Hurricane, coaching Tulsa to a 74-27 record. While at Tulsa, Self coached the Hurricane to consecutive NCAA tournament appearances in 1999 and 2000. In 2000, in addition to coaching Tulsa to a single-season record for victories with a 32-7 record, Self led the Golden Hurricane to its first-ever Elite Eight appearance with a strong motion offense and pressing man-to-man defense.

Self got his first marquis job when he was hired by a Big Ten team, Illinois, after Lon Kruger left the program to accept a job as head coach of the NBA Atlanta Hawks. In 2001, Self's first season in Champaign, he coached a team of mostly Kruger recruits—center Marcus Griffin, forward Brian Cook, Robert Archibald and guards, Frank Williams, Cory Bradford, and Sergio McClain—to a 27-8 record, a share of the Big Ten championship, and an appearance in the NCAA Elite Eight, where they lost to Arizona.

Self coached the Fightin' Illini to a 78-24 record in three years, two Big Ten regular season championships, a Big Ten tournament title and three straight NCAA tournaments, but Illinois never got past the second round in 2002 and 2003, losing to Kansas in the Sweet 16 and Notre Dame in the second round. Self was responsible for recruiting the nucleus of the 2005 Illinois team that was 37-2 and advanced to the national championship game before losing to North Carolina.

Self left for Kansas after the 2003 season, calling it his dream job. His consistent regular-season success there speaks for itself, even though the media questioned his team's performance in the NCAA, based on various upsets in early rounds and a 3-7 record in regional finals.

Self put the issue to rest in 2008 when he coached the Jayhawks to the national championship. Kansas defeated John Calipari's Memphis team in overtime, 75-68, giving the Jayhawks their first national championship in 1988.

Self had an offer to go back to his alma mater after the season, but he stayed put. He signed a ten-year contract extension in 2012 and is currently making a salary of $7.15 million, making him the third-highest paid college basketball coach behind Mike Krzyzewski and John Calipari.

# Rick Barnes
## (1987-Present)

*Tennessee Athletics/UTsports.com*

### Carved in Stone

When Rick Barnes accepted the University of Tennessee (UT) coaching job in 2015, there was no brass band greeting him at the airport.

The sixty-three-year-old Barnes had just been fired by Texas after a highly successful seventeen-year run in Austin. Tennessee was on its fourth coach in a span of five years, after the school fired Donnie Tyndall following just one season because of NCAA charges against him stemming from his previous stop at Southern Mississippi.

### A Winner On Any Court

It took Barnes, who had coached at George Mason, Providence, Clemson and Texas, three years to kickstart the Volunteers (Vols). But he had a blockbuster season in 2017-18, winning the SEC Coach of the Year award after leading the Vols, who were picked to finish thirteenth in the fourteen-team SEC during the pre-season poll, to a 26-9 record, the SEC regular season championship, and a spot in the NCAA tournament. UT advanced to the second round before losing to Cinderella Loyola of Chicago.

The honor earned in Tennessee was Barnes' sixth conference Coach of the Year award in a thirty-one-year career that has spanned and included twenty-three NCAA tournament appearances and three bids to the NIT. Barnes has a 668-358 overall record and had more success than any basketball coach in the history of Texas, a traditional football powerhouse.

Barnes coached the Texas Longhorns from 1998-2015, winning 412 games, taking the Longhorns to the NCAA tournament in sixteen of his seventeen seasons. He coached Texas to its only Final Four in 2003, two Elite Eights in 2006 and 2008, and two Sweet 16's in 2002 and 2004. He coached National Players of the Year T.J. Ford in 2003 and Kevin Durant in 2007, led Texas to its first Number 1 ranking in 2010, won 20-plus games in all but two seasons and twice won thirty games. He was a four-time Big 12 Coach of the Year.

Despite his wins, the administration lost confidence in him as they were expecting more success in NCAA action. Everyone wants consistent success, but Barnes was hurt by losing a number of one-and-done players. He had a difficult time developing continuity with players leaving early. Kevin Durant, Tristan Thompson, and company left. He was dismissed after the Longhorns lost in the first round of the 2015 tournament.

Barnes has shown he is resilient, if nothing else. He has also been successful everywhere he has been. Barnes coached his first team in a Hickory, North Carolina, recreation league while he was still in high school. He said then he wanted to teach high school, nothing else. That all changed when he went to the 1978 ACC tournament in Greensboro, North Carolina. Coaching college basketball became his passion.

Barnes played basketball for four years at Lenoir Rhyne, where he received the Captain's award for leadership in his junior and senior year before graduating in 1977. He was an assistant for two seasons at Davidson and five-years at George Mason under Joe Harrington. In 1985, he took a job as an assistant at Alabama under Wimp Sanderson, and the Crimson Tide posted a 24-9 record, and advanced to the NCAA Sweet 16. The next year, he served as an assistant at Ohio State under Gary Williams when the Buckeyes had a 20-win season and reached the second round of the NCAA tournament. Then, Barnes was on the fast track when he got his first head coaching job at George Mason in 1987, coaching the Patriots to a 20-10 record.

Barnes attracted attention from Providence after he won the Colonial Conference Coach of the Year. He spent six years as head coach of the Friars from 1988-1995, coaching Providence to three NCAA appearances, two NITs and the school's first-ever Big East championship in 1994. During the Barnes era, the Friars averaged 10,596 fans per game at home.

Barnes' climb toward coaching greatness currently at work in Tennessee continued when he took a job with Clemson. Clemson went to never-before-seen heights in four short years, as Barnes coached the Tigers to three NCAA Tournaments and an NIT from 1995-1998 and a Number 2 ranking during its 1996-1997 Sweet 16 season. By the time Barnes left for Texas, he compiled a 74-48 record, including 13 wins over Top 25 teams and the school's best all-time winning percentage (60.7). The Tigers also drew more fans than any other time in school history.

Texas may have let Barnes go, but Tennessee is ready to warm up that brass band, baby!

# Lefty Driesell

## (1960-2003)

*University of Maryland*

## Carved in Stone

Lefty Driesell was way ahead of his time with many creative ideas. He was the first to come up with Midnight Madness and was a recruiting workaholic. I remember one day, early in his career, I was in the Maryland office, talking with his number one assistant (future Hall-of-Famer George Raveling), and I could not believe what George was doing; he was going through a stack of newspapers, reading about perspective prospects. Driesell was always looking for that hidden gem.

Driesell finally made it to the Naismith Hall of Fame at the age of 86.

Man, it took the selection committee long enough to figure it out!

Driesell was the first coach to win more than 100 games at four different NCAA Division I schools—Davidson, Maryland, James Madison and Georgia State. He won Coach of the Year awards in each conference and earned a reputation as "the greatest program in the history of basketball," taking all four of his teams to the NCAA tournament.

At the time of his retirement, he had a record of 786-394 and was the fourth-winningest coach in the history of Division I with 21 seasons of 20 or more wins, and 21 conference or conference tournament titles. He led four of his teams to the Regional Finals, but never advanced to an elusive Final Four.

## A Winner On Any Court

Driesell initially had no intention of getting into coaching after he played for Duke and graduated in 1954. He took an office job with Ford Motor Company and played semi-pro basketball in Virginia, where he once scored 59 points and earned a tryout with the Minneapolis Lakers of the NBA. But he was also given a chance to enter the coaching profession when he was offered the junior varsity coaching position in both basketball and football at Granby High in Norfolk, his high school alma mater. He convinced his wife he could offset a significant pay cut by selling World Book Encyclopedias. Driesell eventually took over the varsity basketball coaching position at Newport News High. His first team finished unbeaten and won the Virginia Group I state title in 1958.

Two years later, he accepted the head coaching job at Davidson, where he won three Southern Conference tournament championships from 1960 through 1969 and developed a reputation for recruiting blue chip players like Fred Hetzel, Dick Snyder, and Mike Malloy to the tiny liberal arts school outside Charlotte.

At one point, NC State coach, Everett Case, was trying to sell Driesell on the idea of joining his staff. "Coach," he said, "I got a better team than you got. Why would I do that?"

Driesell took that idea with him to the University of Maryland. During his first press conference, he announced he wanted to make Maryland the "UCLA of the East." While he never quite reached that status, he did coach the Terrapins to eight NCAA tournament appearances, an NIT championship, two ACC regular season championships and one ACC tournament title. Maryland also attained the Number 1 AP ranking four consecutive years from 1972-1976.

Driesell and his staff—which included George Raveling, Joe Harrington, Jim Maloney, and David Pritchard—turned recruiting into an art form, signing players like Tom McMillen, Len Elmore, and John Lucas. These players were the core of the great 1974 team that lost to David Thompson and eventual national champion, NC State, 103-100, in the ACC tournament finals in one of the greatest games ever played. At one point, there were six future pros on the floor. Maryland was shut out of the NCAA tournament, though, because the field was still limited to conference championship teams. Driesell also recruited Albert King, Buck Williams, Len Bias, and signed Moses Malone, the best college prospect of his career, but Malone was the first player in the modern era to go directly from high school to the pros, making his decision on the day classes were scheduled to begin.

In 1984, Driesell won the school's second ACC tournament championship and the next year he was given a 10-year extension. His life was changed forever, though, when Maryland star, Len Bias, died of a cocaine-induced heart attack shortly after being drafted by the Boston Celtics. An investigation showed Bias was 21 credits short of his graduation requirement, despite having used all his athletic eligibility. That fall, Driesell resigned, becoming the scapegoat for the failure of the administration.

Driesell resumed his coaching career at James Madison in 1988 and remained there until 1996, winning five Colonial Athletic Association regular season championships and leading that team to the 1994 NCAA tournament. Driesell then coached at Georgia State, which he led to four Atlantic Sun Conference regular season championships and one NCAA appearance. He retired from coaching in January of 2003 in the middle of his 41st season.

Driesell's heart always remained at Maryland. In February of 2017, the school, which has left his beloved ACC for the Big 10, hung a banner in the Xfinity Center to honor his career at the university and he accepted the honor.

# Orlando "Tubby" Smith
## (1991-Present)

Joe Faraoni / ESPN Images

## Carved in Stone

My first time becoming aware of Tubby Smith's coaching ability was when I observed him on one of the greatest coaching staffs of all-time. He was an assistant at Kentucky under Rick Pitino where he was joined by Billy Donovan and Herb Sendek. I knew, by simply watching him in practice, he was destined to be a successful head coach.

## A Winner On Any Court

Smith is a true traveling man. In 27 years, he has coached at seven schools—the University of Tulsa, Georgia, Kentucky, Minnesota, Texas Tech, Memphis, and (most recently) High Point University, his alma mater.

Smith has achieved twenty-five winning seasons, capturing a national championship in 1998 when he replaced Rick Pitino at the University of Kentucky. He is one of only two coaches to take five different schools—Tulsa, Georgia, Kentucky, Minnesota, and Texas Tech—to the big dance. In all, he has made fifteen NCAA tournament appearances, advancing to four Elite Eights. His overall record is 597-302.

Smith rose from poverty to become one of the most important pioneers in black coaching.

The now sixty-six-year old Smith was born in Scotland, Maryland, the sixth of seventeen children born to sharecroppers, Guffire and Parthenia Smith. His large family accounts for his unusual nickname. Of all the Smith children, Tubby was fond of staying in the galvanized wash tub where the children were bathed. He tried to shake the name, but it stuck.

Smith was all set to play for Maryland, but the school rescinded his scholarship offer and Smith enrolled at High Point, North Carolina College, scoring 1,589 points in his career before graduating in 1973. Smith worked his way up the coaching ladder:

- He coached high school basketball for six years in Maryland and North Carolina
- Spent time as an assistant at Virginia Commonwealth University (VCU) and South Carolina
- Became an assistant coach at Kentucky under Rick Pitino for two years

During his time at Kentucky, the Cats were rebuilding a program that was locked into NCAA probation and player defections. With only eight scholarship players, none taller than 6'6", Pitino and his staff eventually molded the Cats into a winner. Smith was promoted to associate head coach in 1990, when Kentucky went 22-6 and rose to ninth in the AP poll, despite being ineligible to play in the NCAA tournament for a second straight year.

Smith benefited from his Kentucky experience by being named the head coach at Tulsa in 1991. He coached the Golden Hurricane to a 79-43 record in four years, two consecutive Missouri Valley regular season titles, and two appearances in the Sweet 16 in 1994 and 1995.

Smith was on a fast track. In 1995, he accepted the head coaching job at Georgia, becoming the school's first black head coach. In two seasons, he led the Bulldogs to a 45-19 record, including the first back-to-back 20-win seasons in more than twenty years, plus a trip to the Sweet 16 in 1996.

Smith had his biggest success when he became the first black basketball coach at mighty Kentucky in May of 1997, replacing popular Pitino, who left for a job coaching the NBA Boston Celtics. The Cats were at the top of the basketball world, having won a national title in 1996 and advancing to the championship game the following year. Smith, who inherited seven players from Pitino's final year, kept the legacy alive when he coached Kentucky to its seventh championship during his first year in 1997, without a first-team All-American or future NBA lottery pick. Kentucky beat Utah in San Antonio.

Smith won five SEC championships and five SEC Tournament titles. He led the Cats to six Sweet 16 appearances and four Elite Eights (in 1998, 1999, 2003, and 2005). Smith was named National Coach of the Year in 2003 and SEC Coach of the Year in 1998, 2003, and 2005.

In ten seasons at Kentucky, Smith coached the Cats to a 263-83 record and a winning percentage of 76.0, but he never got back to the Final Four, a major sin in the eyes of the Big Blue nation. They believed his recruiting was subpar and fans questioned his style of play. The Elite Eight double overtime loss to Michigan State in 2005 was the final straw. That May, Smith resigned to accept the head coaching job at Minnesota.

Smith coached the Minnesota Gophers to five post-season bids, including three NCAA appearances. His first season, the team improved from 8-22 to 20-14 in 2007 and reached the Big Ten Tournament semi-finals after defeating Indiana. Smith coached the Gophers to an NCAA appearance in 2009 and again in 2010 and

2013. He could never get to a second weekend. In July 2012, Smith signed a three-year extension but after the Gophers lost to Florida in the round of 32 the next spring, Smith was relieved of his head coaching duties.

If nothing else, Smith was resilient, taking the Texas Tech job in 2012. Smith inherited a team that had failed to make the NCAA Tournament in the seven years prior to Smith's hire. Smith went through two rebuilding years before transforming Tech into a 19-12 team that received an at-large bid to participate in the 2016 NCAA Tournament.

Smith made a move after the 2016 season, accepting the head coaching job at Memphis, where he felt he would have access to better players; he only lasted two years. Following the 2017 season, six of his top eight players transferred and Smith was fired from the position in 2018, despite winning 21 games. We'll have to see what happens this year as Smith is currently back at High Point, where his career started. He was named head coach there in March of 2018 and the school has announced the new arena will be named after him.

# *Dick Vitale's*
## MOUNT RUSHMORE
## OF
## ALL
## SUPPORTING CAST

CAMERON DOLLAR

DONTE DiVINCENZO

LUKE HANCOCK

GERRY McNAMARA

# Cameron Dollar

## (1994-1997)

UW Athletics

## Carved in Stone

Cameron Dollar had no idea he would become an integral piece of UCLA's 1995 NCAA championship team when the Final Four began. He was a sophomore backup point guard who found his way to the West Coast when he was discovered at St. John's Prospect Hall, a high-profile Maryland prep school, by assistant coach Lorenzo Romar. Dollar was a sophomore backup to Tyus Edney, who had become a star during the Bruins' championship run.

Just two weeks earlier, the mercurial 5'10", 150-pound Edney made a last-second, length-of-the-floor drive for a game-winning four-foot bank shot against Missouri in the second round 75-74 victory that saved the Bruins' season, negotiating 85 feet in the final 4.8 seconds with adept ball-handling.

Edney had a great tournament run, scoring 76 points with 38 assists and just nine turnovers when UCLA took the floor against Arkansas in the national finals. But less than three minutes into the championship game, Edney was headed to the bench with a sprained right wrist he initially suffered in the Bruins' national semi-final win over Oklahoma State; he did not return.

## The Honorable Mention

Dollar took Edney's place in the biggest, most important game of the season. Dollar never had time to think about the daunting task of playing against Arkansas' "40 Minutes of Hell" defense.

"It was," he noted, laughing, "too late to think about it."

Perhaps that's why Dollar, who had inbounded the ball to Edney for the game-winning dash against Missouri, never flinched against the Hogs' suffocating pressure as he helped deliver an 89-78 Bruins' victory at the Seattle Kingdome, bringing UCLA its only NCAA championship in the post-John Wooden era.

Asked if UCLA would have won without Dollar's performance, UCLA coach Jim Harrick said, "Absolutely not."

Dollar wasn't the star of that game. All-American forward Ed O'Bannon poured in a game-high 30 points and grabbed 17 rebounds. Freshman Toby Bailey scored 26 against the Razorbacks. But it was Dollar who kept his cool against Arkansas' suffocating pressure, scoring 6 points with 8 assists and only 3 turnovers in 36 minutes against the defending national champions.

"When opportunity knocks," Dollar said. "you'd better be able to answer."

Dollar started in his last two seasons when the Bruins won Pac-10 championships and advanced to a Sweet 16 and Elite Eight. As a senior, he set a school record with 82 steals. Dollar averaged 5.0 points, 3.7 assists, and 2.3 rebounds during his career.

"His leadership qualities were off the charts," Harrick said. "He was always an extension of a coach on the floor."

Dollar always wanted to follow in the footsteps of his father, who coached high school basketball in Atlanta, and become a coach. He wasted little time telling the UCLA staff he wanted to be a college coach and the staff allowed him to sit in on meetings and scouting reports.

At age 22, Dollar became the country's youngest college coach when he was hired as a head coach at Southern California College, an NAIA school now known as Vanguard University. He served ten years from 1999-2009 as an assistant to former St. Louis and Washington coach Lorenzo Romar. Dollar was hired in the spring of 2009 as head coach at Seattle University, which was transitioning to Division I after dropping the sport in 1980. He was fired after eight seasons, but was soon re-hired as an assistant at Washington under new coach Mike Hopkins. He's still there today.

# Donte DiVincenzo
## (2016-2018)

Joe Faraoni / ESPN Images

### Carved in Stone

Donte DiVincenzo was like a wild colt who needed to be tamed when he first arrived at Villanova from Salesianum School in Wilmington, Delaware in 2016.

When Wildcats' coach, Jay Wright, felt the enormously-talented 6'5" redshirt sophomore guard with the 40-inch vertical leap was acting like a superstar in his freshman year, he had to rein him in.

Jay Wright loved teasing him to provide motivation. "I don't remember this, but he said I told him, 'You act like you're the Michael Jordan of Delaware,'" Wright said. "Then the players started saying it. So, I thought they called him that."

### The Honorable Mention

No one is comparing DiVincenzo to Michael, but he did have an MJ moment in San Antonio when he came off the bench as a sixth man to light up the Alamodome. He put up a career-high 31 points, grabbed five rebounds, and contributed three assists and two blocked shots as Villanova defeated Michigan, 79-60, before a crowd of 67,831 to win its second national championship in three years. DiVincenzo also drained five three-pointers, scoring the most points for any player coming off the bench.

Even the King, LeBron James, was excited about Donte's Inferno, proclaiming, "That kid is going to make money."

DiVincenzo shot 10 for 15 from the field and scored 18 of his points in the first half, carrying the Cats to a 38-29 lead. He was an easy choice for Most Outstanding Player. DiVincenzo built his numbers in short spurts of 8 points in two minutes of play, 10 in three, and 10 in three again in the second half.

"The reason he does that," Wright said, "is he can get really hot. But then, when the other team sees that he's hot, they adjust. Then, instead of taking another shot, he'll make the right pass and he'll stop scoring for a couple of possessions. Then he'll go on another burst. It's a unique quality."

DiVincenzo, who was the top Prep Player in Delaware in 2015, was destined to be a star at Villanova. The only question was, 'when?'

As a true freshman, he appeared in eight games before sitting out with a fractured metatarsal bone in his right foot that kept him in street clothes when Villanova won the national championship. He had a great view from the bench when Kris Jenkins drained his game-winning three at the buzzer during a 77-74 victory over North Carolina. "That year versus this year, it was tough not being out there. I think the big thing was not being able to compete with the guys."

DiVincenzo averaged 8.8 points and 3.8 rebounds coming off the bench as a redshirt freshman and was named to the Big East All-Freshman team. In 2018, DiVincenzo was good enough to start, but Wright brought him off the bench as a backup to Phil Booth. DiVincenzo still found ways to make a huge impact, scoring 30 points in an 86-75 win over Butler in February and being named Big East Sixth Man of the Year.

The freakishly athletic DiVincenzo played his way onto the draft radar following the biggest performance of his life. On April 19, he announced he would declare for the 2018 draft without hiring an agent, thereby opening the possibility of a return to Villanova. A month later after participating in the NBA combine, he announced he would remain in the draft and hire an agent, forgoing his final two years of eligibility. He is now a member of the Milwaukee Bucks.

Phil Ellsworth / ESPN Images

# Luke Hancock
## (2010-2014)

Louisville Athletics

## Carved in Stone

Luke Hancock looked like he was going to have a solid college career when he signed to play for Jim Larranaga at George Mason University in the Colonial Athletic Association. The 6'7" forward averaged 10.9 points and was a third team all-conference selection as a sophomore.

Then his whole life changed when Larranaga left, taking the University of Miami job in the ACC and bringing his entire staff with him.

## The Honorable Mention

Hancock decided to leave too, transferring to play for Rick Pitino at the University of Louisville, which had hired his former Hargrave, Virginia Military Academy coach, Kevin Keatts, as an assistant.

Hancock sat out his first year and was named captain of the team before ever playing a game as a redshirt junior. Playing for Pitino, a Hall of Famer, teacher, and clinician, helped Hancock further advance his skills. Hancock was not a starter and averaged just 7.7 point in 2013 as a redshirt junior, but he played a huge role in the Final Four as the Cardinals won the 2013 NCAA tournament.

Hancock was the first reserve ever named Most Valuable Player of the tournament after he put on a pair of brilliant performances against Wichita State and Michigan in the Final Four. Hancock scored 20 points in the national semi-finals against Wichita State. In the title game against the Wolverines. The Cardinals trailed by 12 points late in the first half before Hancock scored 14 straight points for the Cardinals, which cut the deficit to 1 by halftime. He finished 5 for 5 on three-point shooting as Louisville won, 82-76.

Hancock's performance against Wichita had special significance because it was accomplished in front of his seventy-year old father Bill, who was seriously ill with cancer at the time.

Kevin Ware's gruesome broken leg against Duke in the regional finals captivated America, largely because it was played out on national television. Hancock's despair over his father's medical condition had been kept private. That's the way Luke wanted it.

Bill Hancock traveled to the Big East tournament because he wanted to see Luke compete in the Garden. It was on his bucket list, but he only felt well enough to make one game. He did not attend any of the Cardinals' first four games in the tournament.

But the Final Four was different and Hancock's dad summoned the strength to make the trip with his

family from Roanoke, Virginia to Atlanta. Luke told his dad if he didn't feel up to it, he could stay home and watch the game on TV, but Bill was in the front row for Wichita and he and his son embraced after the game.

"How was that, dad?" Hancock said.

It was a touching moment that will go down in Cardinal folklore. Hancock played one more year for the Cardinals, but wasn't drafted. He tried to latch on as a free agent and even played briefly in Greece before he eventually became a successful financial planner.

He enjoyed the ride for the next five years until the NCAA vacated Louisville's title last fall in the aftermath of a highly-publicized sex escort scandal. The banner was removed from the Yum Center rafters.

"It's just disappointing," Hancock told a local radio station. "There are a lot of people who didn't do the wrong things and tried to do the right things and still are wrapped up in this situation. Everybody can, from afar, say it's the worst thing ever. I've tried to be a man of integrity and do the right things. The most disappointing part is people that would question our character because I feel there were good people on the team. I feel bad for those guys."

Hancock's father has since passed away, but the experience still means a lot to the family.

"I wouldn't change a thing about my college decision," he said. "I'm honored to be a Louisville Cardinal and to have played for Rick Pitino, one of the greatest basketball coaches of all time."

*Louisville Athletics*

# Gerry McNamara
## (2003-2006)

*Syracuse Athletics*

## Carved in Stone

Gerry McNamara was one of the heroes of Jim Boeheim's 2003 NCAA tournament championship team as a freshman. The 6'2" guard from Scranton will always be known as Carmelo Anthony's sidekick in Orange folklore.

McNamara was a star in his own right at Bishop Hannan High School in Scranton, where he was named three-time AP Pennsylvania Small School All-State first team and was the AP's Pennsylvania state Player of the Year in 2001 and 2002. He was a gym rat who used to practice at the Holy Rosary Center near his high school gym and transformed himself into a prolific scorer with 2,917 points and exploded for 55 points—41 in the first half—as a senior, as Hannan defeated Trinity High of Camp Hill to advance to the 2002 state finals. He led all scorers with 32 points as Hannan, which has since closed, held off Sto-Rox and won the Class AA state title, 70-68.

## The Honorable Mention

McNamara had offers from schools like Duke and Florida, but chose to attend Syracuse, where he built a cult following of 3,000 fans from his hometown, who used to take sixty buses, accompanied by a police escort, two hours north on I-81 to the Carrier Dome to watch Orange home games. The place was filled with G-Mac sweatshirts.

McNamara started every game for Syracuse in his freshman year, helping lead the Orange to a 30-5 record. He averaged 13 points, 4.6 assists, and 2.2 steals a game, while shooting 35 percent from the three-point line and making 91 percent of his free throws. He was a clutch player even then, nailing a game-winning three-point goal as Syracuse defeated Notre Dame, 82-80, then hitting two three pointers and another jumper as Syracuse defeated Georgetown, 93-84, in overtime.

But he saved his best work for the NCAA tournament run. In a second-round game against Oklahoma State, McNamara scored 14 points and added 6 assists as the Orangemen overcame a 25-8 point deficit. The game's big moment came in the second half. McNamara got elbowed in the forehead, opening a cut on the bridge of his nose. As blood streaked down his face, McNamara came off a screen, caught the pass, and drained a three-pointer to give the Orange their first lead at 40-39, and the flood gates opened. In the national semi-finals against T.J. Ford and Texas, the Orange won behind a career-high 33 points from Anthony and 19 points and four steals from McNamara.

Then he went off in the championship game against Kansas. McNamara made six threes in the first half and scored 18 points when the Jayhawks chose to double-team Anthony.

"In one timeout, I didn't let Jim Boeheim speak one time," Anthony recalled. "I just said, 'We've got to get the ball to Gerry. Let's not run any plays. Let's just find him.'"

Syracuse built an 18-point lead before holding on to win 81-78 behind 20 points by Anthony and a game-saving blocked shot by sophomore forward, Hakim Warrick. Anthony, as expected, was the Most Outstanding Player, but McNamara also made the all-tournament team.

*Syracuse Athletics*

After Anthony left for the NBA draft, McNamara escaped from his shadow to become a popular star who made the all-Freshman team in 2003, All-Big East second team in 2004, and All-Big East first team in 2005 when he led the Orange to the Big East tournament championship. McNamara finished with 2,099 points, 400 three-point goals, 648 assists, and 258 steals, in addition to an 89.1 free throw percentage. He gave the pros a shot, playing minor league ball before getting into coaching, where he is currently an assistant on Boeheim's staff at Syracuse.

# *Dick Vitale's*

## MOUNT RUSHMORE
## OF
## ALL GOLDEN VOICE

### CAWOOD LEDFORD

### WOODY DURHAM

### MAX FALKENSTIEN

### DON FISCHER

# Cawood Ledford

## (1926-2001)

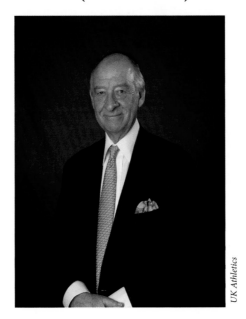

UK Athletics

### Carved in Stone

Cawood Leford, ever the Southern gentleman, broadcast Kentucky basketball for thirty-nine years, from 1953 until 1992, and he will always be considered a beloved treasure in the Commonwealth of Kentucky.

### Smooth Talking

Ledford was the son of a coal miner who grew up in Harlan, Kentucky and served in the Marines in World War II. He earned his degree from Centre College in Danville, and taught high school English. He began his career broadcasting high school basketball and football games for WHFN radio in Harlan, before he began doing play-by-play for University of Kentucky basketball in 1953.

Ledford built a national reputation for his knowledge of the game, gentility, and his excellent command of the English language. He was able to paint a vivid picture of the game and call the action as it happened without missing a beat. His last game as an announcer for a Kentucky basketball game was in 1992 when

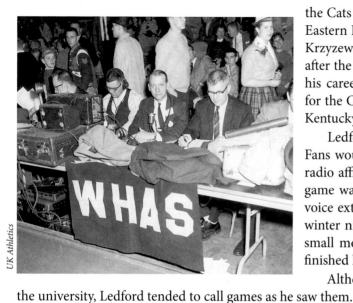

UK Athletics

the Cats fell to Duke, 104-103, in overtime in the NCAA Eastern Regional Final in Philadelphia. Duke coach Mike Krzyzewski walked to the broadcast area immediately after the game's conclusion and congratulated Ledford on his career, which included doing the NCAA Final Four for the CBS Radio network, the Kentucky Derby, and the Kentucky Colonels of the ABA.

Ledford was a giant in his profession. Rabid Kentucky Fans would go to great lengths just to pick up Kentucky radio affiliates, in order to hear his voice, even when the game was televised. They felt Ledford's smooth, familiar voice extended a feeling of warmth and comfort on cold winter nights. They say the lights in the porch houses of small mountain communities would not go off until he finished his broadcast.

Although the Wildcats' broadcasters are employed by the university, Ledford tended to call games as he saw them.

The iconic Kentucky coach, Adolph Rupp, once told him, "By God, Cawood, when you see one of our teams dogging it, by God, burn 'em."

Among his most memorable sayings were "Hello Everybody, this is Cawood Ledford," his sign on; "The Wildcats will be moving from left to right on your radio dial," "He had a notion;" (when a player momentarily deliberated about taking a shot but thought better of it and passed the ball to a teammate); "He went to war on that one;" "Bullseye;" "The Cats are runnin';" "He shot that one from Paducah;" and "It danced around a little bit, but it finally fell."

Ledford was selected the Commonwealth's Sportscaster of the Year twenty-two times and received the coveted Curt Gowdy Broadcasting Award from the Naismith Hall of Fame. A blue banner with his name and a microphone hangs from the rafters of Rupp Arena.

President Clinton paid tribute to Ledford at a 1999 appearance in Hazard, Kentucky, to deliver a speech on Appalachian poverty.

"I was thinking if old Cawood had been a political announcer instead of a basketball announcer, and I could have kept him with me these last twenty-five years, I'd have never lost an election." Mr. Clinton said.

Upon his retirement, Ledford returned to Eastern Kentucky, moving to a farm about ten miles south of Harlan. He lived there with his wife Frances until his passing in 2001.

That year, the University of Kentucky named its basketball court at Rupp Arena in Ledford's honor. The words, "Cawood's Court" and a radio microphone are painted on the floor in commemoration, close to his broadcast location.

During the summer of 2014, Kentucky announced its annual multi-tournament would be called the Cawood Ledford Classic.

# Woody Durham
## (1971-2018)

*UNC Athletic Communications*

## Carved in Stone

Whenever I call a college basketball game, I spend a lot of time before the contest in the media room. I have always enjoyed interacting with writers and broadcasters that cover the teams every day. They always have great stories and information.

I treasured my visits to Chapel Hill.

## Smooth Talking

Woody Durham, a North Carolina native and a1963 North Carolina graduate, was the Voice of the Tar Heels and did play-by-play on radio for UNC football and basketball for forty-one years from the fall of 1971 through the 2011 basketball season.

Durham was the link between fans through this rabid basketball state, when fewer games were televised.

When the TV market expanded, fans would still turn down the sound and listen to Woody's magnetic voice on the radio broadcasts.

Durham was one of the most recognizable figures in the state. Off the air, he represented UNC at multiple alumni and donor functions as an emcee and guest speaker, and he accompanied alumni groups on trips around the world with his wife, Jean. Durham was on the call for thirteen Final Fours and four national championships in 1982, 1993, 2005, and 2009. He was North Carolina Sportscaster of the Year twelve times, was one of just three college broadcasters in the modern era to receive the Curt Gowdy Broadcasting award from the Naismith Hall of Fame and was posthumously inducted in the National Media Hall of Fame in 2018, six months after his death.

Audiotapes and CDs of Durham's most famous calls have been produced, none more famous than when Walter Davis capped off a furious eight points in a seventeen-second rally to beat Duke in 1974 by banking home a 30-foot shot.

"UN-BE-LIEEEVABLE!" Durham screamed into the mike as Carmichael Auditorium exploded.

Some of Durham's expressions during his broadcasts included, "Go where you go and do what you do" and "Go to war, Miss Agnes," a phrase Durham heard from Chuck Thompson during a Baltimore Colts game; and "Good gosh, Gurdy." He is also known for his "How about them Heels?" play call before the end of the 1992 NCAA championship game. Durham repeated the play call for the homecoming ceremony at Kenan Stadium after the members of that team spoke to the crowd.

Durham grew up in Albemarle and was close friends with Bob Harris, the long-time, recently retired voice of the Duke Blue Devils. The two played on the same Little League Baseball team. In 1957, Durham was a guard on the Albemarle High football team; Harris was the team's manager. Durham and Harris also sang together in the Albemarle High chorus.

Durham was working for WFMY-TV in Durham when he caught his big break, becoming the play-by-play announcer for the Tar Heel Football and Basketball Networks in 1971. He took over from the radio network's founder, Bill Currie, "The Mouth of the South," when Currie decided to take a TV job in Pittsburgh. Durham also became the emcee for The Bill Dooley Show and The Dean Smith Show, TV programs that aired through the state. In 1981, Durham was named vice president and executive director of the Tar Heel Sports network.

Durham also gave generously to charities, most notably the Carolina Kids Klassic created with UNC football and basketball coaches to raise thousands of dollars for the UNC Children's Hospital.

Broadcasting became a family affair for the Durhams. Wife Jean was always present at Carolina games, wearing an earpiece so she could hear Woody's calls. Wes, the oldest son, did play-by-play for Georgia Tech and now the NFL Atlanta Falcons, as well as doing TV for Fox. His youngest son, Taylor calls games for Elon College.

Durham was close to the late Dean Smith and Roy Williams, emceeing events like the Fast Break for Cancer, originated by Williams in 2013 and special occasions like the memorial for Smith, who was a frequent golf partner.

# Max Falkenstien

## (1946-2006)

*Kansas Athletics*

### Carved in Stone

Max Falkenstien's golden voice will always be a big part of the fabric of Kansas athletics. In a glorious sixty-year career from 1946 to 2006, the now ninety-three-year-old Falkenstien did radio play-by-play for 1,750 men's basketball contests and 650 football games—a span that included every game played in Allen Field House until his retirement.

### Smooth Talking

Falkenstien is truly unmatched in his field, baby! By comparison, Vin Scully's sixty-seven seasons with the Brooklyn and Los Angeles Dodgers is the record for the longest broadcasting tenure with a single franchise in professional sports.

Falkenstien was honored by the College Football Hall of Fame with the Chris Schenkel award for Broadcast Excellence and was one of three college broadcasters to win the Curt Gowdy Award from the Naismith Hall of Fame. He was selected as "The Best College Radio Personality in the Country" by the Sporting News and received the Distinguished Service Award by the Kansas Association of Broadcasters, the Lifetime Achievement Award from Baker University, and the Ellsworth Medallion—the highest award of the Kansas University Alumni Association

Falkenstien has been around long enough to have met Dr. James Naismith, Kansas' first coach and the man credited with inventing the game. He also knew Phog Allen, for whom the Field House is named. He called one of the greatest NCAA title games, the triple-overtime win by Frank McGuire's North Carolina over Wilt Chamberlain's Jayhawk team in 1957. He was so popular in Kansas that he was hired at one point by Douglas Bank in a public relations and ceremonial capacity.

Falkenstien got his first job in radio at WREN, a Lawrence radio station.

"A guy named Earl Bratten gave me some news copy to read and I got the job," he said.

Falkenstein worked before and after school and on weekends, usually forty hours a week. He graduated from high school in 1942, six months after the Japanese bombed Pearl Harbor. After a semester at Kansas, he enlisted in the Army Air Corps, in hopes of becoming a meteorologist. He left the service in March of 1946.

After leaving the service, he went back to work for WREN. His first assignment was to do the play-by-play for the NCAA district game between KU and Oklahoma A&M. Falkenstein founded the KU Sports Network in 1948, which was subsequently taken over by the university. He broadcast the Jayhawks' national championship games in 1952 and 1988. (Awesome!)

Falkenstien's final broadcast in Allen Field House came on March 1, 2006, in which the Jayhawks defeated Colorado, 75-54. The then eighty-one-year old Falkenstien was honored in a special halftime ceremony, which included friends, family, some former KU players, and a speech from his on-air partner of twenty-two years, Bob Davis. Athletic Director, Lew Perkins, presented Falkenstien with a bronze Jayhawk to commemorate his years of service to the school. His name and number (60, for the number of years he had broadcast for the Jayhawks), were also hung on a banner in Allen Field House. He was the twenty-seventh person so honored by the school and the first non-player.

"I'll look back at this as one of my favorite nights, not because we won the game, but I was here when Max got his name dropped from the rafters," Kansas Hall of Fame coach Bill Self said. "That is special, and he deserves it."

# Don Fischer
## (1973-Present)

*Indiana University Athletics*

## Carved in Stone

Don Fischer has been broadcasting Indiana football and basketball for the last forty-five years. He is the Dean of Big Ten broadcasters and has been selected the state's Sportscaster of the Year a stunning twenty-six times and is a member of the Indiana Broadcasters' Pioneer Hall of Fame.

## Smooth Talking

But the now seventy-one-year old Fischer's celebrated career almost never got off the ground. When Fischer was just starting out in the business, he had a disastrous experience doing play-by-play of his first high school football game in Ottawa, Illinois.

"I set broadcasting back forty-five years; I was horrible, and I knew it," Fischer recalled. "I simply wasn't prepared. I didn't know how to prepare."

When he got back to the station, the station manager was there waiting for him and telling him in no uncertain terms he had three weeks to vastly improve…or else.

Fischer was desperate. He got up the next morning and cold-called Art Kimball, an accomplished high school sports play-by-play man at WLPO in nearby La Salle-Peru. Kimball invited him over after church the next day and covered everything from background reading, rosters, charts, interviews, and game prep. Fischer took notes for five hours. Fischer never forgot Kimball's kindness.

"The stuff he gave me, the information he gave me, I've used the rest of my life," Fischer said.

Fischer, of course, got better and, in 1973, beat out 250 applicants to become the play-by-play man for the Hoosiers. Fischer also repaid the debt. Fischer was in line for a job with WJBC in Bloomington when he accepted the Indiana job. Left empty-handed, the station manager asked Fischer for a recommendation. Fischer immediately recommended Art Kimball, who later became the voice of the Illinois State Redbirds.

It was a dream come true for a guy who grew up as a farmer's son in Rochelle, Illinois, dabbling in construction, selling magazines door-to-door, and doing railroad work. One night, he was sitting in a railroad depot reading Sport Magazine when he noticed an ad promoting a career in sports broadcasting.

Fischer took a gamble, working as an overnight D.J. in Butte, Montana, saving his job in Ottawa, and spending time in Terre Haute, Indiana. There was a possible chance to go to Oregon before he caught his big break.

Fischer has worked with nine football coaches and five basketball coaches, including ESPN personality Lee Corso and the brilliant but occasionally volatile Bob Knight. He called all three of Knights' national championships, including the culmination of Hoosiers' perfect season in 1976. That team had future pros Scott May, Kent Benson, and Quinn Buckner and they defeated rival Michigan in the NCAA title game in Philadelphia.

"I still remember the final minute and a half of that game," he recalled. "That team was so non-demonstrative. They acted like they had been there forever. But they got so excited about being unbeaten and national champions, the guys went nuts. I had tears coming down my cheeks."

Fischer has used a magical six words for the first time at the buzzer: "And Indiana wins the national championship."

Fischer admits he never knew what to expect from Knight when he hosted the coach's weekly radio show. For years, Knight said he wouldn't do a talk show, but then he found out what a potential bonanza it could be financially and he was all for the idea. Suddenly, he was talking it up.

Everything was fine until December in the second year. Somebody called up and told him he was the greatest coach ever, then asked Knight why he was doing something.

"Fischo, let's go to a commercial break," Knight said.

During the break, Knight told him, "That is the last phone call I'm taking on this show."

Questions had to be submitted by postcard or letters. After a while, the letters started slowing down.

"I started making up my own and put names on them," Fischer told former USA columnist Mike Lopresti. "I took the names from my high school yearbook."

Did Knight ever find out? "Heck no," Fischer said. (I guess the cat's out of the bag, now!)

Fischer survived and flourished in Bloomington by being old school. He was always enthusiastic about Indiana University (IU) and knew how to relate excitement to the fans. His most famous call came in 2011 when Christian Watford made a shot to beat Kentucky in Assembly Hall. "Outside to Christian Watford. A three on the way. Ohhh, it went in and Indiana wins the ball game."

Fischer was so popular with IU fans that one of them, Greg Parker, posted a video called, Ol' Fisch" on YouTube, referring to him as the greatest sports broadcaster of all-time.

Fischer doesn't sound like he is ready to retire any time soon. What keeps him going is the thrill of bringing games to life for his listeners.

"The greatest compliment a guy like me can get is for the listeners to say that they were able to visualize the game in their minds," Fisher said. "That's the job, to allow fans to feel the excitement, thrills, and disappointments of the game."

# *Dick Vitale's*
# MOUNT RUSHMORE
## OF
# ALL ZEBRA

# HANK NICHOLS

# JOHN CLOUGHERTY

# TIM HIGGINS

# JIM BURR

# Hank Nichols

NCAA

## Carved in Stone

Dr. Hank Nichols is the most decorated official in the history of college basketball and arguably the best to carry a whistle.

The eighty-two-year-old Nichols, who was inducted as a member of the Naismith Hall of Fame in 2012, officiated ten NCAA Final Fours, a record six championship games, three NIT finals, worked two Olympics, and one European championship. He was the first official to work both the NIT and NCAA tournament finals in a single year and was the NCAA's first national coordinator of officials.

## Vital to the Game

Nichols grew up in Niagara Falls, New York, where he attended Bishop Duffy High and lettered in three sports. He earned a scholarship to Villanova, where he played catcher on the baseball team and started on the freshman basketball team. Nichols led the Cats to the NCAA baseball tournament as a senior in 1958 and was voted the team's MVP. He is a member of the Villanova athletic Hall of Fame.

After graduation, he spent two years in the Marine Corps, followed by three years playing minor league baseball in the Cincinnati Reds organization. In his final season, when he was twenty-seven, he hit .330 as a player-manager in the Western Carolina League.

After leaving baseball, Nichols returned to Villanova to earn a master's degree. From there, he returned to Niagara Falls to teach at a local high school. After dabbling in coaching and teaching for a couple of years, his brother, Bob, convinced him to begin officiating high school basketball games. The Nichols' brothers rose quickly, officiating junior varsity, then varsity, and—eventually—Niagara basketball games.

"One of the first college games we worked together was a freshman game at Niagara when Calvin Murphy was (playing)," Nichols said. "We ended up fouling Calvin out with about six minutes to play. A woman in the stands stood up and hollered, "One thing I know for sure: Two Nichols aren't worth a dime."

Nichols was gathering a solid reputation as an official, but he still felt the need to further his education. He enrolled in Duke to obtain his doctorate and Blue Devils' assistant coach, Hubie Brown, a Niagara native, encouraged him to take the NCAA officiating test and become a full-time official. In 1970, Nichols returned to Villanova to join the faculty and eventually became a professor and the head of the Department of Education for twenty-six years.

In 1974, Nichols worked the first of thirteen consecutive NCAA tournaments. That season, he was one of the officials for the famous NC State-Maryland ACC championship game, which the Wolfpack won, 103-100, in overtime. Towering 7' 4" center, Tom Burleson, was selected MVP of the league's greatest game after scoring 38 points. David Thompson, the league's best player ever, had 29 as the Pack outscored the Terps, who, themselves, had three future NBA first round picks—Len Elmore, Tom McMillen, and John Lucas.

"That was the best game I ever worked," Nichols said. "I just remember getting out of everybody's way. Those players were so good. We just kind of watched them. It was a magnificent game."

In 1975, Nichols worked the first of ten Final Fours, and first of six national championships when UCLA defeated Kentucky to win a tenth national title in twelve years. It was John Wooden's final game as the head coach of the Bruins. The two other memorable championship games Nichols officiated were the 1979 Bird-Magic game between Michigan State and Indiana State, still the highest-rated college basketball broadcast in network history; and the 1983 NC State-Houston game that ended on a slam dunk by Lorenzo Charles that gave the Wolfpack a 54-52 victory.

Nichols was selected to officiate the 1976 Olympics in Montreal and again in 1984 at Los Angeles when he worked the bronze medal game.

In 1987, Nichols became the first NCAA coordinator of officials, a position he held for twenty-two years.

"The goal was to try to get guys across the country to officiate the same way, not to have the ACC be different from the Big Ten and the Big Ten different from the Pac-10. We wanted to teach guys to ref better and be more consistent. We didn't want them to be another factor when teams played on the road. We wanted them to stand tall and figure out tough situations. I think a lot of that has been accomplished."

While in his position, Nichols was also the secretary and editor of the Basketball Rules Committee from 1991-1997. He retired after the 2007-2008 season and was replaced by John Adams.

# John Clougherty

NCAA

## Carved in Stone

When I hear the name John Clougherty, I think about the night my alma mater, Seton Hall, looked like they were going to be the darlings of the college basketball world as national champs in 1989. All of a sudden, a whistle was blown with three seconds left that took away the dream of P.J. Carlesimo and the Pirates. It was one of those unforgettable times. That being said, Clougherty was as honest as could be. He had the utmost respect of everyone in the sport and he believed he made the right call. Seton Hall moved on.

## Vital to the Game

As a kid growing up in the suburbs of Pittsburgh in the 1950s, John Clougherty loved sports, especially football and baseball. He admits he has a soft spot for the Pittsburgh Steelers. He played football and baseball at Duquesne High School.

Clougherty started college at Michigan State as a member of the Spartans' football team, but after two years in East Lansing, he conceded the school was much too big and challenging athletically, so he transferred to Youngstown State. There, he studied to become a teacher. He never dreamed about a career in officiating. The 5'8" Clougherty stumbled into his profession. He worked intramural basketball games for $3.00 a pop.

"I knew I liked it," the seventy-four-year old Clougherty said. "I found out I could tolerate the complaining that goes on."

After the even-keeled Clougherty graduated from Youngstown with honors in 1968, he became a teacher, getting a masters' degree from nearby Kent State the following year. He and his wife, Dorothy, moved to Winston Salem in 1969, when Clougherty accepted a job teaching physical education at Wake Forest. He did some refereeing at local high schools and got his first real break in 1973 when Jack McCloskey, then Wake's head basketball coach, recommended him to the Atlantic Coast Conference. For two seasons, Clougherty officiated small college and ACC freshman games. By the 1975 season, he had worked his way onto the regular roster of ACC officials.

His career took off from there. Clougherty worked ACC games through the 1985 season, the same year he was selected to do the national championship game between Villanova and Georgetown in Lexington. He has gone on to officiate over 2,000 games in thirty years at every conference East of the Mississippi: SEC, Big East, Atlantic 10, Big 12, Sun Belt, and Conference USA. He officiated conference title games in the ACC (1982), Southwest Conference (1981), Metro Conference (1981-85), Sun Belt (1986; 1989-94); he worked the SEC title game fourteen times.

Clougherty's outstanding work led to twenty-six NCAA tournament opportunities and he worked twelve Final Fours and four championship games from 1985 through 2000. He worked internationally in the Central America Games, the European Olympic qualifying tournament, and the World Championships. Clougherty has received the James Naismith Official of the Year award in 1989 and the NIT Officials Award, as well as the Distinguished Alumni Award from Youngstown State.

"It's almost a thankless job," Clougherty said. "They'd like to play without us, but they can't."

Clougherty has seen it all—the start of David Thompson's career at NC State, Michael Jordan's rise to stardom in the ACC, Villanova's perfect game, Danny Manning and the Miracles in 1988, Michigan's overtime victory over Seton Hall in 1989, UNLV's 30-point victory over Duke in 1990 and the Blue Devils' revenge over a perfect Runnin' Rebels team the following year.

"I got a little lucky," Clougherty said of his penchant for being at the right place at the right time.

The respect former Seton Hall coach, P.J. Carlesimo, has for Clougherty speaks volumes. When informed Clougherty was about to be inducted into the North Carolina Sports Hall of Fame, Carlesimo called Clougherty "one of the greatest officials ever" during a story that appeared in the Raleigh News and Observer.

If there is one coach who could hold a grudge against Clougherty, it is Carlesimo. Clougherty made the famous call that decided the Wolverines' 80-79 victory over Carlesimo's Big East Pirates. Seton Hall led Michigan, 79-78, in overtime when Wolverines guard, Rumeal Robinson, dribbled into the lane. The Seton Hall defender put his right hand on Robinson's hip and Clougherty, who was in front of the play under the Michigan basket, blew his whistle.

With just three seconds left, Robinson went to the foul line. He made both shots, and the Wolverines won the title. Clougherty has been asked about that call hundreds of times in the twenty-six years since. There was undoubtedly contact, but in hindsight, Clougherty will admit he should have been more patient.

"Given the timing of the situation and the magnitude of the game, would I have been better off to hold the whistle and let the game play out?" he said. "Yeah. And I don't run away from that."

But, Clougherty said, there was no way to review the call and no room for hesitation. "You do the best you can and that's what I did," he said.

Most Seton Hall fans were and are still livid with Clougherty, but not Carlesimo. "The call was made; there's nothing you can do about it. You can cry about it, but that would detract from what Michigan did," he said.

Carlesimo's graciousness came because "It was John who made the call."

Clougherty earned that kind of respect working in the ACC for ten years and then another twenty primarily in the Big East and SEC before he retired in 2005. He built a reputation for the way he communicated with coaches and players and treated everyone with respect. Clougherty went on to become the ACC's Supervisor of officials, getting the job on the recommendation of none other than the great Dean Smith.

When ACC commissioner, John Swofford, was looking for a supervisor of officials to replace the late Fred Barakat, he asked Smith about the candidates.

Smith told him, "You need to hire a referee. You need to hire John Clougherty."

"Why do you say that?" Swofford asked.

"Because coaches don't know anything about the rules and anything about officiating," Smith said. "You need to hire someone who knows something about officiating, not a coach."

Clougherty held the job for eleven years before retiring in 2016 after forty-one years in the business.

Two of Clougherty's sons are carrying on in his footsteps. Tim is a Big East, ACC, Atlantic 10 basketball referee, while running the family's officiating business, and Conor is an ACC football field judge. Pat, the middle son, played baseball at NC State but never picked up a whistle.

# Tim Higgins

NCAA

## Carved in Stone

Tim Higgins had a very unique passion for putting on his officiating attire He would make small talk before the games. Since we were both from North Jersey, we had plenty of conversations about people we knew.

Higgins is a Jersey guy from Ramsey who originally wanted to be a professional golfer. He grew up caddying at White Beaches Golf Club in Haworth, becoming a scratch handicap in his off hours.

But the head pro there, Ben Parola, told him he wasn't good enough to make the PGA tour.

"I was stubborn," Higgins recalled. "So, he brought in some guys you never heard of who couldn't make it on tour to play me. I shot 71 and lost like $260, which was a lot of money back in the late 1960s. Ben looks at me afterwards and says, 'Alright, smart guy, what are you going to do with your life now?'"

The now seventy-two-year-old Higgins never had much time for school, but it became clear he needed a college education. So, he enrolled at Fairleigh Dickinson.

"I needed something to help pay tuition. The baseball coach, former Orioles catcher John Orsino, put me to work officiating. I started doing kids games for a couple of bucks."

Fast forward three decades.

## Vital to the Game

Higgins went on to become one of the best college officials in the country and one of the most familiar faces in the Big East. He and Jim Burr were part of the Big East's first officiating crew. Higgins figures he has worked 2,000 games over thirty-five years, earned ten trips to the NCAA Final Four with four appearances in the title game before he finally retired at age sixty-six in 2012. His ten Final Fours are more than Jim Calhoun or Jim Boeheim, and he left each of them undefeated, which is not to say Higgins was perfect. He is a game official, so we know it's unlikely he got every call right.

"Timmy is one of the best, if not the best in the land," said Art Hyland, the former Big East coordinator of officials. "He's solid gold."

Higgins worked sixty games a year over twenty weeks in his prime and grossed $50,000 a year. Higgins also held down a full-time job as a vice president of sales for Kamco, a Brooklyn company that sells contractor's supplies and heavy machinery. The hours are flexible. They needed to be!

Higgins was able to keep up with the demands of his other job with regular exercise.

"I exercise every day and I'm in pretty good shape, all appearances to the contrary" he claimed.

He figured he was running 4.32 miles a day during a typical game.

Part of Higgins' strength was his Irish charm, his ability to keep a sense of humor, and blocking out the hecklers in the stands.

"After a while, you learn to tune out basically everything but the game."

He does remember some of the better lines, though. "There was this one UConn fan who got me pretty good a few years ago," he recalled. "I had just done a Connecticut loss to UNC in one of the first ACC-Big East Challenges, and it was the following weekend in Hartford. We're standing around during warm-ups and this young kid says very politely, "Mr. Higgins. Excuse me, Mr. Higgins. He seemed harmless and polite. So, I turned around to address him and he says, "Yeah, Mr. Higgins, I just wondered if you could take your pants down, so I could see Dean Smith's autograph. Wham. He was gone."

Higgins has had more success with coaches and players. "With coaches, you let them make their point, and then you expect them to move on," he said. "There are certain words and phrases which everybody knows will result in an automatic technical. And then there are technicals that result from accumulated BS. As for the players, I'm always talking to kids. They're terrific almost without exception. Mostly, we just tease each other. I give them a longer leash than the coaches to express themselves."

Higgins has a reputation for being unbiased, but he was involved in a major controversy at the 2011 Big East tournament when he and veteran officials, Jim Burr and Earl Walton, worked a seemingly innocuous second round game between St. John's and Rutgers. With 1.7 seconds left and St. John's ahead, Justin Brownlee stole the ball, but he appeared to travel after the catch. The officials didn't see it because they had left the court without checking the monitor for the clock situation. NCAA coordinator of officials John Adams called it "unacceptable" that they would not work to the finish of the game and all three were suspended for the rest of the tournament.

Even the great ones miss a call. Higgins can live with the abuse he gets for the life he's had. "I miss the games," he said. "I miss the guys. But I don't miss the travel. It's torture. Nothing goes out on time, nothing comes back on time. But you know something, I'm a lucky guy. I walked into locker rooms a thousand times and I'd hear some of the guys say, 'Oh, man. That was hard.' And I'd think, Yeah, right, we are making a living doing this. How lucky are we? I was blessed, man."

# Jim Burr

NCAA

## Carved in Stone

Over the years, I have enjoyed a great relationship with several officials. I respect the men in the striped shirts, blowing the whistle and taking charge of the game I love. One official I have truly enjoyed interacting with is Jim Burr. I can remember the start of one season, I had a question about a rule change and the way officials would handle it. I was calling a game at Madison Square Garden and, in preparation, I went over to the officials' locker room. Burr was there and he was happy to sit down and explain to me his interpretation of that new rule. As a broadcaster, I am fortunate to have referees come over during a play stoppage to help explain a controversial call or to tell us exactly what they saw. It helps us out on the telecast and gives the fans a good perspective.

## Vital to the Game

On the court, Burr has enjoyed a special career. He has been calling games for a long time and that longevity as an authority figure on the court is impressive.

"He reffed all the big games," Jim Boeheim, told the Albany Times Union. "He had Syracuse-Georgetown for twenty-five years in a row, probably. He didn't care who won. He never did. He was fair. He got the calls right."

Burr's first season as an NCAA official was 1976-1977, which coincided with Hall of Famer Boeheim's first year as head coach at Syracuse.

I think back to the 1996 Big East final at the Mecca of college basketball. It was a night filled with hoops hysteria with Georgetown's ultra-quick Prime Time Player, Allen Iverson, versus the sweet shooting talent of Huskies star, Ray Allen.

The Garden was rocking and rolling that night. The scalpers were out in full force. Two future NBA superstars did battle and Burr helped make sure the contest was well-officiated. It was a Maalox Masher which went down to the wire. In that scenario, the zebras have a lot of pressure. Burr always came through. One way you know an official is doing his job well is, very simply, when we as announcers don't talk much about them. That was certainly true that night.

Burr later admitted, "The (Big East) games were hard. Back in the '80s and '90s, every night was a dogfight. It was hard. Those games were really hard. The old Big East games, coaches, competition, I don't know if you'll ever see that again."

The crème de la crème of officials get picked for the Final Four. Burr has been a regular there, starting in 1985 in Lexington, Kentucky. Overall, he officiated in seven championship games: 1991, 1994, 1995, 1998, 2000, 2002 and 2006. How consistently was he among the best? He was at the Final Four from 1990-1995, 1997-2000 and 2004-2006.

That is a model of consistency blowing the whistle, my friends.

# ACKNOWLEDGEMENTS

Over the years I have been very blessed to have so many people in my life. This book, like many others that I have been involved in, would not happen without the support that I have received from my NUMBER ONE TEAM, which starts with my wife Lorraine, and my daughters Sherri and Terri and their wonderful families.

I also must give a sincere thanks to my "second family," all of my colleagues at ESPN over the past four decades.

Finally, let's face the reality that this book would not have been completed without the dedication and work ethic of Dick "Hoops" Weiss, the Hall of Fame journalist, and the vital statistics and research by my good friend, Howie Schwab. Dick and Howie worked together as a smooth tandem and spent many hours researching and collecting all the stats and info that allowed me to come up with my choices for the various categories. Yes, even if I weren't on ESPN calling a game, I simply say that Hoops Weiss and Howie are AWESOME, BABY! With a capital A!

- Dick Vitale

I would like to thank the following people for all their assistance and support in this project: First, my wife Joan, who has co-authored books with me in the past and put up with my ever-changing moods for the three months I needed to complete the manuscript; Dick and Lorraine Vitale, two of the finest people I have ever known; Howie Schwab, an ultimate sports encyclopedia who was an immeasurable help with this and every other book I have done with Dick; and his wife Suzie, who was kind enough to put up with my constant phone calls for assistance; Bob Ryan, one of my best friends and a true Hall of Fame sportswriter who was kind enough to write the foreword for this book; publisher Mike Nicloy of Nico 11 Publishing and Design; good friends Elaine Ryan, highly talented, prolific author and close friend, John Feinstein; Mike Flynn, a visionary in women's basketball and the CEO of Blue Star Sports; Joe and Betty Anne Cassidy, Scott and Suzanne Schenker; Jeanine Reynolds and her children Tim, Andrew, and Matt; Karl Grentz and his wife, Theresa, the best basketball player of her generation; TV icon Lesley Visser; Liza Lank; Lea Miller, who is the driving force behind Battle for Atlantis, and her husband, Jim Tooley, who runs USA Basketball; my attorney Rick Troncelliti; basketball savant Pat Plunkett; Dave Pauley; American commissioner, Mike Aresco, who always fights for the underdog; John Akers, the editor of Basketball Times; Steve Richardson from the FWAA and Joe Mitch of the US Basketball Writers: Dave Goren of the ASMA; journalism colleagues, Dick Jerardi, Mike Kern, Roger Rubin, Ray Didinger, Alan Cutler, and Adam Berkowitz; Brian Morrison, Dr. David Raezer, Sam Albano, Jerry McLaughlin, Larry Pearlstein, Mark Whicker and Robyn Norwood; the late, great Larry Donald, Mike Sheridan, and John Paquette of the Big East; and Steve Kirchner from the ACC; Danny Gavitt and David Worlock of the NCAA; Sean Ford and Craig Miller of USA Basketball; all of the folks in the Big 5; four-footed friends, Charlie and Sadie; and The Guys and the coaches and players in college basketball who have made coverage of the sport so much fun for me over the years. Some of the background and statistics for this book was put together with the help of books I co-authored with Dick Vitale over the past thirty years, particularly *Dick Vitale's Top 50 Players and Moments in College Basketball*.

- Dick Weiss

I have loved college basketball for over forty years, attending my first major college game in 1975, Syracuse vs. St. John's at Alumni Hall. Doing this book is a labor of love and I thank Dick Vitale, Hoops Weiss and Mike Nicloy for the opportunity to be involved in such a great project.

I want to acknowledge my mother and father, who have always provided love, guidance, and support. I also acknowledge my wife, Suzie, who inspires me to be a better human being each day. Thanks to my family and Suzie's as they make life special.

Enjoy the book. I am sure it will provoke bar arguments!

- Howie Schwab

# ABOUT THE AUTHORS

**D**ick Vitale is college basketball's top analyst and ambassador. His thorough knowledge of the game is brought forth in an enthusiastic, passionate, sometimes controversial—but never boring—style.

In 2018, Vitale began his *fortieth* season at ESPN. He joined the worldwide leader in sports during the 1979-80 season, just after the network's September 1979 launch when he called the networks first-ever major NCAA basketball game, Wisconsin at DePaul, on Dec. 5, 1979. Since then, he's called over one thousand games.

ESPN Images

Vitale has authored thirteen books, including *It's Awesome, Baby! 75 Years of Memories and a Lifetime of Opinions on the Game I Love, Dick Vitale's Living a Dream*, both co-authored with Dick Weiss, *Getting a W in the Game of Life*, co-authored with Reji Laberje, and Children's book *Dickie V's ABCs and 1-2-3s*.

### Hall of Fame Career

In 2008, Vitale received the sport's ultimate honor when he was selected as an inductee into the Naismith Memorial Basketball Hall of Fame.

Vitale has been selected for a total of thirteen halls of fame: National Italian American Sports Hall of Fame, the Elmwood Park, N.J., Hall of Fame (his hometown), the Sarasota Boys and Girls Club Hall of Fame (inducted in inaugural class of 2001), the Five-Star Basketball Camp Hall of Fame (2003), the University of Detroit Hall of Fame, the Florida Sports Hall of Fame in 1996 (he's a resident of the state), the East Rutherford, N.J., Hall of Fame (1985), the National Collegiate Basketball Hall of Fame (2008), the Naismith Memorial Basketball Hall of Fame (2008), Sarasota Community Archives Hall of Fame (2009), the Little League Museum Hall of Excellence (2012), the National Sportscasters and Sportswriters Association Awards (NSSA) Hall of Fame (2013), Wooden Cup Award (2017) and the National Sportscasters Hall of Fame (2018).

He continues to participate on selection committees for both the Naismith and Wooden Awards and is a member of The Associated Press voting panel for the Top 25. He is also a voter for the Hall of Fame's Bob Cousy Awards.

Vitale graduated from Seton Hall University with a Bachelor of Science Degree in Business Administration. He also earned a Master's Degree in education from William Paterson College, and has 32 graduate credits beyond the Master's Degree in Administration.

Vitale's roots are in teaching the game he's loved since a child. Following graduation from college, he got a job teaching at Mark Twain Elementary School in Garfield, N.J., where he also coached junior high school football and basketball. He began coaching at the high school level at Garfield High School, where he coached for one season (1963-64). He then earned four state sectional championships, two consecutive state championships, and 35 consecutive victories during his seven years at his alma mater, East Rutherford, NJ, High School (1964-70).

He joined Rutgers University for two years (1970-72) as an assistant coach, helping to recruit Phil Sellers and Mike Dabney, two cornerstones on an eventual NCAA Final Four team (1976).

Vitale then coached at the University of Detroit (1973-77), compiling a winning percentage of .722 (78-30), which included a 21-game winning streak during the 1976-77 season when the team participated in the NCAA Tournament. Included in the streak was a victory in Milwaukee over Al McGuire's eventual national champion Marquette team. In April 1977, Vitale was named Athletic Director at the University of Detroit and later that year was named the United Fund's Detroit Man of the Year. In May 1978, he was named head coach of the NBA's Detroit Pistons, which he coached during the 1978-79 season, prior to joining ESPN.

### Philanthropy

Vitale is on the Board of Directors of The V Foundation, a non-profit organization dedicated to finding a cure for cancer and founded in 1993 by ESPN and the late Jim Valvano (an organization with has since raised over $200 million for cancer research). He hosts the annual "Dick Vitale Gala" in Florida benefiting the V Foundation, which has raised $25.2 million to date, gathering numerous celebrities to raise money and honor individuals such as Mike Krzyzewski, Bob Knight and Pat Summitt, Billy Donovan, Tom Izzo, Jay Wright and Nick Saban, and Robin Roberts.

For many years he's awarded five scholarships annually to the Boys & Girls Club of Sarasota, Florida. His involvement with the organization was highlighted in April 1999 with the "Dick Vitale Sports Night," an annual banquet that has raised more than $1 million. In April 2000, in recognition of Vitale's support for the Boys and Girls Club, it was announced that a new building would be named The Dick Vitale Physical Education and Health Training Center. A statue of him stands in front of the Training Center. Vitale was inducted into the Sarasota's Boys and Girls Club Hall of Fame at the 2001 Dinner. In 2002, Sarasota magazine named him one of the area's most influential citizens.

Dick Vitale was born in Passaic, New Jersey, and resided in his youth in Garfield and Elmwood Park, New Jersey. He and his wife Lorraine now reside in Lakewood Ranch, Florida (Sarasota-Bradenton area), and have two daughters, Terri and Sherri, who both attended Notre Dame on tennis scholarships, and who both graduated with MBAs from the Golden Dome. Terri and her husband Chris have two children, Sydney, 17, and Ryan, 15. Sherri, and her husband Thomas have three children; twins Jake and Connor, 16, and Ava, 13.

The Vitale's proud involvement with Notre Dame includes the endowment of the Dick Vitale Family Scholarship, presented annually to Irish undergraduates who participate in Notre Dame Sports and activities that do not provide financial aid. Recipients over the years have included the school's Leprechaun mascot, cheerleaders, and band members.

Dick is a popular figure even outside of sports television. He's made cameo appearances in several movies such as *The Naked Gun, Hoop Dreams, Blue Chips, The Sixth Man, He Got Game, Love and Basketball,* and *Jury Duty.*

**D**ick Weiss has worked for the Philadelphia Daily News, New York Daily News, and Blue Star Media since 1970. He has covered 46 NCAA Final Fours and co-authored 14 books with basketball personalities like Rick Pitino, John Calipari, and Dick Vitale. Weiss has received the Curt Gowdy Media Award from the Naismith Hall of Fame, the Bert McGraine Award from the Football Writers of America and the College Football Hall of Fame, the first Big East Media award, the preseason NIT award, the Edwin Pope award from the Orange Bowl, and the Lew Klein Award from the Temple Journalism Hall of Fame. Weiss was recently inducted into the National Sportswriters and Sportscasters Hall of Fame and is a member of the College Basketball Writers Hall of Fame, the Philadelphia Sports Hall of Fame, the Philadelphia Big 5 Hall of Fame and the Pennsylvania Hall of Fame (Delco Chapter). He is a past president of the Football Writers of America Association and the U.S. Basketball Writers' Association. He and his wife Joan, an editor and author, reside in Havertown, Pa.

**H**owie Schwab began his career of covering college athletics back in 1980 at College and Pro Football Newsweekly. He worked at ESPN for 26 years and enjoyed stints at Sports Jeopardy and Fox Sports, where he most recently served as the network's college basketball bracketologist. Schwab also hosted podcasts called The Schwab Speaks and The Schwabcast. He and his wife, Suzie, reside in Fort Lauderdale, Florida